Y0-FCF-009

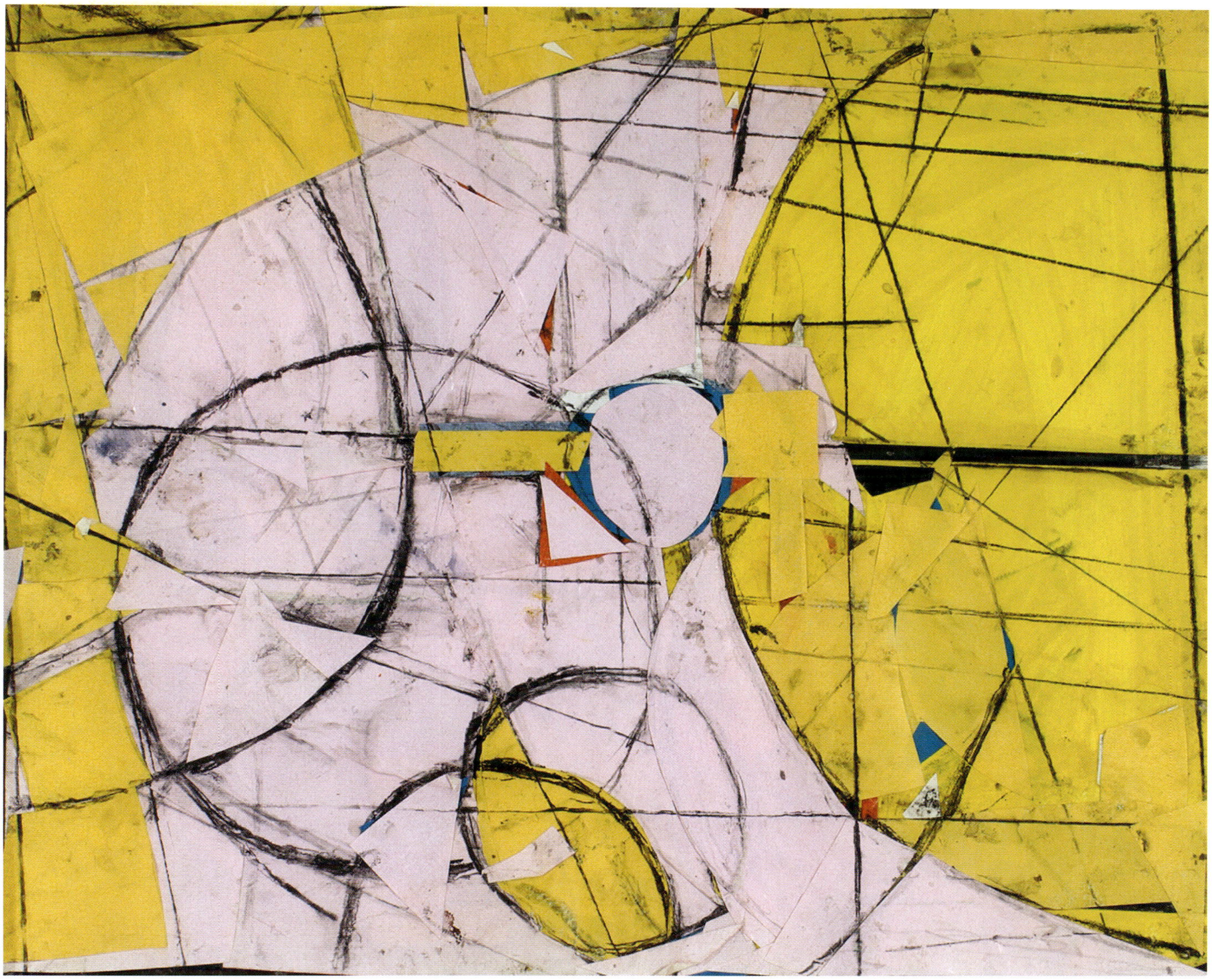

macrocosm/ microcosm:

abstract expressionism in the american southwest

Fred Jones Jr. Museum of Art
University of Oklahoma

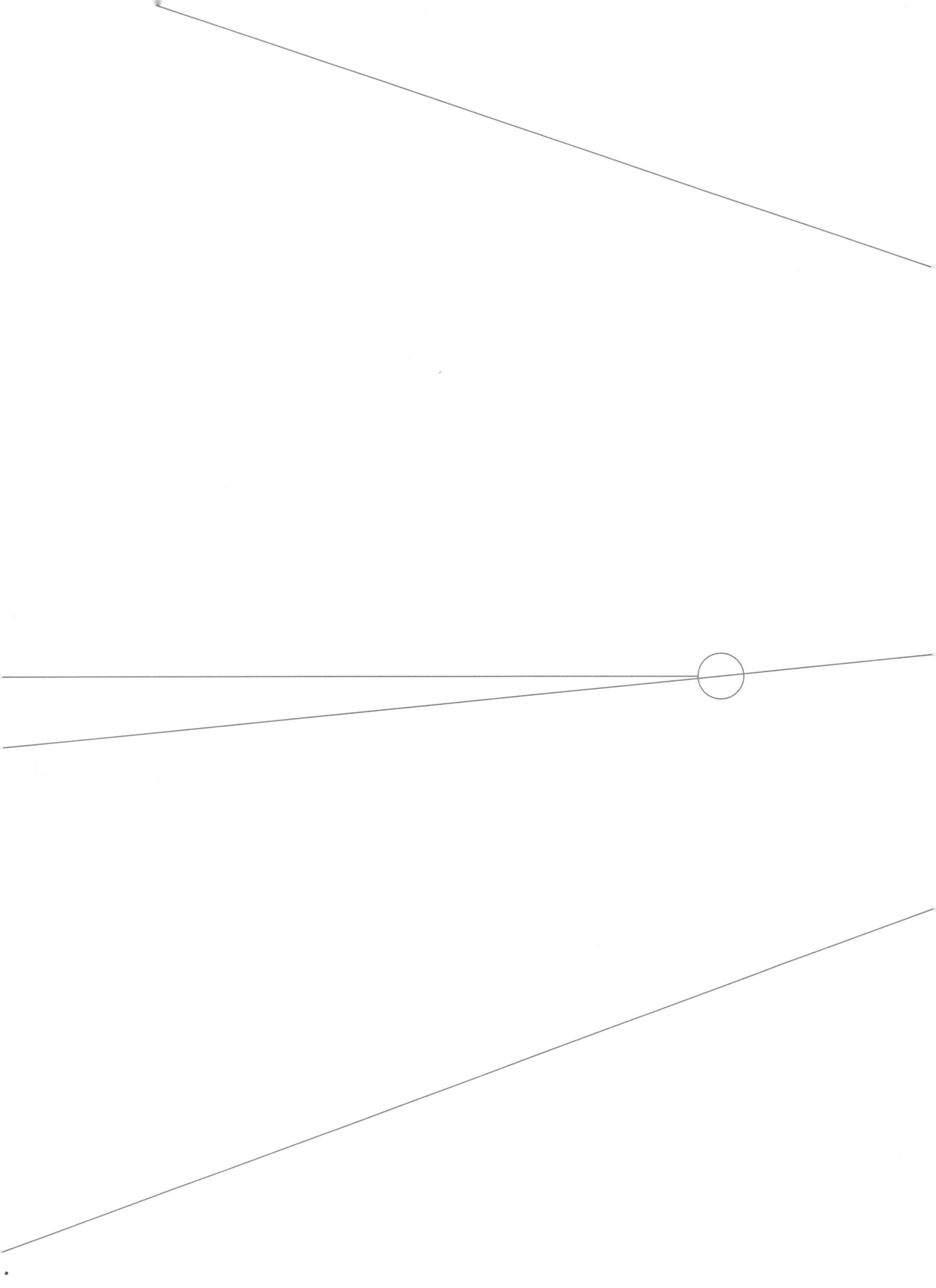

macrocosm/
microcosm:
abstract expressionism in the american southwest

Contents

Errata:

- p. 16, fig. 4. Albuquerque is dated 1951, and the lender should be listed as "Oklahoma City Museum of Art."
- p. 25, fig. 14. Credit line should be listed as "Collection of Nathaniel Abbey; reproduction permission courtesy of the artist."
- p. 63, fig. 55. Wilbert "Bill" Verhelst's life dates should be listed as (U.S., 1923-2012).
- p. 73, fig. 66. Robert Smithson's life dates should be listed as (U.S., 1938-1973).
- p. 81, fig. 71. Research conducted by Susie Kalil and the Museum of South Texas following publication of this catalogue revised the date of *The Blessings of Gravity* from the 1970s to 1994.

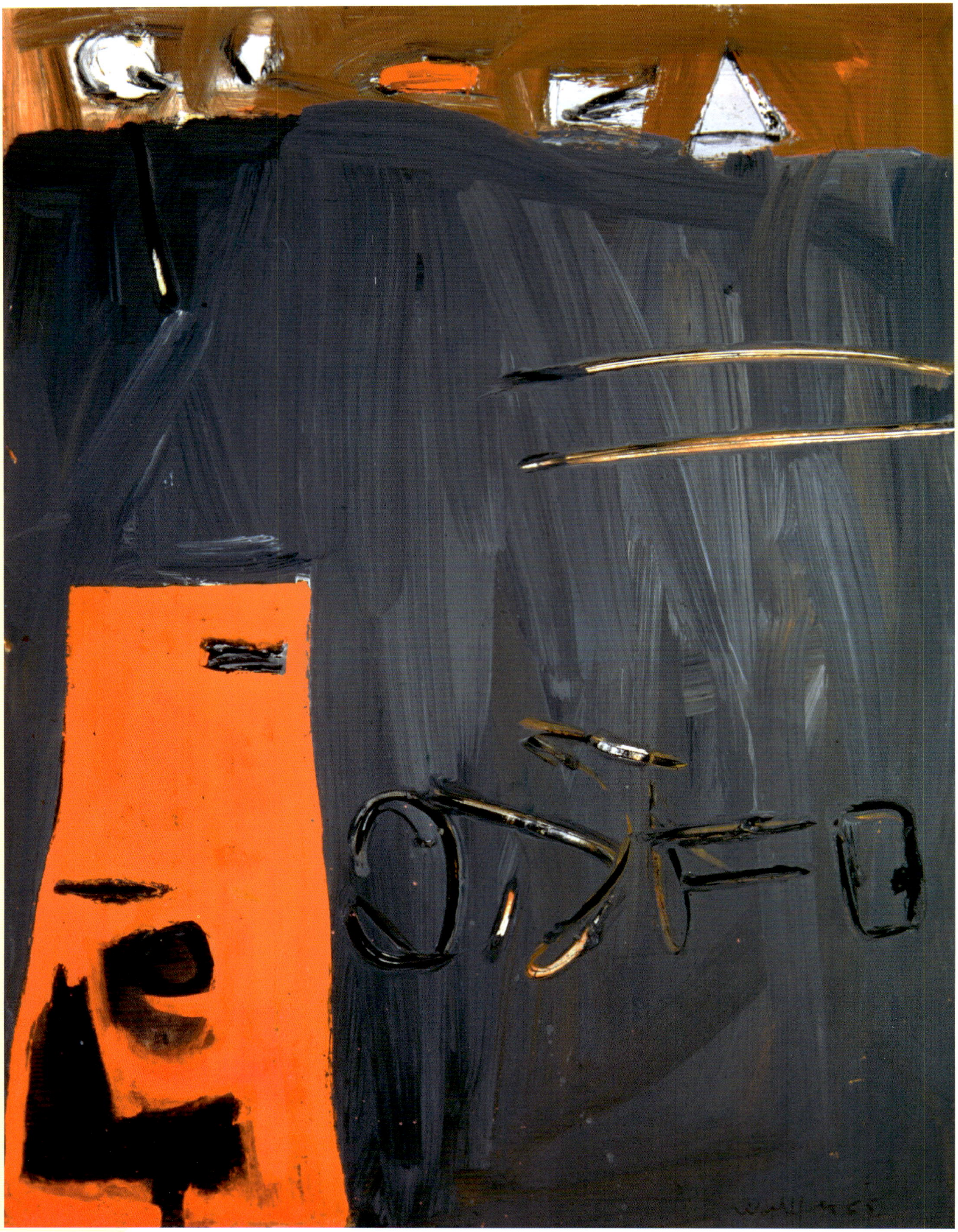

Preface

Emily Ballew Neff
Wylodean and Bill Saxon Director and Chief Curator

In recent years, the Fred Jones Jr. Museum of Art, in tandem with the University of Oklahoma's School of Art and Art History, has become a leading institution in the study of the art and culture of the American West. In the area of museum exhibitions, shows such as Bruce Goff: A Creative Mind; The Eugene B. Adkins Collection: Selected Works; and Oklahoma Clay: Frankoma Pottery have explored how architects, artists, and designers have responded to and interpreted the West throughout the twentieth century. Macrocosm/Microcosm: Abstract Expressionism in the American Southwest continues this investigation, adding an important and long overdue chapter on Abstract Expressionism in the Southwest.

The critical analysis of Abstract Expressionism focuses largely on the New York School and, to a lesser extent, the California School of Fine Arts, where Douglas MacAgy built a short-lived but experimental program that included Clyfford Still, Richard Diebenkorn, and visiting artist Mark Rothko. Action painting, Color Field, and Post-painterly abstraction outside of Manhattan or the Bay Area fare little better in the scholarly literature, with the exception of a handful of insightful monographs or studies focused on individual states. Similarly, the discussion of modernism in the American Southwest frequently emphasizes developments prior to World War II, leaving the vitality of the visual arts in the region after 1950 relatively uncharted.

In this important exhibition and catalogue, Mark Andrew White provides critical attention to mid-century modernism in the Southwest from the 1950s to the early 1970s, during the halcyon days of Abstract Expressionism. Influential artists from the east and west coasts, such as Diebenkorn, Elaine de Kooning, and Edward Corbett, worked in the Southwest during these decades and exchanged ideas and techniques with artists who made their home in the region. All of the artists, whether visitors or residents, responded like so many artists before them to the expansive spaces and distinctive geography of the Southwest. In the early decades of the twentieth century, the spirit of place as a concept abounded, as artists and geographers argued that land and landscape were something more than mere topography. The quality of light, the sculptural solidity of its landforms, the striking colors, and the human imprint of indigenous, Spanish, and Anglo cultures, altogether defined the genius loci of the Southwest, a heady combination that lured hundreds of artists and writers to the region. But, as White argues, unlike these earlier American artists, mid-century painters and sculptors also examined new concepts of space beyond their immediate, physical surroundings, as significant advances in nuclear science, astrophysics, and space exploration coincided with artistic production. The vast reaches of the macrocosm and the infinitesimal extent of the microcosm shaped how these artists understood the very nature of space itself and expressed it in their art. In the following pages, this exhibition catalogue shows us how.

Acknowledgments

Exhibitions and publications are rarely conceived and executed without the valuable assistance of colleagues, donors and other important contributors. This publication was made possible with funds from Nancy and George Records, who have long been faithful friends of the Fred Jones Jr. Museum of Art. We extend our heartfelt gratitude for their patronage of this project and the museum.

The University of Oklahoma, thanks to the vision of President David L. and Molly Shi Boren, enjoys the support and encouragement of the entire university and Norman community. Their unwavering generosity has been of enormous benefit to museum.

Research on this project first began in late 2009, and numerous individuals have been of tremendous help in the completion of both the exhibition and catalogue over the ensuing years. We would like to thank the artists and their families for their tireless patience in answering countless questions and securing works for the exhibition. We owe a special debt of gratitude to Rita Deanin Abbey, William Conger, Duayne and David Hatchett, Jim Henkle, Mary McChesney, Richard Stout, and Karl B. Williams, without whom this exhibition would not have been possible in its current form. Carolyn Fitz also deserves our appreciation, not only for her interest in preserving the legacy of her father, Dord Fitz, and the artists he represented, but also for the donation of his papers, which were invaluable to this project, to the Western History Collection at OU.

Many others have been generous with their time and knowledge over the course of this exhibition, and we would like to thank the following for their assistance: Marty Avrett, Alexandra Benjamin and the Mandelman-Ribak Foundation; Dean Bloodgood; Jina Brenneman, Curator at the Harwood Museum of Art; William Camfield; Andrew Connors, Curator of Art at the Albuquerque Museum; the Richard Diebenkorn Foundation; Katie Robinson Edwards, Curator at the Umlauf Sculpture Garden and Museum; Brewster Fitz and Carol Moder; Mary Alice Gibner; Hugh Grant, Director of the Kirkland Museum of Fine and Decorative Art; Chris Herron, Collection Manager and Deputy Curator of the Kirkland Museum of Fine and Decorative Art; Michael Howell, Collections Manager and Registrar of the Colorado Springs Fine Arts Center; Jim Levis Fine Art, Inc.; Blake Milteer, Executive Museum Director and Chief Curator of the Colorado Springs Fine Arts Center; Jonathan and Talitha Nichols; James Nottage, Vice President, Chief Curatorial Officer and Gund Curator of Western Art at the Eiteljorg Museum; Charles Peveto; William Reaves Fine Art; the Karan Ruhlen Gallery; W. Jackson Rushing III, Adkins Presidential Professor of Art History and Mary Lou Milner Carver Chair in Native American Art History at OU; Amber Sharples, Executive Director, and Clint Stone, Visual Arts Director, of the Oklahoma Arts Council; Verna Lee Shirley; Linda Hooper, Director at the Manny Silverman Gallery; Robert Summers; Chip Ware; the Washburn Gallery; and Lou Wynne.

Words cannot express my gratitude to Emily Ballew Neff, Wylodean and Bill Saxon Director and Chief Curator, for her considerable support of this project. And finally, we would like to acknowledge the work and dedication of the museum staff who assisted in the planning and development of this exhibition: Michael Bendure, Director of Communication; Tracy Bidwell, Head Registrar; Brad Stevens, Chief Preparator; and Becky Zurcher Trumble, Director of Administration and Financial Operations.

Macrocosm/Microcosm promises to further the critical dialogue on both Abstract Expressionism and modernism in the American Southwest, and its value has only been enhanced by the help of those mentioned.

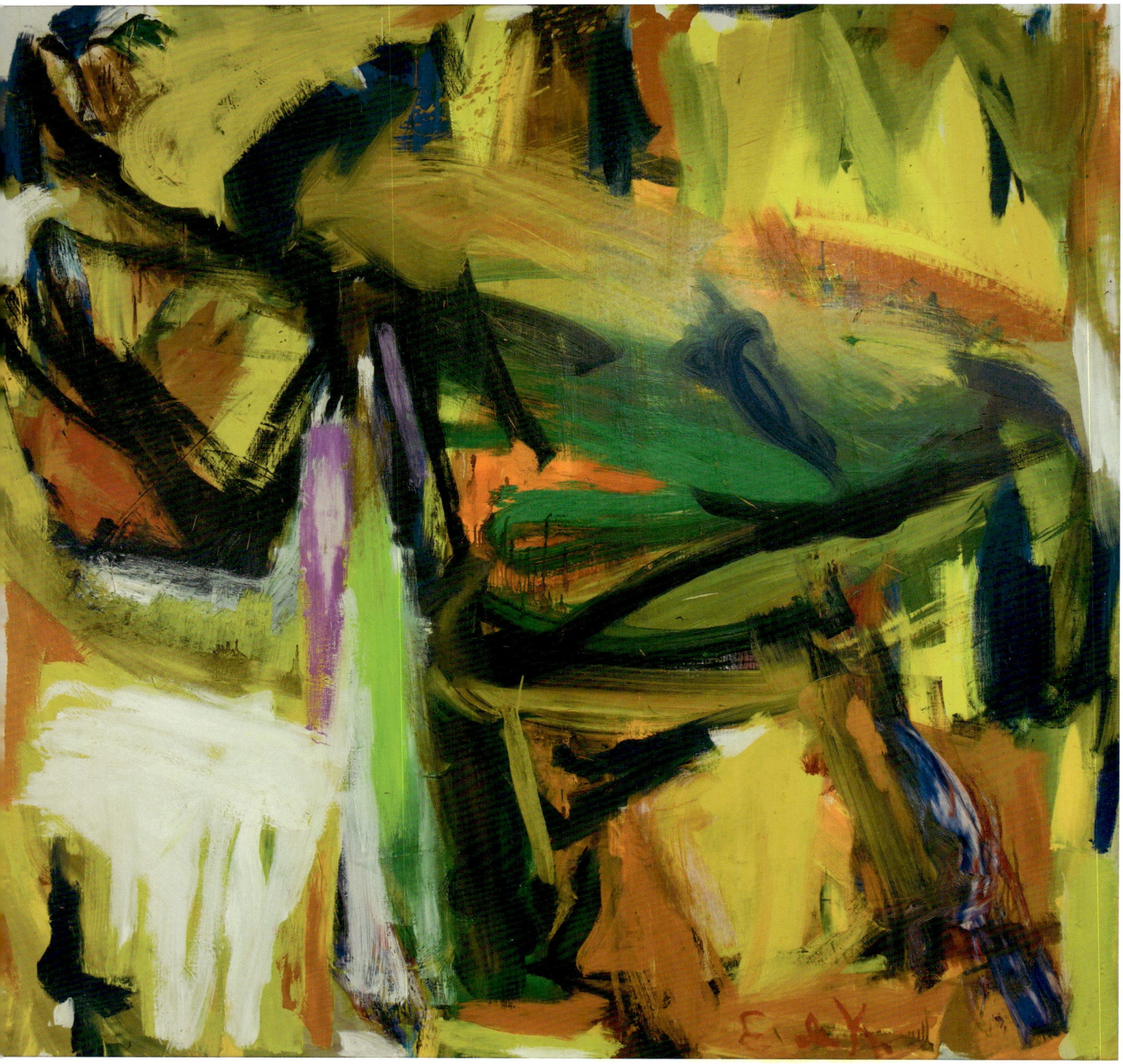

1 **Elaine de Kooning** (U.S. 1918–1989)

Albuquerque, 1960
oil on canvas, 82 1/2 x 77 3/4 in.
Collection of Linda and Robert Schmier; reproduction permission courtesy of the Elaine de Kooning Estate.

Macrocosm / Microcosm:
Abstract Expressionism in the American Southwest

Mark Andrew White

In 1962, the Amarillo *Globe-Times* interviewed artist and critic Elaine de Kooning, regarding her perception of art in the American Southwest. De Kooning had been visiting regularly since 1957 when local artist and gallery owner, George Edward "Dord" Fitz, had invited her to exhibit and teach a workshop. She had broadened her experience of the region in 1958 as a visiting professor at the University of New Mexico (UNM). Given her familiarity with both the artists at UNM and those represented by Fitz, she advanced the informed opinion that "The Southwest is developing an art style all its own, one with a feeling of quiet and remoteness. It is entirely different from the turbulent art of the east and west coasts." Those distinguishing features of quiet and remoteness, or perhaps silence and seclusion, not only differentiated the Southwestern modernists from Abstract Expressionists working in either New York or the San Francisco Bay Area, but also suggested a deep affinity for the expansive, open spaces of the Southwest. De Kooning, whose previous paintings had been responsive to urban life in New York City, admitted that the scintillating, sprawling Southwest had stirred a new direction in her work: "Suddenly I abandoned gray and my painting became bright with color. This wonderful space had its effect after those crowded city streets. I'd always painted vertically on rectangular canvases; now I paint horizontally for the feeling of wide spaces."[1] She had already confided to Fitz that both she and her husband, acclaimed painter Willem de Kooning, considered the paintings she produced in the Southwest her best to date.[2]

The expansive spaces, bright light, and vivid coloration of the Southwest obviously influenced Elaine de Kooning in a profound way, and she began painting metaphorical landscapes with titles such as *Colorado, Oklahoma,* and *Albuquerque* (1960; fig. 1). She was hardly alone in her perception of the Southwest and its artists, however. In the 1950s, the American Southwest became a confluence for Abstract Expressionists from the New York School and the San Francisco Bay Area.[3] In this volume, Abstract Expressionism may be understood as an ontological investigation that is not restricted to a cultural center, such as New York City, with peripheral practice in other parts of the country, and as a broader intellectual and emotional program that provided artists with a means of responding to and informing the American experience at mid-century.

For Abstract Expressionists in the Southwest, the seemingly vacant yet astounding immensity of the Southwest prompted many to pause in contemplation of both the limitless cosmos above and the nuanced variations of the natural world below. Photographer Ansel Adams described it best years earlier on a trip through New Mexico: "The skies and land are so enormous and the detail so precise and exquisite that wherever you are, you are isolated in a glowing world between the macro and micro—where everything is sidewise under you and over you, and the clocks stopped long ago."[4] The peculiarity of Southwestern space prompted in Adams a metaphysical confusion in which he felt adrift in a seemingly infinite span of space and time.

Like Adams, de Kooning and other visitors to the Southwest at mid-century also turned inward to scrutinize the self and their place in the universe. Using gestural brushwork and veils of color to depict the vast spaces and distinctive coloring of the landscape, they joined with local artists in Arizona, Colorado, New Mexico, Oklahoma, and Texas to create a distinctly modern view of the Southwest that expressed the aesthetic and cultural concerns of postwar America.

As if the geographic spaces of the Southwest were not vast enough, artistic sensitivity to space changed dramatically with the scientific and technological advances of the postwar era. The establishment of the Los Alamos National Laboratory (LANL) in New Mexico in 1943 linked the Southwest to the expansion of human knowledge into the microcosmic spaces of the atom. Conversely, the aeronautics industry developed rapidly in the Southwest following World War II and offered an increasing number of Americans a different, more expansive view of the country through air travel. In 1958, this macrocosmic awareness only broadened with the creation of the National Aeronautics and Space Administration (NASA), through which space launches were organized and controlled in Houston. Photographic images of the earth, as seen from space, and of celestial phenomena increased understanding of the extent of the universe.

Prompted by a culture of innovation and experimentation in the postwar period, Southwestern modernists took notice of these scientific developments and responded using the language of Abstract Expressionism. In this respect, the artists included in this catalogue helped to expand how Abstract Expressionism addressed both the Atomic and Space Age in meaningful ways, adding both richness and complexity to the innovative and experimental approaches initiated in New York and San Francisco.

Macrocosm/Microcosm demonstrates that space, broadly speaking, became a persistent theme among disparate artists from different geographic points in the Southwest. Whether they worked independently, or in one of the more closely knit art communities in Albuquerque, Taos, Houston, or Norman, Oklahoma, they all responded to the enormity of space, whether infinitely large or infinitely small. Most studies of mid-century modernism in the Southwest have focused on the history of individual cities or states, but this exhibition and catalogue argues that these artistic developments were far from isolated.[5] Modernists in the Southwest may have worked at great remove in cities as far-flung as Denver, Stillwater, and Tucson, but travel and exhibitions provided opportunities for interaction and influence. These modernists may have shared broad interests in the geography of the region with those artists of an earlier generation, such as the Santa Fe and Taos colonists, but their work exhibits a tension between local and regional concerns and thoroughly cosmopolitan expression.

A Cosmopolitan Southwest

The 1950s witnessed a great deal of critical interest in artistic developments in regions across the country, particularly in the Southwest. This was not a renewal of nationalist interests that supported the Regionalist style in the 1930s, but a recognition that culture existed west of the Hudson River. Curators, art historians, and periodicals scanned the nation for young artists, conscious perhaps that the West had helped to foster the likes of Jackson Pollock and Clyfford Still.

Most notably, Dorothy Canning Miller, Curator of Painting and Sculpture at the Museum of Modern Art (MoMA), looked beyond Manhattan for artists to include in her influential *Americans* series of exhibitions. She noted that both *Americans 1942* and *Fourteen Americans* (1946) included contemporary artists from different parts of the United States, and she followed suit in *Fifteen Americans* (1952). Her aim was not a survey of regional variations in contemporary art, with New York City being one region among many, but an attempt to demonstrate the cosmopolitanism of cultural expression in the U.S. Miller explained in the foreword to *Fourteen Americans* that all the artists included expressed the "moods and intentions of our time," and she concluded that "the idiom is American but there is no hint of regionalism or chauvinistic tendency. On the contrary, there is a profound consciousness that the world of art is one world."[6] Miller's use of the term "one world" indicates that she, like many in 1946, appreciated the pervasive spirit of internationalism following World War II and sought to include her fourteen Americans in a cosmopolitan community of culture regardless of their locale.

Miller traveled the country in search of new talent. She became familiar with Texan Ben L. Culwell in 1945 during his brief stay in New York and subsequently exhibited his World War II work in *Fourteen Americans*. In Albuquerque in late 1951, she visited Richard Diebenkorn, who was completing his Master of Fine Arts at the University of New Mexico, and he encouraged her to continue to Taos, where she met Clay Spohn and Edward Corbett. Corbett's work was included in *Fifteen Americans*.

This interest in artists working outside New York was not exclusive to Miller, and James Johnson Sweeney also looked afield. Sweeney and Miller had been colleagues at MoMA during the 1940s, before he accepted the directorship of the Solomon R. Guggenheim Museum in 1952. The Guggenheim collection and exhibition program broadened considerably under Sweeney, who looked not only to contemporary European painters associated with Art Brut and Art Informel but also to artists working across the U.S. He organized *Younger European Painters: A Selection* in 1953 after traveling through Europe, and the exhibition later toured the U.S., stopping at the Dallas Museum of Fine Arts, among other venues, during February 1955. He followed that exhibition with *Younger American Painters: A Selection* in 1954. The organization of that exhibition required him to take a circuit through North America with stops in Dallas, Santa Fe, Los Angeles, San Francisco, Berkeley, Portland, Seattle, Minneapolis, Chicago, and Toronto. Sweeney began his search in Dallas and, when the local press asked about his selection process for the exhibition, he explained, "Perhaps my aims are too personal, but I am looking for work that has no counterpart in, or similarities to, painting and sculpture now being done in New York. That I am ignoring."[7] *Younger American Painters* featured a number of artists connected with the Southwest, such as Richard Diebenkorn, who had recently completed his MFA, and Texans James Wesley "Jack" Boynton and McKie Trotter.[8]

Sweeney's interest in modernism in the Southwest continued after his appointment as director of the Museum of Fine Arts, Houston, in 1961. The year following his arrival, he organized *The Southwest: Painting and Sculpture* as a replacement to the venerable *Annual Exhibition of Works by Houston Artists*, which he cancelled in favor of a regional exhibition. The Southwest, by Sweeney's definition, ran from southern California to Arkansas and as far north as Colorado. Juried by Sweeney, James Brooks, and Alexander Calder, the exhibition surveyed the most progressive work done in the Southwest. That region was hardly isolated, and Sweeney observed, "An acquaintanceship with the remarkably broad field of contemporary pictorial and sculptural exploration was evident. Facilitated travel and communication had unquestionably made its inroads to geographical limitations."[9] Greater accessibility to air and automotive travel allowed artists to witness developments in other parts of the country and abroad, and a proliferation of arts periodicals ensured the spread of aesthetics and ideas.

To some degree, the spread of modernist aesthetics had been achieved years earlier with other regional exhibitions, the most notable of which was the *Annual Exhibition of Western Art* at the Denver Art Museum. The annual exhibition showcased contemporary art west of the Mississippi, regardless of style or theme, but in the late 1940s, it became a venue for some of the most progressive work in the Southwest. For the 54th annual show in 1948, the museum awarded a purchase prize to Max Ernst's decalcomania painting, *Time and Duration*, and awarded a prize the following year to *Discovery*, a surrealist painting by University of Oklahoma professor John O'Neil.

Modernist abstraction came to dominate the *Annual Exhibition of Western Art* in the 1950s and prompted the juror of the 57th annual, Lester Burbank Bridaham of the Art Institute of

Chicago, to justify the stylistic character of the exhibition to a presumably concerned audience: "Remember, we are living in an atom age—a period of deep unrest and emotional tension. Our future is uncertain. The artist is deeply conscious of these forces now at work."[10] Bridaham paraphrased the justifications used by Abstract Expressionists such as Jackson Pollock and Adolph Gottlieb to assert that western modernists, like their eastern counterparts, used styles expressive of the anxiety of the age.[11] This did not mean, however, that western artists were beholden to New York, and Otto Karl Bach, Director of the Denver Art Museum, clarified: "The fact that these Western Annuals in Denver are removed from the pressures of fashion and a New York market, also gives them a grass-roots validity not always evident in other competitive showings."[12] For Bach, the annual exhibitions evinced some tie to place or locale that helped to differentiate western artists from those in Manhattan.

Critical interest in the Southwest, and other regions, intensified in the 1950s, and commentators consistently recognized that artists working across the country were cognizant of international developments in art and responded to the concerns of the age by using styles and techniques shaped by their locale. *Art in America* devoted several issues in the 1950s and '60s to lesser-known artists working across the country with its series "*New Talent in the U.S.A.*" Likely prompted by the exhibitions of Miller and Sweeney, *Art in America* intended to explore regions across the nation for a sampling of latest developments, and critics and museum professionals around the country were asked to discuss artists of note. For the inaugural issue in February 1955, critic and contributor James Thrall Soby observed that "the quickening of means of communication in the art world" had provided American artists in the 1950s a better knowledge of international developments regardless of their location.[13] The Southwest section was compiled by Jerry Bywaters, director of the Dallas Museum of Fine Arts, who chose several artists for inclusion, most notably John O'Neil and McKie Trotter. Unfortunately, the series ended in the early 1960s, although one of the final issues did include selections by Miller.

"*New Talent in the U.S.A.*" hoped to draw greater attention to modernist tendencies across the country and, like the Western Annuals and the exhibitions of Sweeney and Miller, to demonstrate the cosmopolitanism of American artists. Southwestern artists received favorable notice in all of these projects for their idiosyncratic approach to the salient concerns of the day. Expanded means of communication certainly encouraged the spread of modernist aesthetics into the more remote regions of the country but, by the mid-1950s, the Southwest had already become a confluence of influences from the east and west coasts.

Where East and West Converge: New Mexico

Art historian David Witt has characterized Taos as a "crossroads between New York and San Francisco," yet Albuquerque and other cities in the Southwest witnessed a similar convergence in the 1950s.[14] Like Taos, Albuquerque benefited from an influx of artists from New York City, some of whom had studied with Hans Hofmann, and from San Francisco, where cutbacks at the California School of Fine Arts (CSFA) prompted the resignation and dismissal of many of the most progressive faculty. Regardless of their points of origin, modernists from the coasts brought styles and techniques to the Southwest that they adapted in order to express the distinctive features of their new environs. Exhibition and travel created lines of influence and dialogue that spread quickly between Albuquerque and Taos and points in Colorado, Oklahoma, and Texas (fig. 2). By the mid-1950s, Abstract Expressionism, as it had been dubbed, had a strong presence across the Southwest.

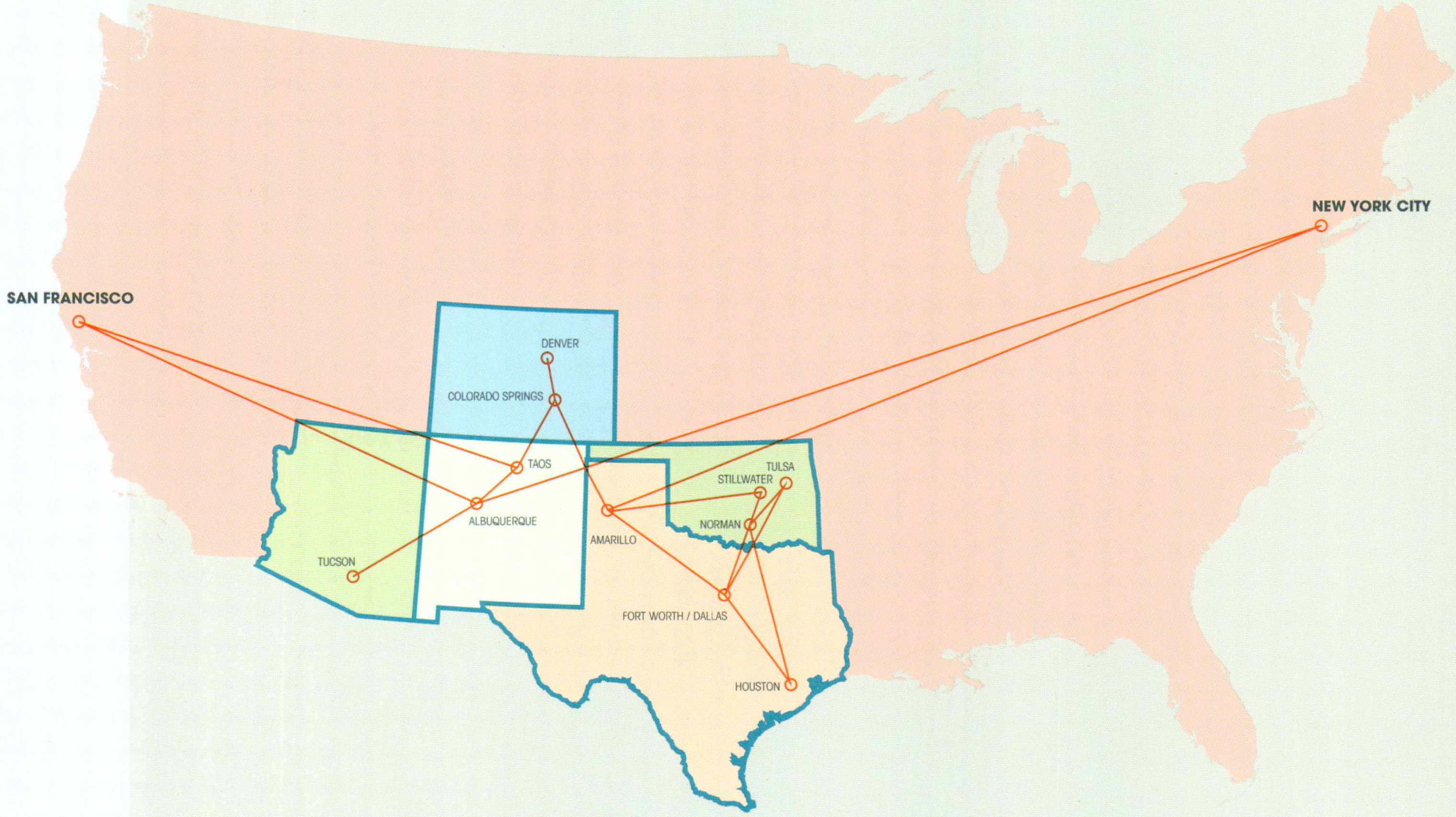

2 Centers of Abstract Expressionist activity in the Southwest and lines of communication and influence

One of the most important points of influence developed at the University of New Mexico in Albuquerque, where modernist Raymond Jonson encouraged aesthetic experimentation. Elaine de Kooning characterized him as "the force that created a climate that enabled art to endure in a desert," in recognition of his acceptance of new approaches and his support for young artists. He taught at UNM for most of the 1940s before officially joining the faculty in 1949, and he then convinced the university administration to construct the Jonson Gallery, which opened to the public on January 8, 1950. The gallery not only served as his living space but also as a campus laboratory for students and young artists to exhibit their work, thus providing one of the few forums for contemporary art in the Southwest in the early 1950s.[15]

Jonson had been working non-objectively since the 1930s and practiced a meticulous, hard-edged style that drew influence from Wassily Kandinsky, the Bauhaus, and Constructivism. Jonson never quite embraced the improvisational character of gestural abstraction, even though he titled many of his works from the 1950s as improvisations. Nevertheless, he had looked

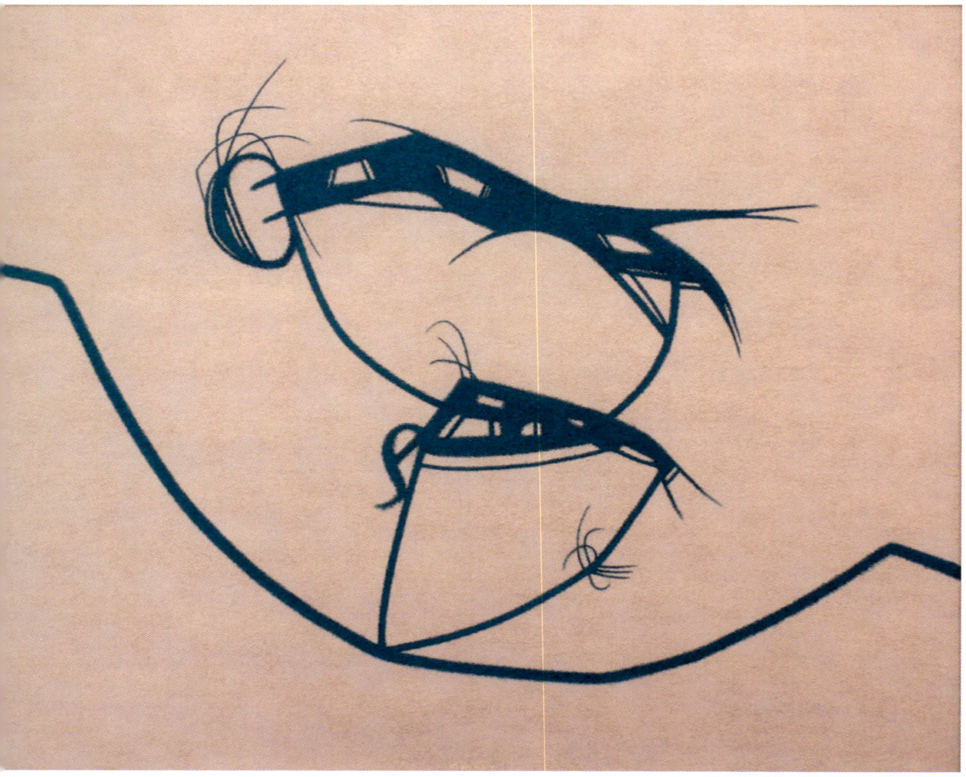

3 **Raymond Jonson** (U.S., 1891–1982)

Oil No. 13, c. 1953
oil and sand on masonite, 32 x 40 in.
© The Raymond Jonson Collection, The University of New Mexico Museum of Art, Albuquerque. Photo credit: Matthew Madison Rowe, Addison Rowe Gallery, Santa Fe.

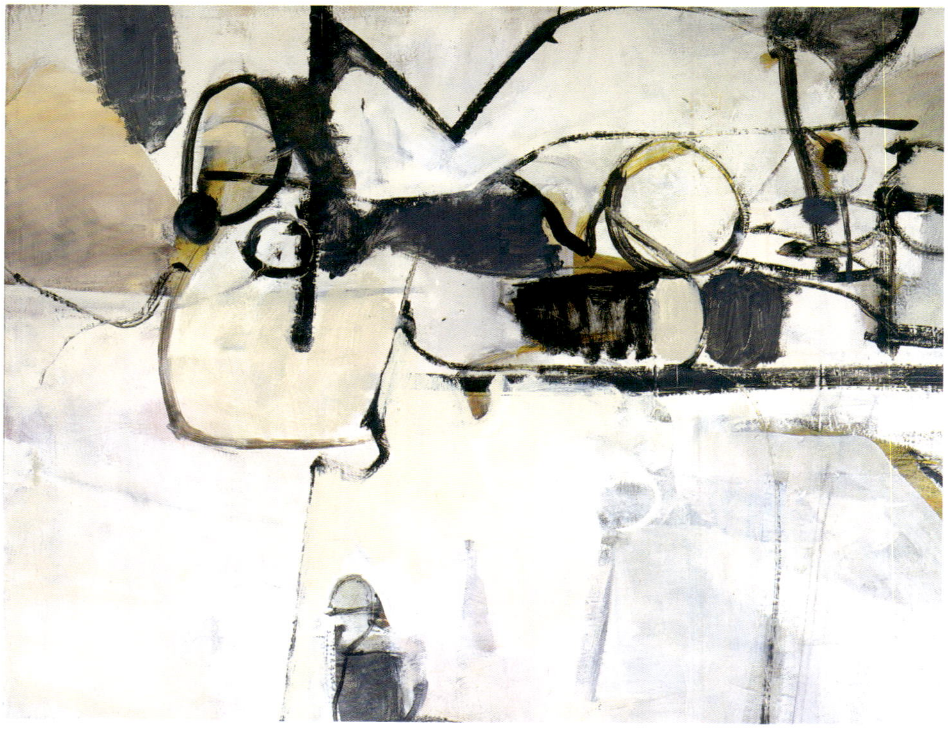

4 **Richard Diebenkorn** (U.S., 1922–1993)

Albuquerque, 1953
oil on canvas, 41 5/8 x 51 1/2 in.
The Oklahoma City Museum of Art, Museum purchase, Washington Gallery of Modern Art Collection, 1968.136;
© The Richard Diebenkorn Foundation.

to the Southwestern landscape for inspiration routinely in the 1920s and '30s and, by mid-century, he had developed a sensitive approach to form and materials that evoked the essence of the Southwest. He drew upon the vivid coloration, rough textures, and open spaces of the region in his *Oil No. 13* (1953; fig. 3), which conjures associations with petroglyphic imagery. A vaguely anthropomorphic form, suggestive at once of human, animal, and insect anatomy, dominates much of the space and may have a provenance in Mimbres pottery or rock art.[16] The surrounding field carries the color of pink sandstone, an association Jonson furthered through the addition of grit and other aggregates to emulate the surface of rock. Whereas the influence of petroglyphs and Native ceramics on *Oil No. 13* should not be overlooked, Jonson's concern for materiality in the painting is more than a vehicle for modernist exploration of Indian motifs.[17] The painting may be read in other ways, not solely as an interpretation of iconic forms, but as a looser network of lines and shapes with geographical connotations. Jonson's lines may represent cracks and fissures on a rock face or, if envisioned from above, even ravines and canyons produced by erosion and tectonic forces. Mesas and plateaus shaped by nature, a staple of his early artistic diet, might have been the origin of the mysterious forms of *Oil No. 13*. With this reading of the painting, Jonson's space becomes metaphorically vast, especially in the curving line in the lower third that extends off each end of the canvas, inferring a segment of a much larger geological body.

The conjunction of Jonson's interest in materiality and landscape is unsurprising, considering the artistic climate at UNM in the early 1950s, and a recent crop of students with a similar bent may have swayed him. Richard Diebenkorn enrolled at UNM in 1950 under the Servicemen's Readjustment Act or G.I. Bill to complete his MFA, having served as an instructor at the CSFA before budget cuts forced his departure. He found a sympathetic presence in Jonson and recalled, "I visited his place fairly often and we would talk, and he was the only one who was really, had any kind of understanding of what I was doing."[18]

Diebenkorn, like Jonson, had been working non-objectively but with a gestural immediacy unlike the latter's more disciplined approach. The CSFA had been a hothouse for experimentation through a fertile mixture of influences from a progressive faculty that included Clyfford Still, Hassel Smith, Corbett, and Spohn. Diebenkorn cultivated the accidental and improvisational in paintings that are replete with gestural strokes, paint drips, and bold color contrasts he described cumulatively as "honest-to-God chaos."[19] Diebenkorn's Bay Area paintings suggested landscape, through both the use of place names as titles and the loose reference to local color and topography, but it was not until the move to Albuquerque that he acknowledged his debt to his surroundings.

Living on an outlying ranch east of the Rio Grande and south of Interstate 40, he developed a more profound empathy for nature: "Temperamentally, perhaps I had always been a landscape painter, but I was fighting the landscape feeling. For years I didn't have the color blue on my palette because it reminded me too much of the spatial qualities in conventional landscapes. But in Albuquerque I relaxed and began to think of natural forms in relation to my own feelings."[20] Disdainful of traditional landscape, Diebenkorn's New Mexican paintings avoided recognizable forms in favor of colors, masses, and details that responded empathetically and metaphorically to the local environment. *Albuquerque* (1951; fig. 4), painted a year after his relocation, uses nuanced whites and blacks warmed and cooled by subtle earthen browns and greens, as if his entire palette had been blanched by the intense light of the Southwest. These passages of amorphous color, vaguely geometric in shape, help to organize a composition otherwise defined by a crude, seemingly random intersection of calligraphic lines and rough masses. He eradicated the suggestion of a ground plane entirely to make use of the entire visual field in his intuitive response to the Southwest, and the controlled chaos of the painting bespeaks his interest in the plasticity of his medium and the myriad possibilities of color.

Diebenkorn's improvisational marks, when combined with the less active passages towards the bottom of the canvas, create a sense of space that seems paradoxically sprawling and contained, or vacant and populous, similar in some respects to Jonson's *Oil No. 13*. For poet and critic James Schevill, the inference to landscape was obvious in the compositional effects: "It is this sharp, crude, dramatic division of space that has given many viewers an impression of the loneliness, the jagged opposition and the distance of western landscapes."[21] Diebenkorn, in turn, later acknowledged the influence that the vast spaces of the Southwest had on his Albuquerque paintings: "The scale is, there is something that really is kind of overwhelming and most immediately apparent [when] one is there, I think."[22]

The Southwest shaped Diebenkorn's approach to nature and space, and other students at UNM responded in similar ways, albeit through a different set of stylistic influences. Charles Littler and Rita Deanin Abbey were colleagues of Diebenkorn's at UNM but were drawn ultimately to the circle of Hans Hofmann. Littler attended UNM from 1949 to 1950, and then the Hans Hofmann School of Fine Arts from 1951 to 1952, eventually serving as his instructor's secretary the two following years. Hofmann's formal approach and his endorsement of Action painting led Littler to produce gestural interpretations of the Provincetown landscape by 1952.

Littler eventually returned to the Southwest in 1957, where he accepted a position at the University of Arizona in Tucson, and he brought the lessons of Hofmann with him.[23] *Desert I* (ca. 1960; fig. 5) exemplifies his early style with its vigorous brushwork and vibrant but limited palette. Variations of blue and green form a loose network of masses and tangled strokes suggest desert foliage against a field of pale sands. *Desert I* borders on representation, through both the shadow of a monolithic mesa and the high horizon line that creates a subtle vertigo as it climbs to the right. Littler employed Hofmann's lessons on the psychological effect of colors to suggest spatial recession, and the dark horizontal seems to recede dramatically from the lighter field in the lower register of the painting.[24] When paired with the high horizon, the effect is one of great distance.

Littler eventually abandoned landscape for the figure, but Abbey drew inspiration from the visual and essential characteristics of the Southwest for much of her career. She earned her Bachelor of Fine Arts and Master of Arts at UNM in 1952 and 1954, and spent summers with Hofmann in Provincetown after the award of each. In 1953, she relocated to Taos, following her MFA exhibition at the Harwood Foundation. Living outside of town, she focused on painting, and Hofmann's lessons informed her *Taos Solitude* (1953; fig. 6). The title clearly references her physical isolation in the high desert terrain of Taos, but it also implies seclusion and a meditative silence, resulting from her communion with her surroundings. Like Littler, she uses warm and cool colors of varying intensity to suggest psychologically the projection and recession of the painting's rough forms. Despite the strength of her palette, Abbey lightened her color with generous amounts of white, effectively "quieting" the painting. Both stylistically and thematically, *Taos Solitude* encourages introspection and demonstrates Abbey's sensitivity to her environment.

In Taos, Abbey exhibited at both the Harwood Foundation in 1953 and later in 1960–61 at La Galeria Escondida, one of the few forums for contemporary art in northern New Mexico outside of the Jonson Gallery. Eulalia Emetaz opened the gallery in 1946, and it attracted modernists living in Taos, as well as those in the surrounding region.[25] Initially, Emetaz exhibited an earlier generation of modernists working in Taos, such as Andrew Dasburg and Ward Lockwood, but an influx of artists from the coasts in the 1940s and early 1950s broadened her representation. Beatrice Mandelman and Louis Ribak arrived from Manhattan in 1944, prompted by advice from his former instructor and mentor John Sloan. Ribak opened the Taos Valley Art School in 1947, which attracted students on the G.I. Bill and also helped to encourage the development of modernism in Taos. Mandelman would later reflect that in the 1950s Taos became a point of contact between the East and West Coasts, resulting in "a certain vitality and a certain originality."[26] The pair had worked under the Federal Art Project and had been committed to an art of social engagement, but their relocation to northern New Mexico and association with other modernists would produce dramatic changes in their work.

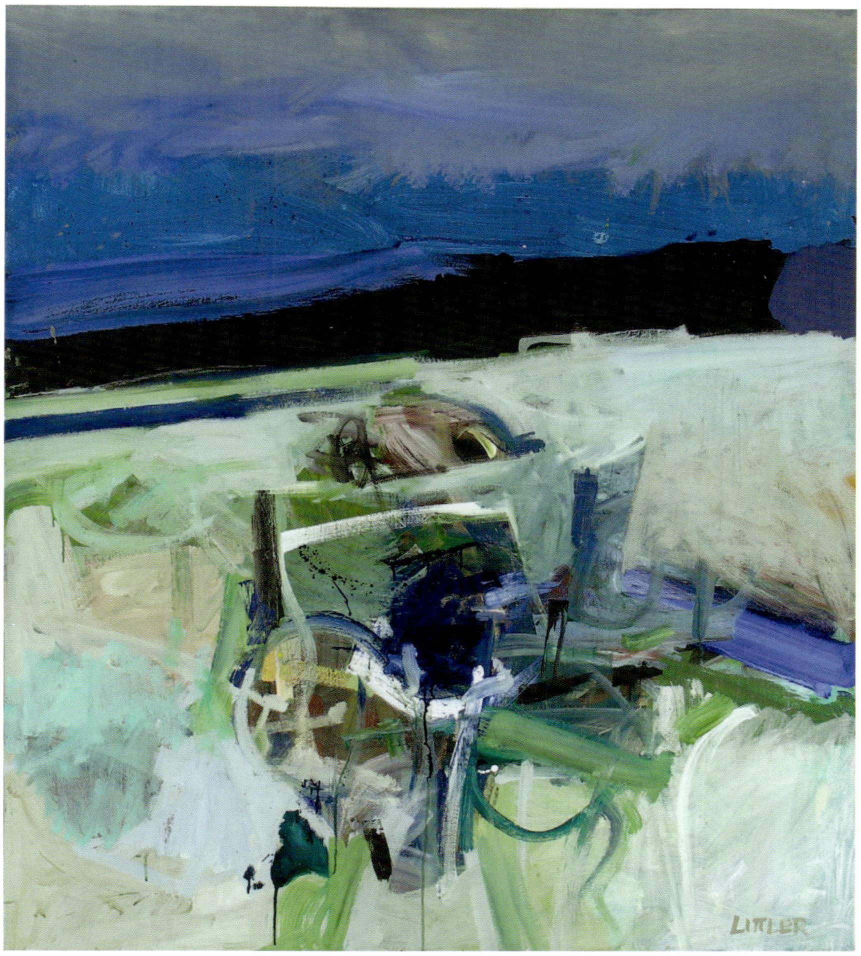

5 **Charles Littler** (U.S., 1928–1991)

Desert I, ca. 1960
oil on canvas, 60 x 55 in.
The University of Arizona Museum of Art, Tucson;
gift of the Phoenix Art Museum.

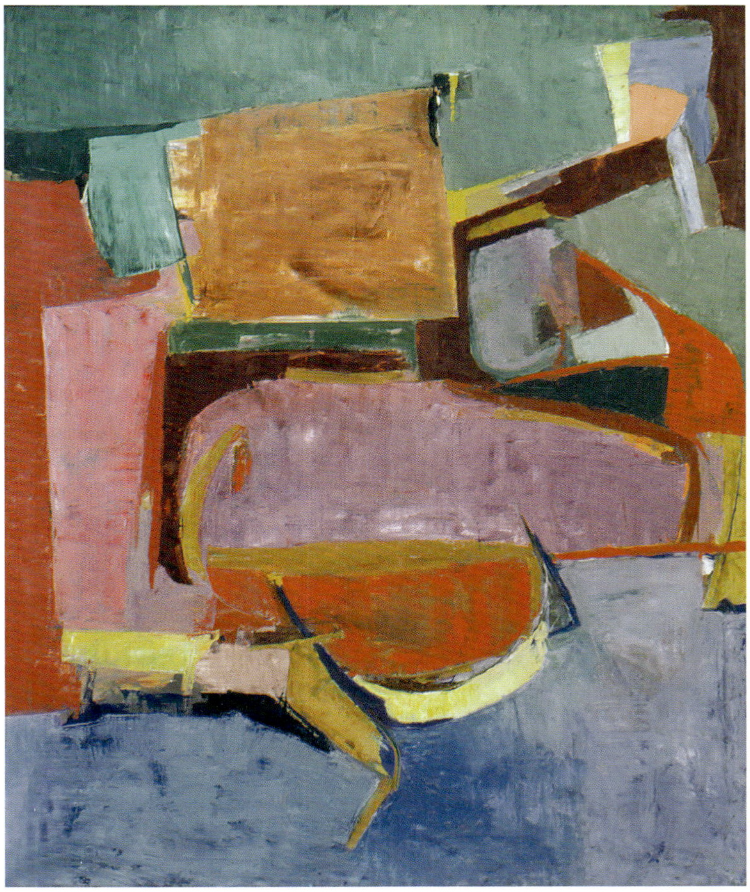

6 **Rita Deanin Abbey** (U.S., b. 1930)

Taos Solitude, 1953
oil on canvas, 50 x 43 in.
Collection of the artist; reproduction
permission courtesy of the artist.

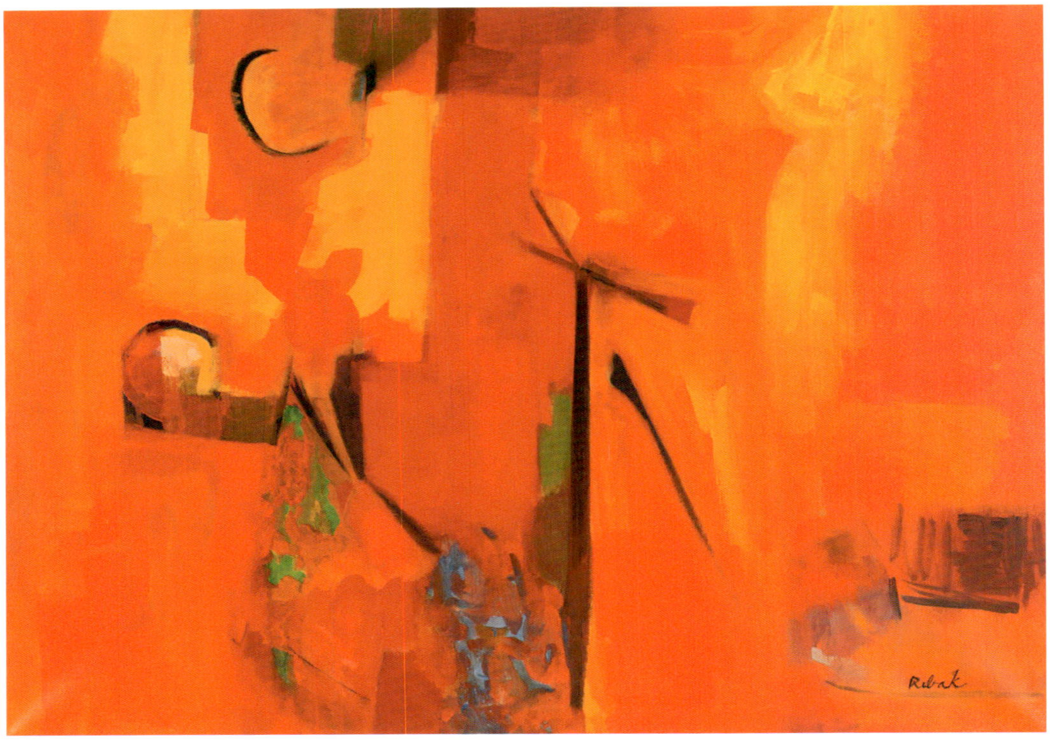

7 **Louis Ribak** (U.S., born Lithuania, 1902–1979)

Red Canyon Rising, late 1960s
acrylic on canvas, 52 x 68 1/2 in.
Fred Jones Jr. Museum of Art, the University of Oklahoma, Norman, Oklahoma; gift of the Mandelman-Ribak Foundation, 2011.

Initially, both Ribak and Mandelman worked representationally in an expressionist vein but turned to non-objectivity in the 1950s, influenced by the new environment and possibly other modernists in the orbit of La Galeria Escondida. Ribak, who suffered from a respiratory ailment, later acknowledged that the Southwest not only improved his health but also resulted in substantive changes in his work: "I started freeing myself from muddy colors and appreciating space organization as far as the physical look of a two dimensional area, a painting or a drawing. It was very beneficial for my health and my art. . . . Also the expanse—the mountains, the gorges, the arroyos, the rock formations."[27] A profound appreciation for the expansive space and geological variety of the Southwest marked Ribak's mature career and resulted in paintings such as *Red Canyon Rising* (late 1960s; fig. 7). Ribak likely found his inspiration at sunrise in one of the many canyons surrounding Taos, like the Rio Grande Gorge, and composed the painting with amorphous passages of brilliant color, evocative of the geological formations produced by centuries of wind and water erosion. An analogy may be found in Ernest Blumenschein's *Rio Grande Gorge (Strength of the Earth)* (1944–49; fig. 8) in which the artist attempted to bring sensible form to the chaotic array of geometric and organic shapes and diverse hues of red, yellow, orange, blue, and green found in the yawning gorge.

Ribak, however, eschewed representation in favor of an empathetic approach. Like Jonson and Diebenkorn, Ribak relied on dark, calligraphic marks that allude at once to cracks, as well as crevasses. Forms extend off the edge of the pictorial space suggesting a continuation of these metaphorical features into the unbounded space beyond the painting. But color dominates the visual experience, especially the oscillating red, an exaggeration of the region's sandstone. *Red Canyon Rising* bears some similarity to the work of Still or Robert Motherwell, two artists that Ribak had probably met in the 1950s.[28]

Mandelman also recalled that the New Mexican environment had affected the direction of her work, particularly in the "use of space, the feeling of prehistory, of a place geological. I did not want to reach out to the world. I've spent my life in a hermetically isolated, quiet way."[29] The desire for introspection and isolation, paired with a sense of the antediluvian, led Mandelman to produce spare, minimal paintings in the 1950s characterized by textural passages, collaged elements, and large areas of relatively unbroken color. A palpable silence and solitude haunts the sparse composition of her *Moonlight* (ca. 1955; fig. 9). With a nod to the work of Joan Miró, Mandelman situated biomorphic

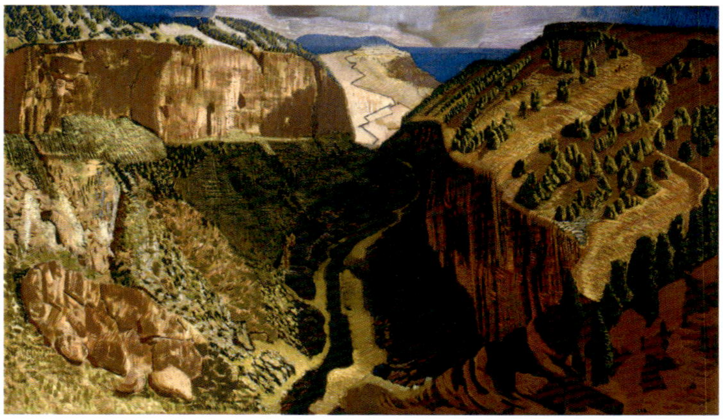

8 **Ernest Blumenschein** (U.S., 1874–1960)

Rio Grande Gorge (Strength of the Earth), 1944–49
oil on canvas, 27 x 47 in.
Fred Jones Jr. Museum of Art, the University of Oklahoma, Norman, Oklahoma, and the Philbrook Museum of Art, Tulsa, Oklahoma.
© Courtesy of the Blumenschein Estate.

forms within a nocturne of black, blue, and gray. Drips, smears, stains, and other marks made seemingly by chance or accident in *Moonlight* infer a viscous, mutable environment, changing slowly under lunar light. Like other Abstract Expressionists, Mandelman conceived of nature as a slow, continual process of terrestrial and cosmic change, metamorphosis, and flux.[30] She was clearly aware that the New Mexican environment had been shaped centuries earlier by volcanic eruptions, which left behind striking landforms and volcanic rock strewn chaotically across the landscape.

Mandelman's liberal use of black and other dark tonalities may have been the influence of San Francisco transplant Edward Corbett, who began an influential series of black paintings in 1950. Corbett first visited Taos in 1947, partly through the encouragement of his colleague Clay Spohn who had been there in 1945. When Corbett received an Abraham Rosenberg Foundation Fellowship in 1951, he relocated to Taos, after resigning his position at the CSFA in anticipation of a faculty reduction, and he studied briefly at Ribak's Taos Valley Art School. Emetaz offered him a solo exhibition that same year. Spohn also departed the CSFA in 1951 and joined Corbett in Taos.

Corbett began his black paintings while living on Point Richmond in the Bay Area, and he had little difficulty translating that aesthetic approach to his new environment. He saw painting itself as "an act of loneliness. Unbelievable solitude," and black helped to convey the introspection and isolation he found in both his craft and the Southwest.[31] Drawing, rather than painting, commanded much of his attention during his New Mexican period, and he explored the textural and tonal possibilities of charcoal, pastel, and crayon in works clearly inspired by his surroundings. In his *New Mexico #34* (1954; fig. 10), delicate gradations of gray and black form roughly horizontal bands, similar in appearance to strata or lateral fractures. Corbett's powdery media alludes to the dry desert terrain, an association only furthered by the linear cracks or fissures that extend from one layer of the image to the next. *New Mexico #34* seems elemental in its formal simplicity, and art historian Susan Landauer has asserted that Corbett "seems to have been

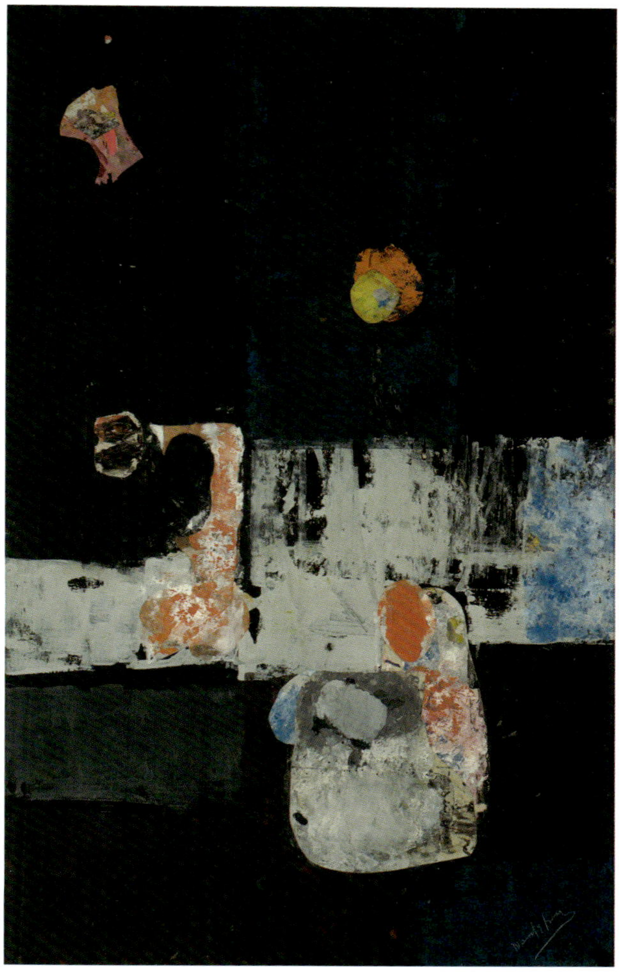

9 **Beatrice Mandelman** (U.S., 1912–1998)

Moonlight, ca. 1955
casein with collage on cardboard, 43 3/4 x 28 in.
The Harwood Museum of Art, Taos.

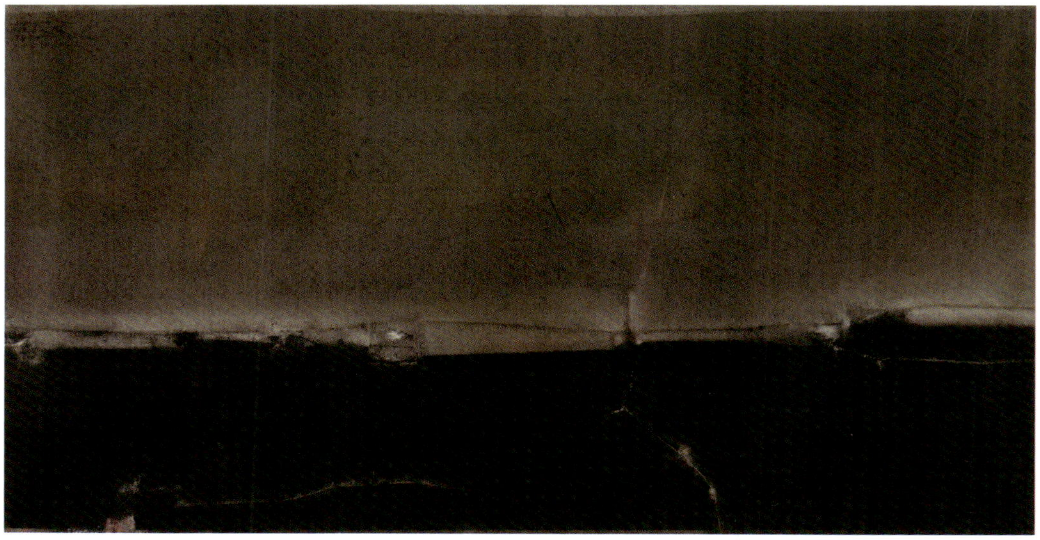

10 **Edward Corbett** (U.S., 1919–1971)

New Mexico #34, late 1954
charcoal, conte crayon, and crayon on paper, 13 5/8 x 26 1/6 in.
The Hirshhorn Museum and Sculpture Garden, Smithsonian Institution, Washington, D.C.; gift of Joseph H. Hirshhorn, 1966.
Photo credit: Cathy Carver.

fascinated by [New Mexico's] primordial element, the inhuman image of eternal nature."[32] Like Mandelman, Corbett admitted an innate empathy for the immensity and mutability of the Southwestern landscape:

> *I have a strong emotional attachment to the American Southwest—to the people and their culture, the language, the architecture, the food: but mainly I have an emotion about the landscape, the immense changing spaces of mountain and plain. The emotion is important in my life as an artist. I believe my first moments of significant self-awareness, of imaginative life, were when I became speculatively involved with the dramatic nature around me; when I tried to understand the peculiar, almost giddy state of mind caused by seeing a mountain peak 70 miles away in Sonora, and the round white clouds just touching it. I am still trying to explain this state of mind. But I admit, now, that the explanation is secondary; the wonder is the thing, and the longing that follows it to say something perceptive and human about one's experience of a fabulous impersonal reality.*[33]

The Southwest, as his statement indicates, initiated his early appreciation for nature and left him with a speculative bent. Accordingly, silence and a contemplative mood not only permeates *New Mexico #34* and other drawings from the period but also the poetry he wrote in Taos. For example, the last stanza of his poem *By This Empty Window* associates the northern New Mexican landscape with a pervasive peace:

> *Silence, as sudden as its ending. Silence of rock and pinon [sic], above,*
> *where wings go; of the silent morning sun; of the smoke-haze in the*
> *silent valley; silence of water murmuring beyond hearing; silence of*
> *this sky asleep against this earth.*[34]

In Corbett's poem, every element of the landscape is mute and encourages a sense of solitude. *New Mexico #34*, in turn, also conveys quiet and isolation. The drawing serves as an ontological investigation of Corbett's emotional engagement with the vast spaces of the Southwest, with the visible traces of its geological formation, and with its changing physical character. He sought a viable and suitable formal means to express that engagement and especially his sense of awe. Despite clear sympathies for the Southwestern terrain, Corbett staunchly denied that he painted either "evocation of landscape" or "landscapes of my mind."[35] Like many artists included in this exhibition, Corbett insisted that his paintings were principally arrangements of form and color, and viewers should not seek some identification with landscape in his work. Nevertheless, Corbett responded to his environment on some level, and his interest in space and silence certainly corresponds to traits others discovered in the Southwest.

Corbett's CSFA colleague, Clay Spohn, also found inspiration in the "vast feeling of spacelessness" of the Southwest upon relocating in 1951.[36] Spohn hoped his move to Taos would provide the seclusion necessary for serious painting and, like Corbett, he sought an "articulate and coherent" means of translating his experiences. He tended towards archetypal, elemental themes in his work of this period, going so far as to list basic concepts for examination such as the tree, the desert, the cloud, the mountain, and the forest.[37] Such an approach is evident in *Blue Abstraction* (1950s; fig. 11), in which somewhat isolated patches of yellow, orange, red, and green float against an atmospheric field of blue. Nature took form in his work as a network of detached gestural passages, as though he sought to represent individually each experience of the myriad phenomena of his environment. *Blue Abstraction* avoids recognizable representation of nature, but each of the colorful forms derives from the northern New Mexico landscape, whether the nearby mountains or the vast sky of the Southwest. Although Spohn's formal approach is similar in some respects to Ribak's *Red Canyon Rising*, the verticality of *Blue Abstraction* demonstrates a concern not for the panoramic expanse of the terrain but for the dialogue between land and sky.

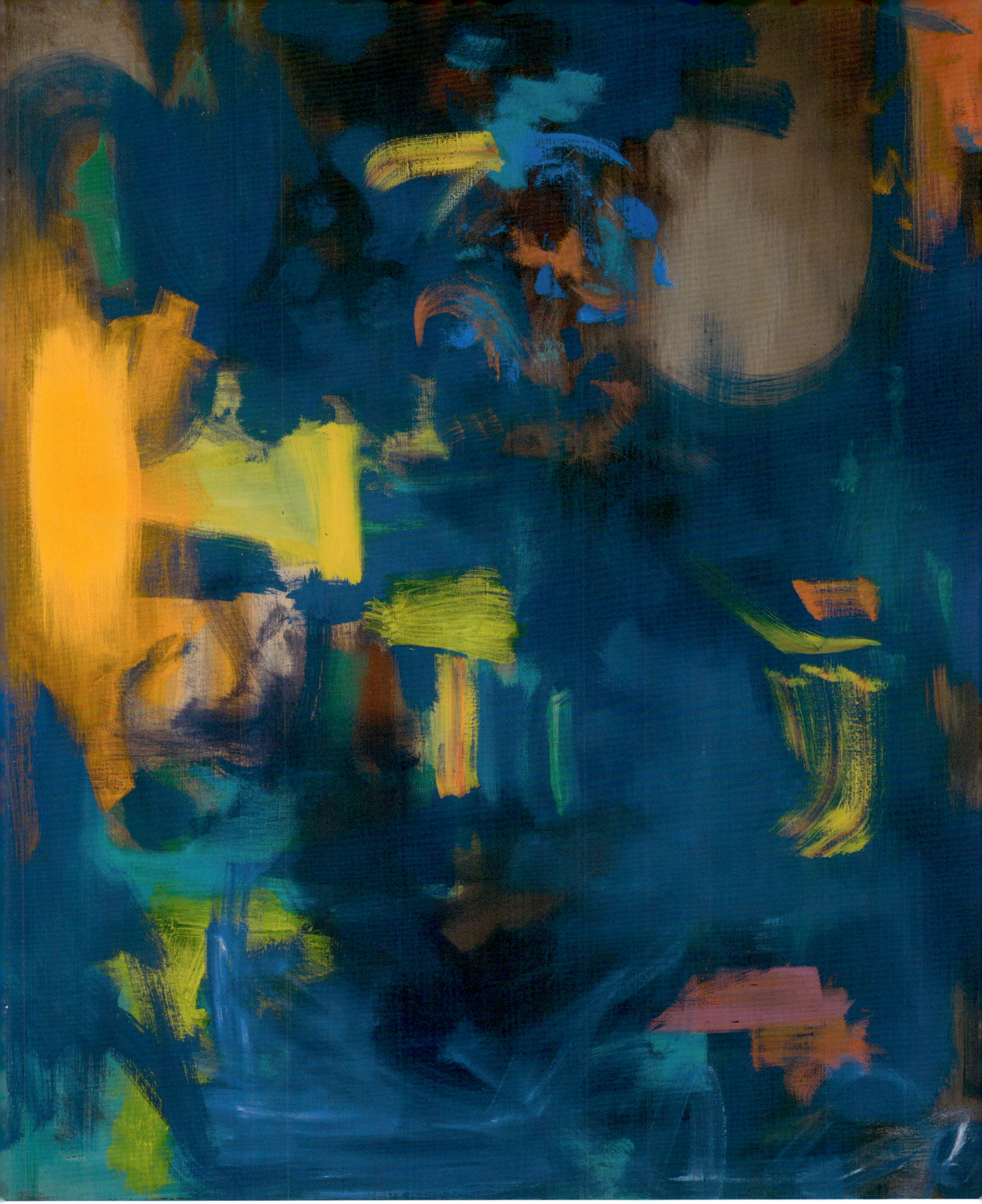

11 **Clay Spohn** (U.S., 1898–1977)

Blue Abstraction, 1950s
oil on canvas, 50 3/4 x 42 3/4 in.
The Roswell Museum and Art Center, Roswell.

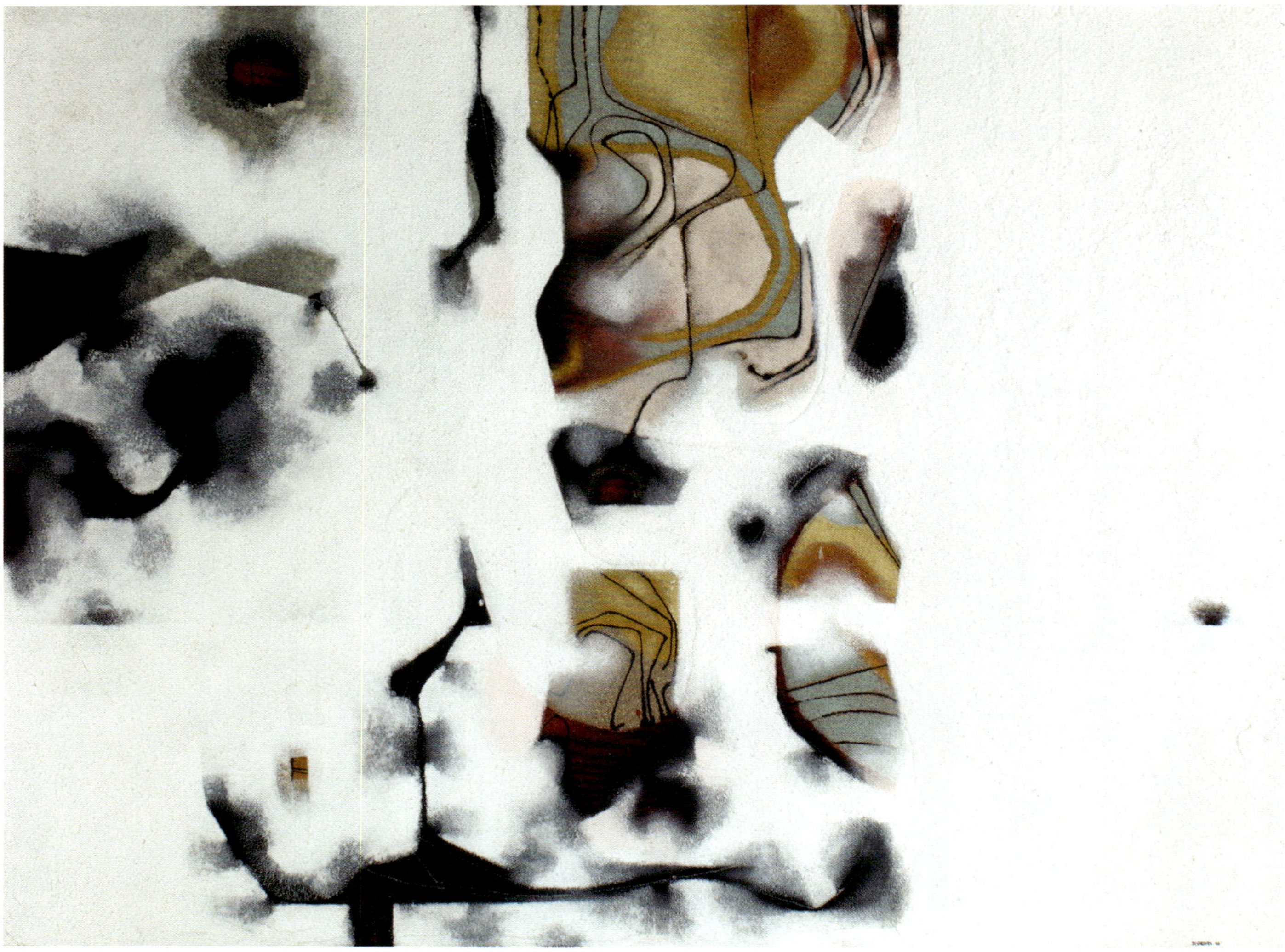

12 Robert McChesney (U.S. 1913–2008)

Arena No. 35, 1959
enamel and sand on canvas, 49 x 67 in.
Fred Jones Jr. Museum of Art, the University of Oklahoma, Norman, Oklahoma; gift of Mary McChesney.

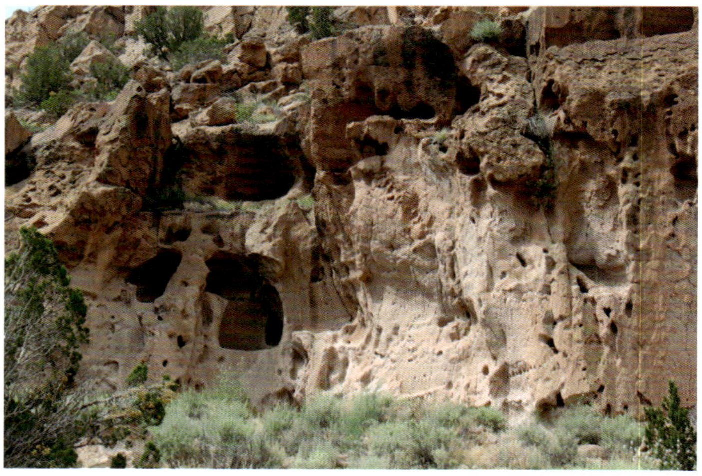

13 Tuff formations, Bandelier National Monument. *Photograph by author.*

Corbett and Spohn joined with Ribak and Mandelman to create the nucleus of a modernist colony in Taos, and La Galeria Escondida provided a sympathetic venue for high modernism. For example, Diebenkorn accepted an invitation from Emetaz to exhibit in 1951, and he returned periodically because of Corbett and Spohn.

Their former CSFA colleague, Robert McChesney, and his wife, the writer Mary Fuller, visited in 1951 and, even though they chose to settle in Petaluma, California, McChesney maintained contact with his colleagues in New Mexico and frequently showed his work at La Galeria Escondida. The couple sojourned in Taos during the 1950s on trips to Mexico. McChesney acknowledged the role these trips through the deserts of Mexico and the Southwestern U.S. played in his work, yet it was not until the inception of the *Arena* series in 1958 that the results were clearly evident. Named for the Spanish word for sand, the *Arena* series acknowledges both the geographical and geological influence of the region. McChesney's technique joined texture and form in a clear homage to the physical character of the terrain. For example, he created *Arena No. 35* (1959; fig. 12) by introducing sand into wet enamel and then applying a thin layer of paint, which flowed through the grit. He accentuated the viscous effects by lightly sweeping the surface with a dry brush. The results suggest igneous formations in the process of change as lines, colors, and forms flow into one another and then dissipate into the larger expanse of white. McChesney's inclusion of sand infers an entire geological process in which mountains, boulders, and rocks are formed and then gradually eroded to particulate through the influence of wind and water.[38] Given the largely pale field and the allusions to erosion in *Arena No. 35*, the painting also recalls the pocks, cavities, and odd weathering of volcanic tuff formations throughout the Southwest and Mexico (fig. 13).

Geology, not as a science but as a source of aesthetic ideas, appealed to many of the Southwestern Abstract Expressionists, all of whom saw nature as unpredictable and subject to constant change. The protean environment of McChesney's *Arena No. 35* has a parallel in the subterranean apparitions of Rita Deanin Abbey's *Painting in Black and White* (1952; fig. 14). Prior to the completion of her MFA, she began a series of paintings derived from the limestone formations in Carlsbad Caverns National Park. The caves became an important tourist attraction following their election to national monument status in 1923 and national park in 1930. *Painting in Black and White* takes an anthropomorphic view of formations, which by virtue of Abbey's gestural approach, move and stretch in the darkness. Subtle tones of red and ochre add further animation to the forms, especially the circular orbs that stare like watchful eyes from the darkness. Many of the limestone formations have whimsical names such as "The Eternal Kiss"

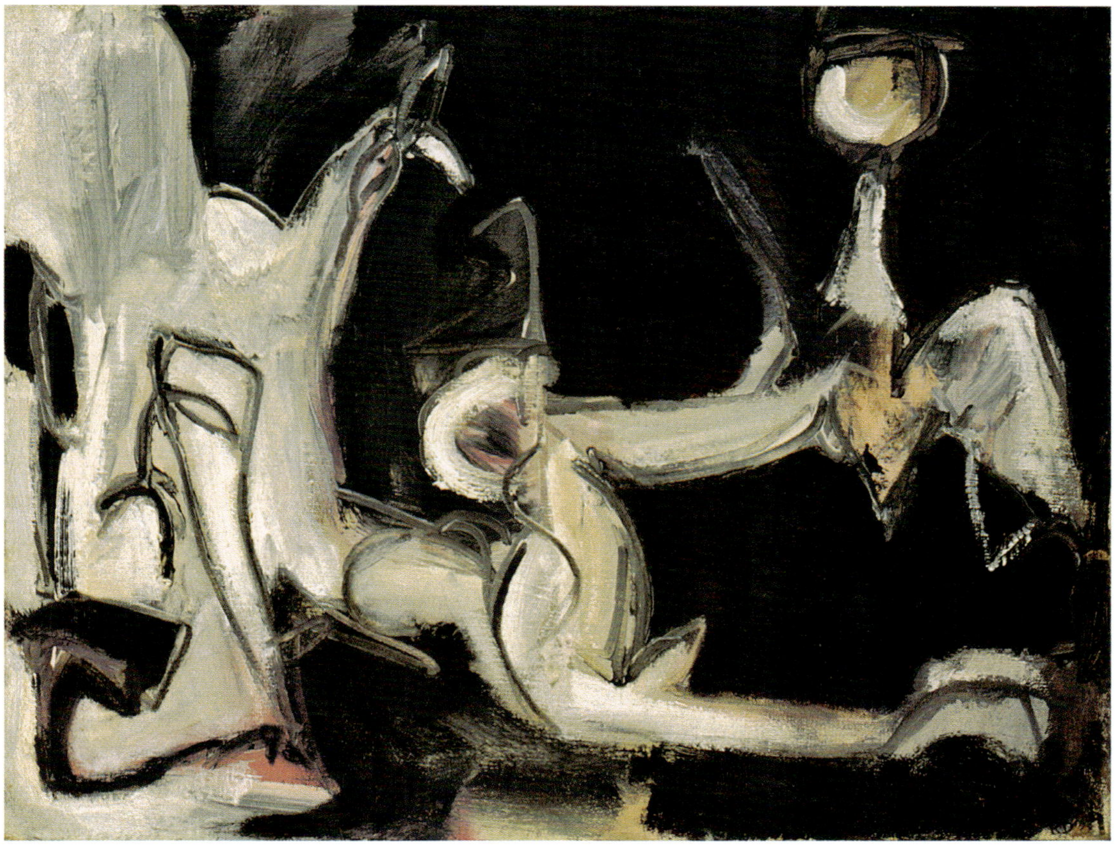

14 **Rita Deanin Abbey** (U.S., b. 1930)

Painting in Black and White, 1952
oil on canvas, 18 x 24 in.
Collection of the artist; reproduction permission courtesy of the artist.

or "Caveman," so it is unsurprising that Abbey also approached the subject metaphorically. Yet, her depiction of the formations does not suggest a fixed identification. The fluidic immediacy of Abbey's technique infers continual change as water, calcium carbonate, and other minerals sculpt a world beneath the earth's crust.[39]

Taos lured other modernists during the 1940s and '50s. Having studied at Teachers College, Columbia University in 1941–42 and then UNM in 1946, Agnes Martin attended the University of New Mexico Summer Field School of Art in Taos in 1947. She later completed her Master of Arts at Teachers College, Columbia University in 1952 and decided to settle in Taos. Befriended by the modernists there, she worked at first in a biomorphic Surrealist style inspired by the work of Arshile Gorky and William Baziotes, but she experimented as the decade progressed with formal approaches clearly influenced by the work of her colleagues.[40] Martin's *Untitled* (1954; fig. 15) compares to the work of Diebenkorn and Corbett in its spare palette of white, ochre, and black and its seemingly chaotic composition. Automatic drawing produced those crude lines that recall in character the landscapes she drew at the Summer Field School in 1947. Arrows, intersections, and radiating curves tie disparate sections of the composition together and encourage the viewer to follow specific trajectories and courses across the rough sections of white and ochre. Martin's lines seem to describe points of reference and contours akin to those found on a topographical map, which is unsurprising considering she enjoyed hiking and camping in the mountains of northern New Mexico and found ample inspiration there in the early years of her career.[41]

Martin's arrival in Taos in 1952 coincided with that of Fort Worth artist Jack Boynton, who also joined Emetaz's growing stable of artists. Boynton visited Taos regularly in the early 1950s, showing at La Galeria Escondida until 1956, but he chose to live in Texas, where he drew much of his inspiration.[42] The ostensibly infinite reach of the Southern Plains and the elemental division of sky and land absorbed Boynton in the 1950s. Like Corbett and Littler, Boynton used the horizon to infer immeasurable distances and spans, yet the horizon also acts as a compositional fulcrum by which he explored the dramatic interplay of atmosphere and terrain.[43] His *Thunderstorm* (1955; fig. 16) explores that relationship with its low horizon and the nebulous theatrics above. A cobalt field extends across the center of the composition, breaking unevenly to reveal a dark space above. Near the emphatic horizon below, a frenetic scribble of white, suggesting lightning, illuminates the field and streaks the ground plane. Boynton's inspiration was likely the massive cumulonimbus clouds that build over the plains in spring and fall, resulting in dramatic and sometimes destructive storms. Frequently, those clouds and storms loom over the horizon and seem nearby through a curious effect of scale and perception, even though the meteorological event may be miles away. Boynton employs this ambiguity in *Thunderstorm*, leaving the viewer uncertain as to whether the event is near or far. Art historian Douglas MacAgy, who had overseen the flowering of the CSFA in the late 1940s and later assumed the directorship of the Dallas Museum of Contemporary Art in 1959, recognized in *Thunderstorm* and later works "an interplay of mass and space on a grand scale. There is no middle ground. It is an odd ambivalence: in effect the far and the near are indivisible." Boynton's Southwestern space compares to that of Georgia O'Keeffe's "the faraway nearby," or that seeming collapse of the distant and the proximate.[44] *Thunderstorm*, like so many of the works of his New Mexican and Texan colleagues, addresses that conflation of the macro and the micro.

16 James Wesley "Jack" Boynton (U.S., 1928–2010)

Thunderstorm 1955
oil on canvas, 34 x 48 in.
The Museum of Fine Arts, Houston, 31st Annual Houston Artists Exhibition, museum purchase prize, 1955; reproduction permission courtesy of the MFA, Houston, and Sharon Boyrton.

15 **Agnes Martin** (U.S.,1912–2004)

Untitled, 1954
oil on board, 36 1/8 x 47 3/4 in.
University of New Mexico Art Museum, Albuquerque, New Mexico; anonymous gift in honor of Vernon Nikkel.
© 2014 Estate of Agnes Martin/Artists Rights Society (ARS), New York.

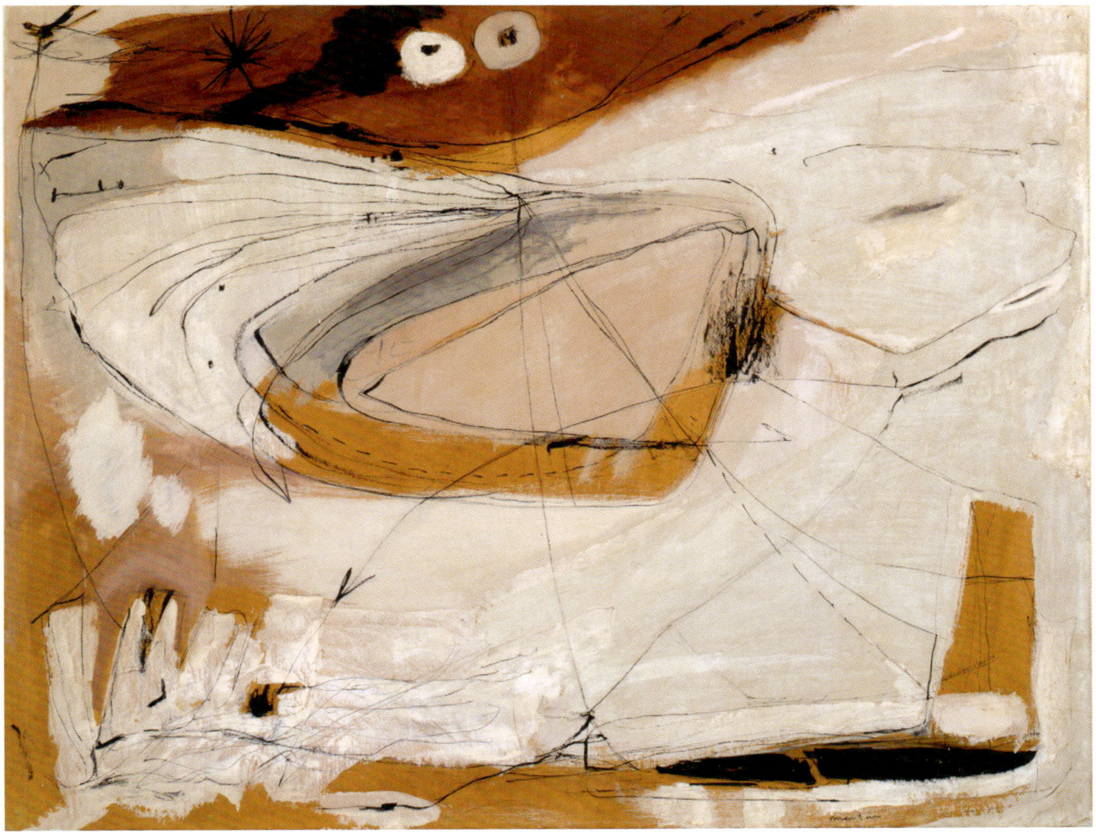

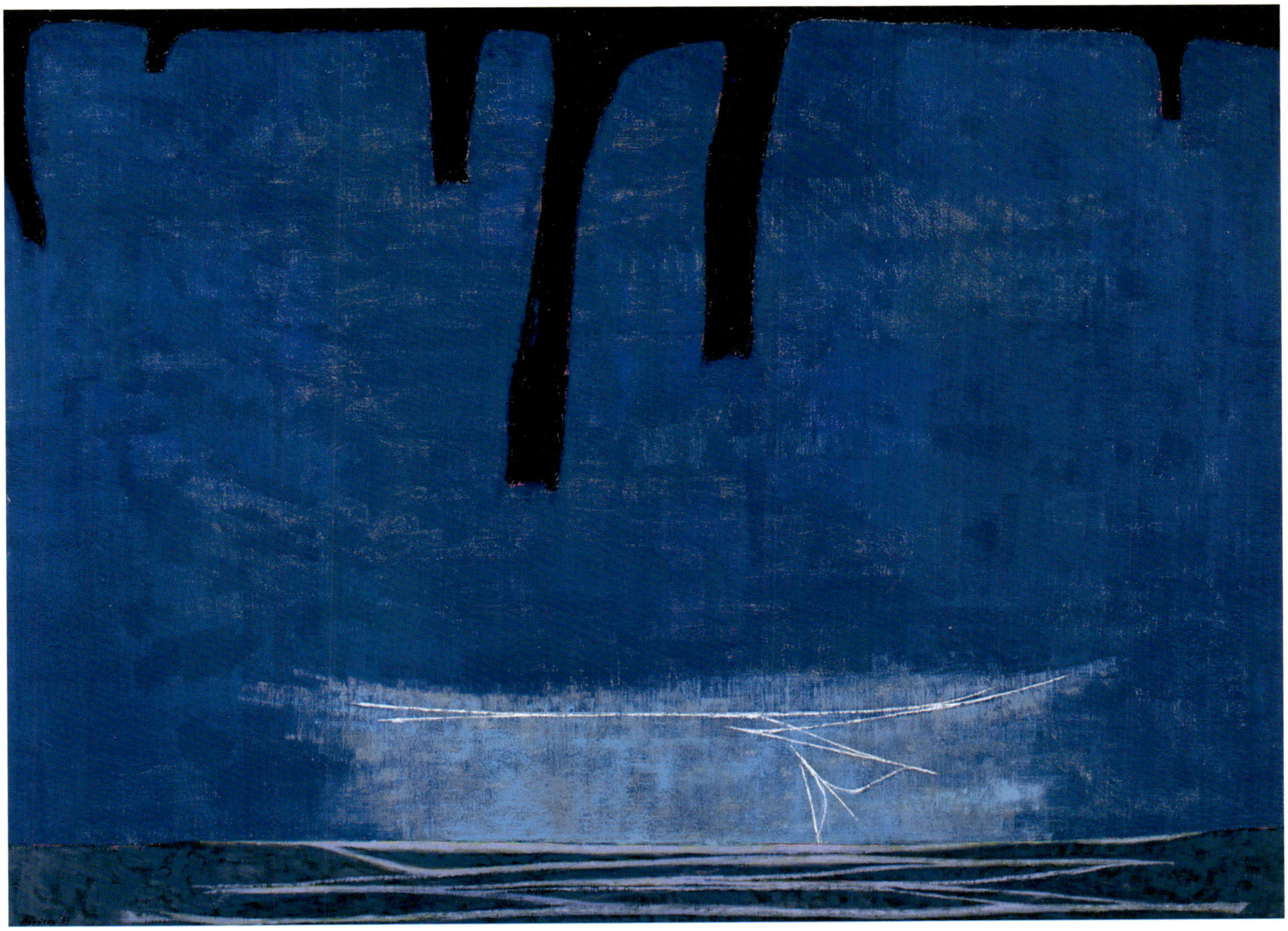

17 **Charles Truett Williams** (U.S., 1918–1966)

Lava, ca. 1951
volcanic stone, 25 x 16 x 11 in.
The Modern Art Museum of Fort Worth, Museum Purchase; reproduction permission courtesy of Karl B. Williams.

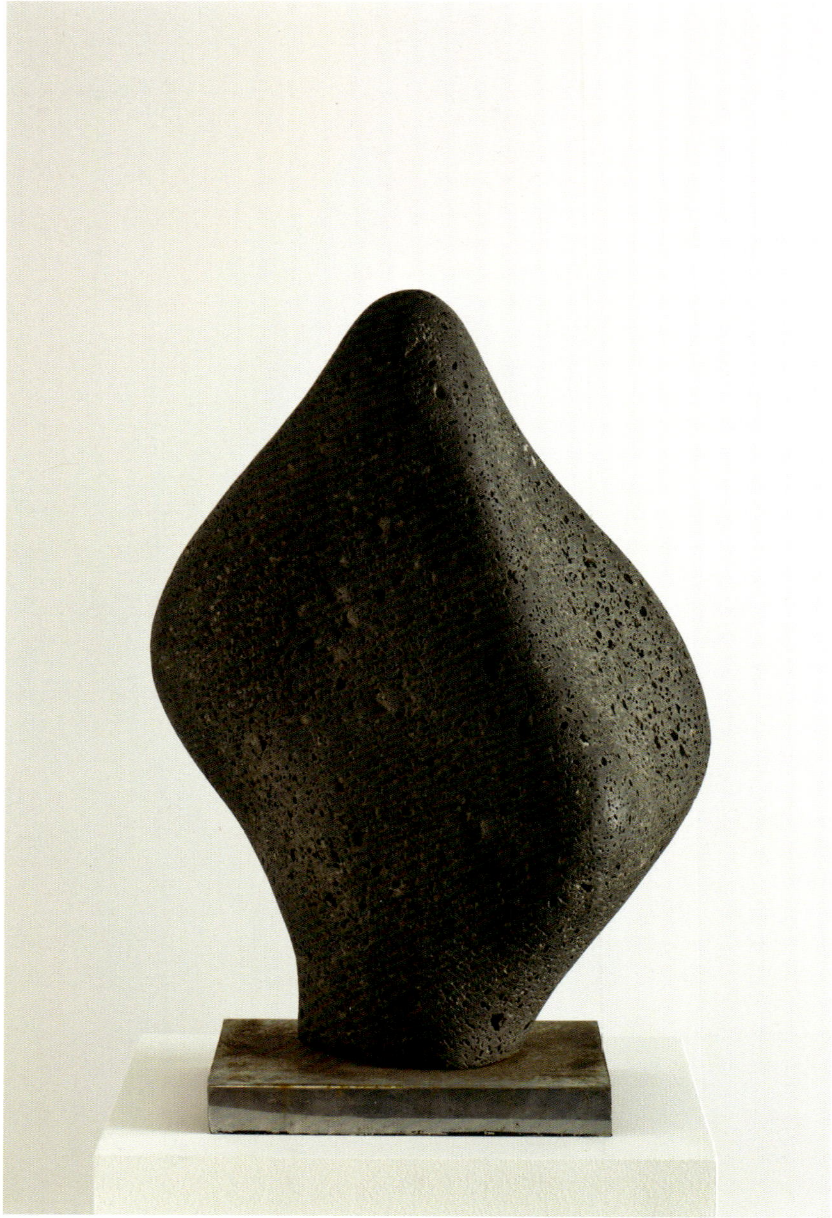

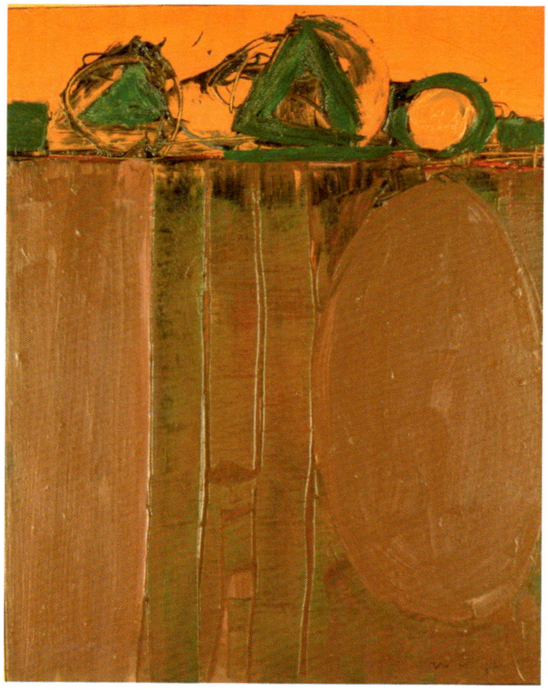

18 **Emerson Woelffer** (U.S., 1914–2003)

The Hatch, 1956
oil on canvas, 21 x 18 in.
The Colorado Springs Fine Arts Center; Artwork Courtesy of the Otis College of Art and Design Emerson Woelffer Collection.

Boynton's association with the Taos colony provided an essential link between modernists groups in New Mexico and Texas. Boynton's colleague in Fort Worth, the sculptor Charles Truett Williams, also visited Taos regularly in the early 1950s, and Boynton attempted to secure a showing for him at La Galeria Escondida, although it is unclear whether Emetaz ever chose to represent his work.[45] Regardless, Williams translated the salient qualities of the Southwest in his sculpture *Lava* (ca. 1951, fig. 17), which he sculpted from a piece of the scattered volcanic debris he discovered outside Taos. His medium speaks to the tumultuous geological history of the area more literally than the work of either Mandelman or McChesney, and his biomorphic approach to the porous stone emphasizes its molten origins in the undulation and curvature of the surface. *Lava* suggests a viscous body undergoing formation, shaped by galvanic forces.

Where East and West Converge: Colorado

Williams, and to a greater degree Boynton, helped to establish important ties between modernists in Fort Worth and Taos in the early 1950s but, at the same time, Taos modernists also forged connections to those in Colorado. That relationship began in 1951 when Mitchell Wilder, the director of the Colorado Springs Fine Arts Center, announced the premature expiration of the Taos art colony in an article for *Atlantic Monthly*. Offended by the allegation, the modernists asked Wilder for an exhibition to prove the vitality of the colony. The resulting exhibition, *Taos Painting: Yesterday and Today*, opened in March 1952 and included a sampling of work from the older and younger generations, although it favored younger artists. The show's curator, Fred S. Bartlett, recognized "a flavor of locality" in their work, even though he admitted their styles clearly demonstrated awareness of national and international trends.[46]

Taos Painting was likely the event that introduced the colony artists to Emerson Woelffer, who had joined the faculty of the Fine Arts Center in 1950 at the invitation of Wilder. Woelffer had studied at the School of the Art Institute of Chicago in the 1930s and then spent the years between 1942–49 teaching at the Institute of Design in Chicago, where he had been hired by László Moholy-Nagy. By the time Woelffer relocated to Colorado Springs, he was already working with automatism and archetypal imagery, filling his canvases with cryptic marks and mysterious personages. He remained in Colorado Springs until 1956 and, towards the end of his tenure, he began a series of paintings defined by a high horizon and littered with ideographs. *The Hatch* (1956; fig. 18), for example, is dominated by a monolithic expanse of rust, tinged with warm and cool colors, and structured by a series of vertical bands and a large ovoid, which may be interpreted as the hatch of the title. That expanse terminates in an emphatic horizon above which Emerson has sketched several gestural circles and triangles against a field of radiant orange. The forms and colors of the painting are understandably analogous to the mountains, foliage, and chromatic sky of Colorado Springs, and Woelffer and his wife Diana lived outside the city in a renovated shanty built out from a cave in the Austin Bluffs. *The Hatch* makes reference in both title and imagery to the terrestrial surface and the subterranean, yet he also positions both the landscape and the painting as a gateway to an unspecified, enigmatic experience. *The Hatch* encourages the viewer to plumb the depths of the arcane signs to find profound emotional, psychological, and spiritual significance.

Woelffer's sympathy to Abstract Expressionism helped him establish camaraderie with the modernists in Taos, and he communicated regularly with Corbett, Spohn, Martin, Mandelman, and Ribak.[47] That relationship provided additional connections between the Southwest and the New York School as Woelffer invited both Motherwell and Mark Rothko to Colorado Springs. Motherwell accepted an invitation to teach in spring 1954 but produced no work in response to the Colorado environment during that appointment. He was pleasantly surprised, noting that Woelffer "already had created a fine body of Abstract Expressionist work by the time I first encountered him in 1954." Critical discourse on Abstract Expressionism was still limited in the early 1950s, Motherwell opined, and the style was often subject to "violent rejection" in most artistic circles throughout the country, making Woelffer's presence in Colorado

Springs remarkable.[48] The two became lifelong friends, and Motherwell was vocal regarding the import of Woelffer's work. It is unclear whether the Taos modernists had the opportunity to meet Motherwell, but Rothko did visit Santa Fe and probably Taos, since he already knew Corbett and Spohn from his days as a guest instructor at the CSFA between 1947–49.[49]

Woelffer's influence in Colorado Springs attracted a number of aspiring artists. Kenneth Goehring arrived from Detroit in 1945 and studied at the Fine Arts Center from 1948 to 1950, prior to Woelffer's appointment, but he readily acknowledged Woelffer's impact.[50] Goehring populated his *Landscape #1* (1958; fig. 19) with superimposed ideographs likely derived from figures, mountains, and trees. An undulating horizon bisects the composition and an enlarged sun looms over the confusion of forms below. That opposition between earth and sky, also present in Woelffer's *The Hatch*, became a consistent theme among many artists in the Southwest, and also appeared in the work of Janet Lippincott.

Born in New York, Lippincott used the G.I. Bill to enroll at Emil Bisttram's Taos School of Art in 1949, but dissatisfaction with his instruction led her to the Fine Arts Center in the early 1950s. Woelffer encouraged her to experiment with new techniques, including using large brushes and spreading her canvas on the floor.[51] By the time Lippincott settled in Santa Fe in 1957, she was working in an Abstract Expressionist style. She gravitated to the modernist colony in Taos and formed close friendships with Spohn, Mandelman, and Ribak. The paintings she produced during this time bear the influence of Woelffer, especially her *Southwest Landscape* (ca. 1962; fig. 20). Similar to *The Hatch*, Lippincott's *Southwest Landscape* employs a high horizon and a palette reminiscent of the region. She crafted the angular forms with wide brushstrokes and a gestural immediacy. The contrast of dark masses at center and yellow, green, and orange projections at the periphery of the composition suggests the juxtaposition of ravines and rock formations.

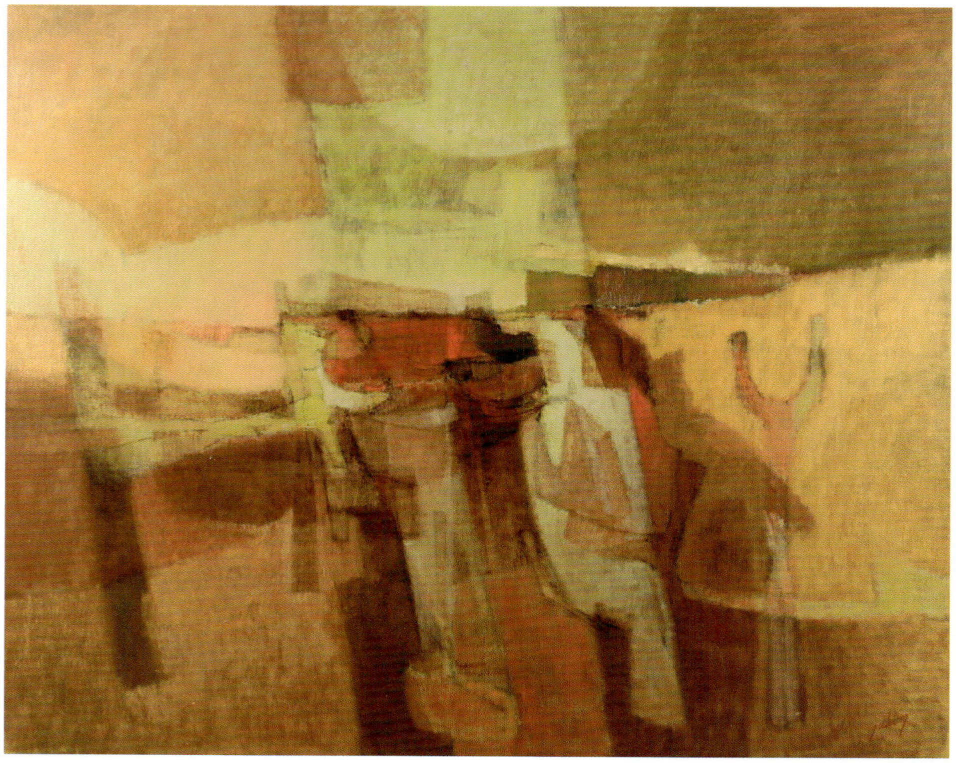

19 **Kenneth Goehring** (U.S., 1919–2007)

Landscape #1, 1958
oil on canvas, 38 x 48 in.
The Colorado Springs Fine Arts Center

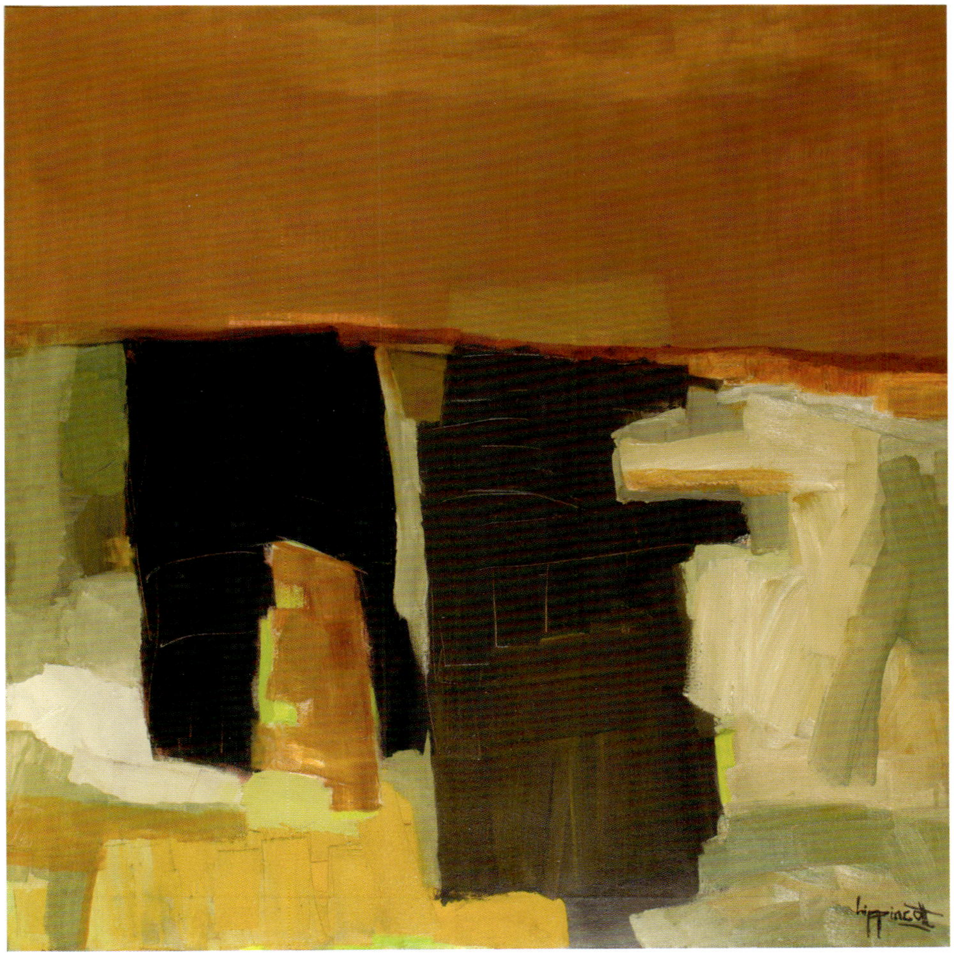

20 **Janet Lippincott** (U.S., 1918–2007)

Southwest Landscape, 1962
oil on canvas, 60 x 60 in.
Fred Jones Jr. Museum of Art, the University of Oklahoma, Norman, Oklahoma; reproduction permission courtesy of the Karan Ruhlen Gallery.

Woelffer's brief tenure at the Fine Arts Center helped strengthen ties to both Taos and New York City, while another modernist in Colorado Springs, Charles Bunnell, fostered additional connections to Amarillo, Texas. Bunnell had studied with Ernest Lawson and Boardman Robinson at the Broadmoor Art Academy and worked representationally until the early 1950s, but his interest in the transcendental aspects of world religions and his friendships with Jackson Pollock and Hans Hofmann encouraged his transition to non-objectivity. Finding inspiration in the snow-capped peaks of the Rocky Mountains, Bunnell applied paint in textural, vaguely geometric passages suggestive of the mountainous terrain near Colorado Springs.[52] His 1955 untitled painting (fig. 21) evokes a rugged space through the use of broken lines of black, blue, and red impasto and angular pinnacles of white and gray against a luminous field of yellow. Though the painting is relatively small in size, the loose arrangement of forms infers a scale and breadth larger than the confines of the image. Bunnell's dealer, fellow artist Dord Fitz, once owned the painting and observed that the modest dimensions of such works did not undermine their metaphorical measure: "The scale is such that a painting sixteen inches by twenty inches may seem galactic in size."[53] Fitz used cosmic language as a nod to Bunnell's transcendental aspirations, which are given form in the lines and angles that direct the eye upward to some heavenly space. A meditative silence pervaded Bunnell's paintings, Fitz argued, and contemplation of the unspoken significance of the painting promised spiritual revelations: "Mr. Bunnell is speaking of the area of silence that lies between the component parts of positivity. There in the secret darkness man will find God."[54]

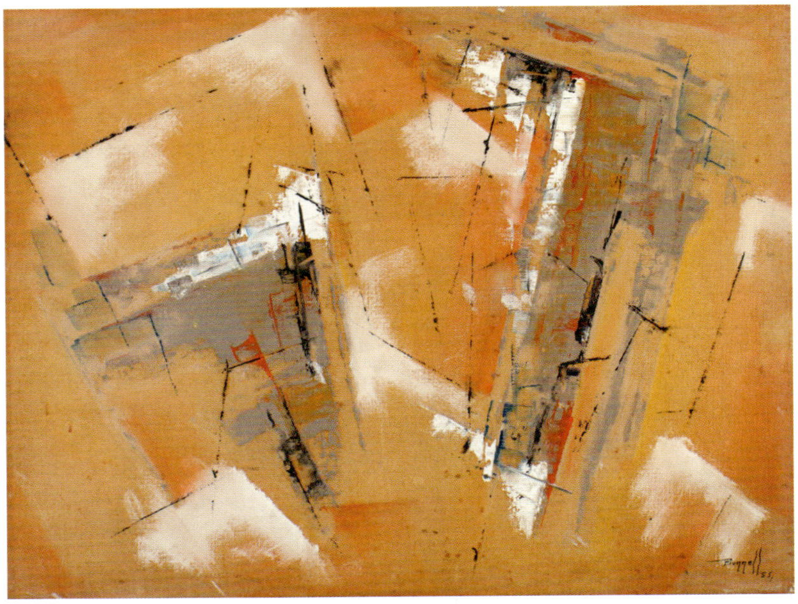

21 **Charles Ragland Bunnell** (U.S., 1897–1968)

Untitled, 1955
oil on board, 16 x 20 in.
Fred Jones Jr. Museum of Art, the University of Oklahoma, Norman, Oklahoma; gift of Jonathan and Talitha Nichols.

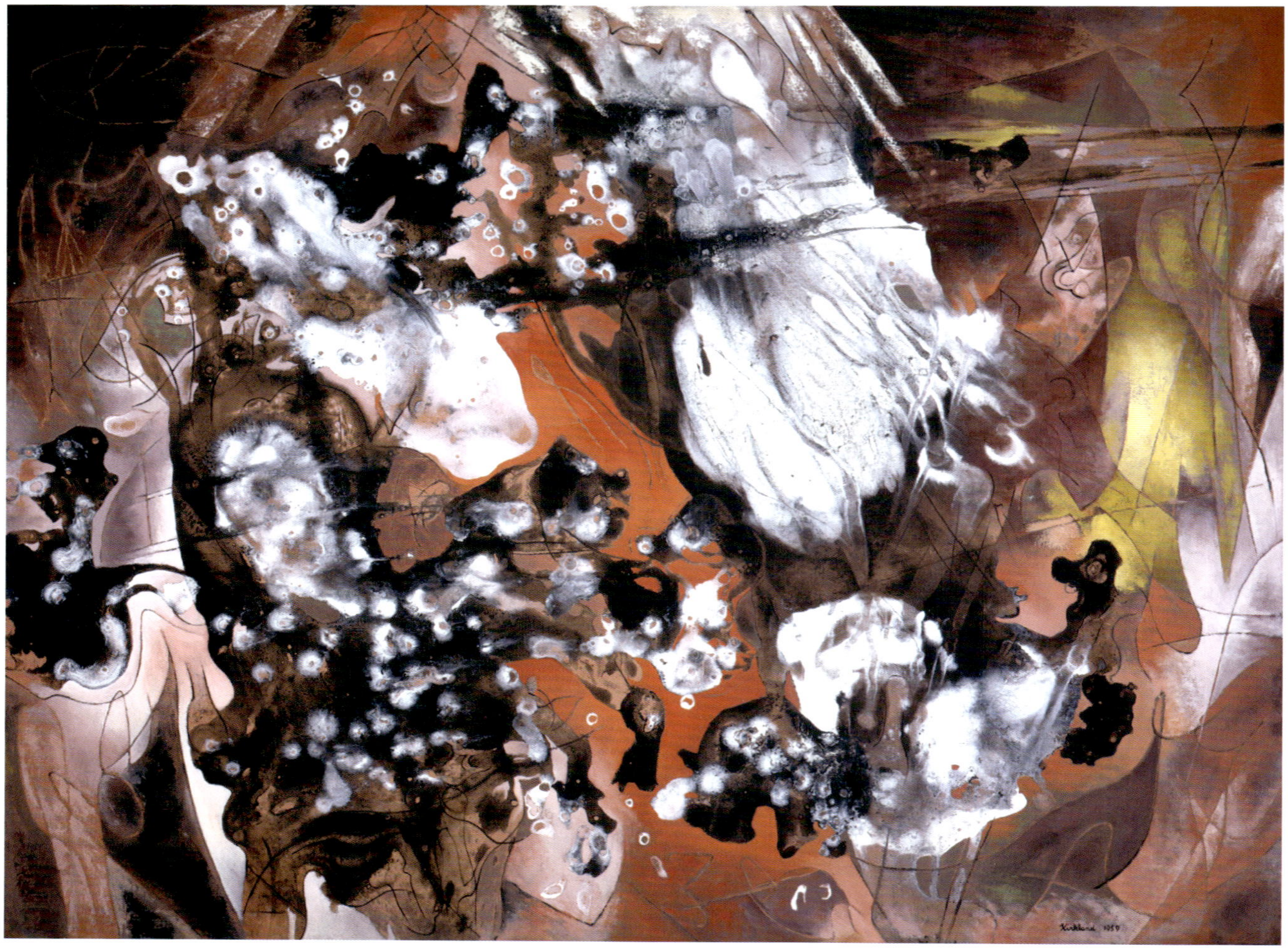

22 **Vance Kirkland** (U.S., 1904–1981)

Nebula Near Mars, 1959
oil and water on linen, 44 x 60 in.
Collection Kirkland Museum of Fine and Decorative Art, Denver; reproduction permission courtesy of the Kirkland.

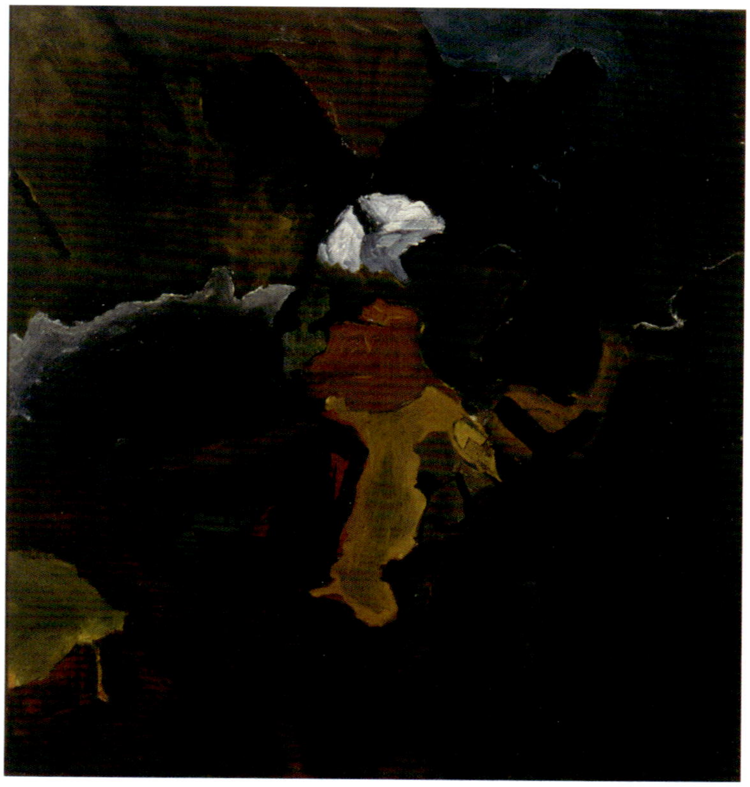

23 **Charles Strong** (U.S., 1918–1999)

Rocky Mountain Quartet #1, 1960
oil on canvas, 74 1/2 x 69 1/4 in.
Collection of Lyn Bleiler-Strong; reproduction permission courtesy of Lyn Bleiler-Strong.

Bunnell was hardly alone in finding spiritual awareness in the Rockies. Other modernists to the north also used the mountains as both motifs and vehicles for emotional and spiritual exploration and, like Bunnell and Woelffer, developed relationships with artists across the region. Denverite Vance Kirkland was less interested in the mountains themselves than the perspective of the night sky they offered him. Wary of the picturesque Colorado landscape that "had already destroyed so many artists," Kirkland began a series of large, nebulae paintings inspired by celestial phenomena: "I had reached a point when I did not want to spend any more of my time looking at nature. I had to rise above it and beyond it. I took myself up and away from the landscape because I thought at the time, at least the sky is very clear and I can paint farther away."[55] Kirkland envisioned cataclysmic explosions across immense distances drawn loosely from his observations of the night sky. His *Nebula Near Mars* (1959; fig. 22) is an imagined epic of viscous forms and amorphous bodies radiant with energy. He had less interest in astronomical realities than in the slow course of cosmic evolution or "all the things that have been happening in space over 25 billion years."[56] Using a resist technique that involved oil paint, water, and denatured alcohol, Kirkland combined the results of largely unpredictable chemical reactions with lyrical lines and subtle color gradations to create a volatile image that vacillates between the accidental and the deliberate.[57] Glass and paper pressed against the wet surface helped Kirkland create some of the patterns in a method akin to that of Ernst's decalcomania paintings.

Kirkland had made his reputation in the 1940s with surrealist and magic realist imagery of driftwood, rocks, and other detritus from the landscape, and he had been included in important exhibitions such as the Art Institute of Chicago's 1947 show *Abstract and Surrealist American Art*. The strength of his surrealist work led to representation at New York's prestigious Knoedler & Co. in 1946. Kirkland visited New York City regularly thereafter, which eventually exposed him to Abstract Expressionism and likely led to his embrace of non-objectivity in 1951.

Whereas Kirkland generally took his cue from New York, artist Charles Strong looked to San Francisco. Strong studied briefly at the Coronado School of Art in San Diego and Colorado State College of Education in Greeley before abandoning his training for work at a molybdenum mine in Climax, Colorado. A mining accident in 1959 dissuaded him from the profession, and that fall he enrolled at the CSFA, where the legacy of Clyfford Still persisted. Strong met Still the following summer, during Still's summer session at the University of Colorado. Still's textural surfaces and colossal canvases influenced the direction Strong's work would take for much of the 1960s and clearly inspired the Strong's series of four paintings, the *Rocky Mountain Quartet* (fig. 23). Painted upon his return to San Francisco in 1960–61, the series of four paintings derived from the mountainous landscape near Strong's home in Greeley. Blacks and grays, enlivened by glowing patches of red, orange, and yellow, dominate much of the series as references not only to the metamorphic granite of the Rockies and the local flora, but also as allusions to the tectonic forces that have long since shaped the Continental Divide. Although Strong's painterly stroke and coarse surface owe a debt to Still, the turbulent, dynamic compositions are also an homage to Albert Pinkham Ryder. Strong recalled a visit to the National Collection of Fine Arts (now the Smithsonian American Art Museum), where he saw multiple examples of Ryder's work: "I was impressed by the power of them, being small paintings and having extraordinary sense of scale, and this dense kind of painted surface where he worked on them over and over again."[58] Ryder's layered surfaces and his ability to suggest capacious space in a relatively small painting through compositional effects clearly contributed to the aesthetic Strong developed in the *Rocky Mountain Quartet*.

Although Strong had little connection to either Woelffer or Taos artists like Corbett and Mandelman, the *Rocky Mountain Quartet* demonstrates clear affinities to their respective treatments of the Southwestern landscape in color and form. Strong's study at the CSFA was coincident with the arrival of Boynton, who taught between 1960–62 at the CSFA (renamed the San Francisco Art Institute in 1961). It is unclear how much interaction Boynton and Strong might have had, but such intersections help to illustrate the connections modernists in the Southwest developed during the 1950s and '60s.

Where East and West Converge: Dord Fitz and Elaine de Kooning

Boynton and other Texans, like their counterparts in Colorado and New Mexico, were just as informed about developments on the coasts. Artists in Amarillo, Dallas and Fort Worth, and Houston were in contact with artists, critics, and curators in both New York and San Francisco, and Boynton, Culwell, and Trotter had already received national attention through exhibitions and publications. Texan artists also had a great deal of influence within the region and established dialogue with others in Colorado, New Mexico, and Oklahoma.

Amarillo artist and dealer Dord Fitz maintained a close affiliation with artists in the Southwest, as well as those in the New York School. Bunnell and Boynton showed frequently at the Dord Fitz Gallery and, in 1957, Fitz planned an exhibition of New Mexican modernists from Albuquerque, Santa Fe, and Taos, but it is unclear which artists he visited on his tour of the state.[59] That same year, Fitz curated the Tri-State Fair Art Exhibition, which included artists from New Mexico, Oklahoma, and Texas.

Fitz's promotion of mid-century modernists was not limited to the Southwest and, in 1956, he contacted members of the New York School about the possibility of showing their work. Through his acquaintance with Jeanne Reynal, who had attended a showing of Fitz and his students at the Burr Galleries in New York City, Fitz was encouraged to approach Milton Resnick but did so unannounced. Resnick's initial consternation at the uninvited guest eventually gave way to admiration, and Fitz came to know many of the New York School, including the de Koonings, Rothko, Franz Kline, Louise Nevelson, and others. This exposure led Fitz, who had already been working abstractly, to experiment with Action painting. *The Way* (1956; fig. 24) is composed of a largely white field under which Fitz constructed a mosaic of blues and reds that sway the white cool and warm alternately, resulting in a gestural play that draws the eye to the surface while also implying atmospheric depth. A yellow stripe, which reads as both a sequence of calligraphic forms and as some sort of plasmic ribbon, extends from the left edge to the right with the implication that it continues indefinitely. The dark Charybdian mass at right seems to be in a state of flux, either broadening or collapsing. Fitz's title suggests a path, direction, or course of action with the implication that some communion with the formal elements promises a vaguely spiritual or emotional reward.

Fitz, a supporter of Jungian theory, invested the forms with archetypal significance in the belief that exploration of the mind and spirit promised some understanding of cosmic mysteries. As he once theorized: "The Life Force moves throughout the cosmos and is omnipresent. Inherent with it are infinite mind and infinite spirit. Soul is an entity that inhabits many planes of existence simultaneously, including the physical plane."[60] Given his statement, it appears that Fitz saw creation as both multidimensional and theistic, and painting provided a means of spiritual engagement. Fitz clearly felt sympathy with some elements of the New York School, since his rhetoric compares to that of Rothko and others, and his new stylistic direction bears some similarity to that of Kline and Gottlieb. The Way also demonstrates a parallel to work of Kirkland, since Fitz clearly derived some inspiration from his ruminations on the cosmos above. Just as the Rockies provided Kirkland a platform for examining the night sky, the High Plains, where the unbroken horizon gives way to the limitless sky, acted as the physical plane for Fitz's artistic and spiritual investigation of the infinite.

Fitz's contact with the New York School came to fruition with an exhibition he organized for September 1957 titled *7 Contemporary Painters*, which featured Kline, Resnick, Elaine de Kooning, Miles Forst, John Grillo, Patricia Passloff, and Joe Stefanelli. The exhibition introduced de Kooning to the Southwest, and she became a frequent guest of Fitz in ensuing years, holding workshops and painting portraits for local collectors.

De Kooning's influence in the Southwest expanded in 1958 when she accepted a position as Visiting Professor of Art at the University of New Mexico. There she met Jonson, who had retired from teaching in 1954 but continued to manage the Jonson Gallery, and a group

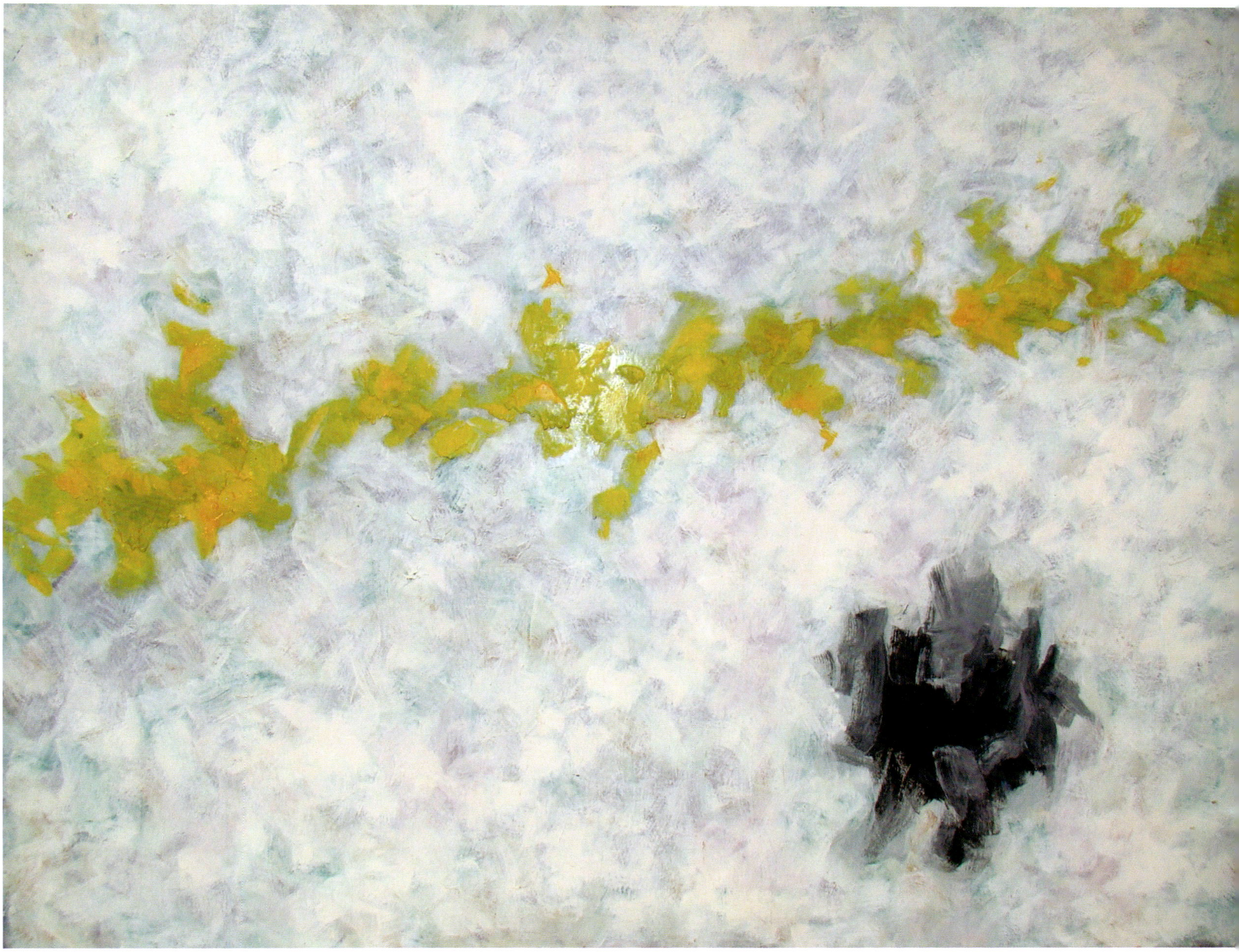

24 George Edward "Dord" Fitz (U.S., 1914–1989)

The Way, 1956
oil on Masonite, 47 1/2 x 64 in.
Collection of Jonathan and Talitha Nichols.

of students, in his orbit, who were receptive to experimentation. She also encountered the New Mexican landscape, which would have a decisive impact on her work. The shifting colors of New Mexican light prompted both an invigorated palette and a large format that allowed de Kooning to investigate her empathetic response to the environment. As she explained, "When I went West, the color experience of New Mexico convinced me that 'feeling' was the thing. Nowadays, when an artist discovers 'the sky,' it's like a bride who has never done any housework raving about her first vacuum cleaner. It's just not news. However, there were the skies and the twilights and they were inescapable and tremendous."[61]

That discovery of the sky informed the chromatic diversity of *Albuquerque* (1960; fig. 1) which includes all primary and secondary colors as well as countless variations. She used slashing, active brushwork, most of which directs the eye upward, save for a largely horizontal thrust at right. Even the drips and scrapes direct the viewer's eye to the sky, as though de Kooning acknowledged her inspiration. Nevertheless, the compositional energy in *Albuquerque* is cacophonous resulting from de Kooning's shifting perception of the city and surrounding environment. As she explained, "Color and space are actors, changing role from hour to hour, constantly in flux. Light resounds and reverberates over the city, drastically magnifies and diminishes the buildings, brings the surfaces of the mountains aggressively close or thrusts them off to legendary distances."[62] Like Ansel Adams, she experienced a conflation of the macro and micro in *Albuquerque*, which she translated using abrupt juxtapositions of brushstroke and color.

During de Kooning's year in Albuquerque, she took an active interest in many of the students there. She argued that modernist painting in New Mexico possessed elements from both the east and west yet remained singular: "Here is a strongly introspective art, stubbornly original and personal, yet not eccentric. Revealing an awareness of East- and West-Coast painting, the work of New Mexican artists reflects neither. None of the slashing brushstrokes and drips of the former, none of the brilliant colors of the latter."[63] The Albuquerque artists were neither a school nor a colony, she posited, although Jonson had assumed a role similar to that of Hans Hofmann and the New York School.

De Kooning's support for the New Mexicans eventually resulted in an exhibition she helped to organize at the Great Jones Gallery in New York City in February 1960.[64] It included Jonson and a number of students, including William Vaughn Howard and William Conger, both of whom had benefited from de Kooning's influence. Howard produced colorful, gestural works such as his 1960 untitled painting (fig. 25). Similar in many respects to Willem de Kooning's paintings from the 1950s, like *Gotham News* (1955; Albright-Knox Art Gallery, Buffalo, N. Y.), Howard's painting was equally influenced by the legacy of Diebenkorn, whose Albuquerque work could still be viewed at the Jonson Gallery. The deserts of New Mexico must have had some influence on Howard, who had spent much of his early days as a student in 1948 hiking and painting with Agnes Martin.[65]

Conger came to UNM in 1957 after a year at the School of the Art Institute of Chicago, where he had ample opportunity to study Abstract Expressionism in the museum's collection. Upon arriving in New Mexico, he, too, found inspiration not only in the gestural works of de Kooning and Diebenkorn, but also in the desert landscape. As Conger later recalled: "The vastness of the Southwest landscape made a lasting impression on me. Nature seemed to heave and move on a huge scale. Nothing was hidden. Wherever you looked, you saw new and ancient nature side by side. A meditative or awed response seemed to be the only way to comprehend the bigness, the variety, the daunting presence of the landscape. It encouraged a broad way of painting; it mocked little gestures, small shapes, weak colors. New Mexico was not a place for purely intellectualized art. Instead, it inspired a romantic, transcendent abstraction imbued with fear."[66]

Like so many other artists, Conger saw the Southwestern desert as a bewildering disjunction of limitless expanse and endless detail. An awareness of geological time and the variability of the landscape only accentuated his sublime response. Conger looked to the techniques of Abstract Expressionism as the only means of translating his transcendent experience of New Mexico. Action painting, with its malleability and spontaneity, allowed Conger to explore both the incongruities and unpredictability he perceived in the New Mexican landscape, using a stylistic approach he later characterized as "the polarity of chaos and order."[67] His *Action Painting* (1958; fig. 26) alternates between calm passages of relatively undifferentiated color and more agitated sections of color contrasts and vigorous brushwork. To achieve "a glowing surface" akin to the brilliant light and atmosphere of the Southwest, Conger experimented with Ponsol Colors, which allowed for greater translucency and staining.[68]

De Kooning admired Conger's work and described him as "a real 'comer'" to Fitz, who was apparently seeking new talent in New Mexico.[69] It is unclear whether Fitz exhibited the work of Conger or any of the other New Mexicans, but the connections de Kooning fostered between Fitz and the New Mexicans helped to create a sense of community among modernists across the Southwest. Fitz actively promoted the broadening circle of modernists with whom he was in contact through exhibitions and educational programming. And he organized an exhibition in 1958 of Boynton, Bunnell, de Kooning, and Dallas sculptor Heri Bert Bartscht that included a panel discussion on modern art.[70]

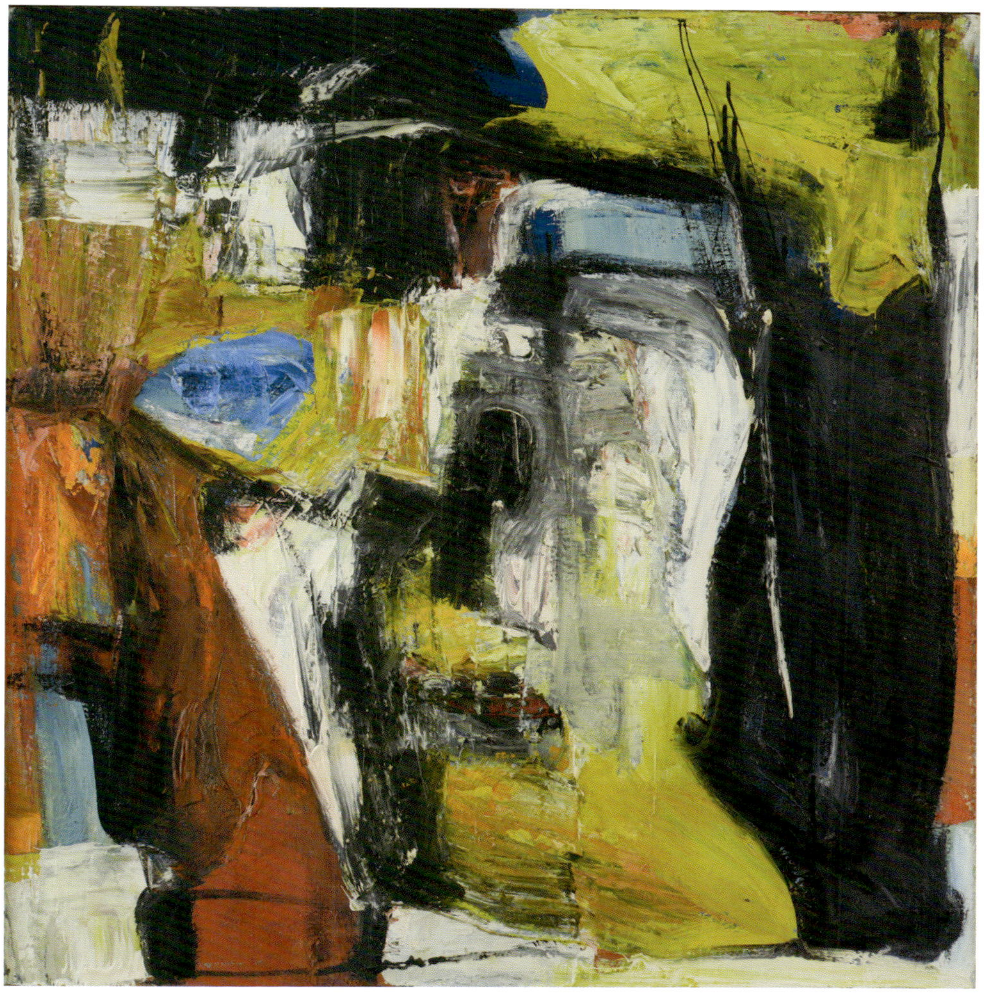

25 **William Vaughn Howard** (U.S., 1921–1986)

Untitled, 1960
oil on canvas, 35 x 36 in.
Bequest of Raymond Jonson, The Raymond Jonson Collection, University of New Mexico Art Museum, Albuquerque 82.211.1147.

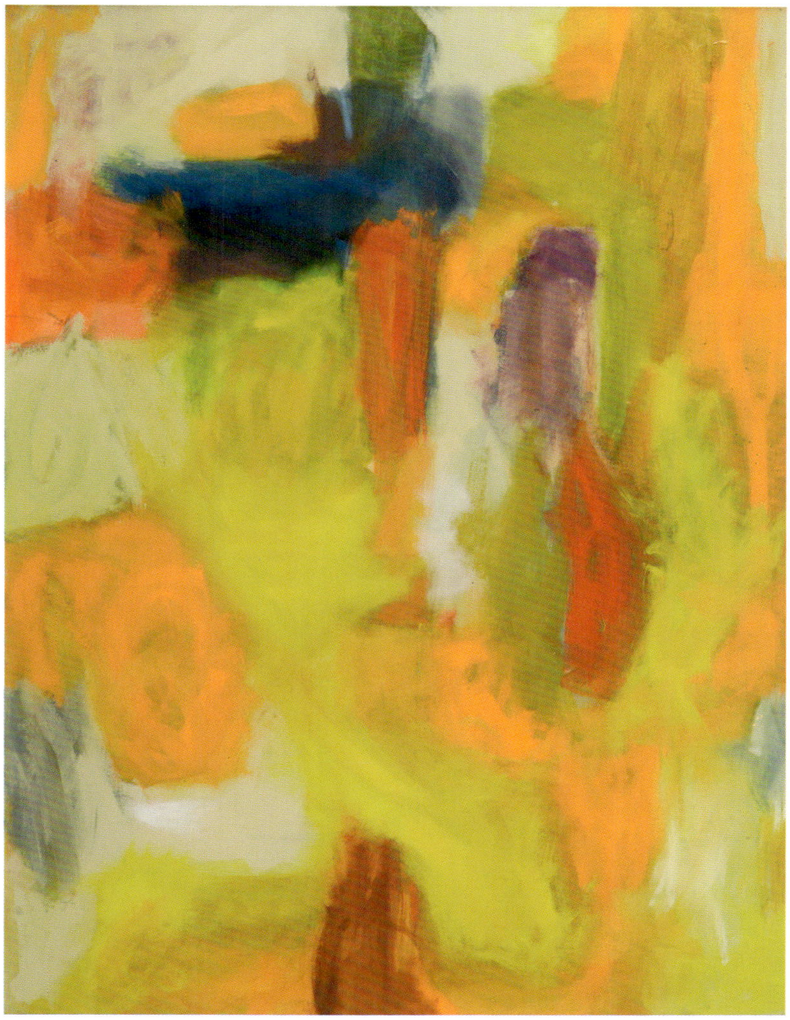

26 **William Conger** (U.S., b. 1937)

Action Painting, 1958
oil on canvas, 65 x 85 in.
Bequest of Raymond Jonson, The Raymond Jonson Collection, University of New Mexico Art Museum, Albuquerque 82.211.1147; reproduction permission courtesy of the artist.

Where East and West Converge: Texas and Oklahoma

Jack Boynton also had connections to modernists in Dallas and Fort Worth, Taos, and eventually San Francisco and Houston. Boynton began his career in Fort Worth and received his MFA in 1955 from Texas Christian University, where he had been a protégé of McKie Trotter. Trotter taught initially at Texas Wesleyan College in 1948 before leaving for TCU in 1953. Along with Charles Williams, he became one of the leading practitioners of modernism in the region in the 1950s, and his formal interpretation of the Southwestern landscape clearly influenced Boynton. Much of Trotter's work at mid-century relied on an almost architectural arrangement of tectonic masses that suggested a sweep of primordial terrain. Jerry Bywaters saw his paintings as "placeless" yet somewhat evocative of the "dry and vast spaces" of the plains outside Fort Worth.[71] Trotter frequently used the term "earthscape" in titling these works, partly as an attempt to avoid specific associations with place and also to imply an indefinite span. In his *Earthscape with Sea* (1963–64; fig. 27), irregular, ruddy masses, separated by tributaries of blue and green, emulate the platting of land, as though the painting depicts an aerial view of terrain, although a great swath of red prevents a purely cartographic reading. A blue stripe at the upper left clearly references the sea of Trotter's title. Both the palette and the implication of expansive space in *Earthscape with Sea* demonstrate parallels to the work of Boynton and others working in the Southwest during this time period.

27 **McKie Trotter** (U.S., 1918–1999)
Earthscape with Sea, 1963–64
oil on canvas, 46 x 50 in.
William Reaves Fine Art, Houston.

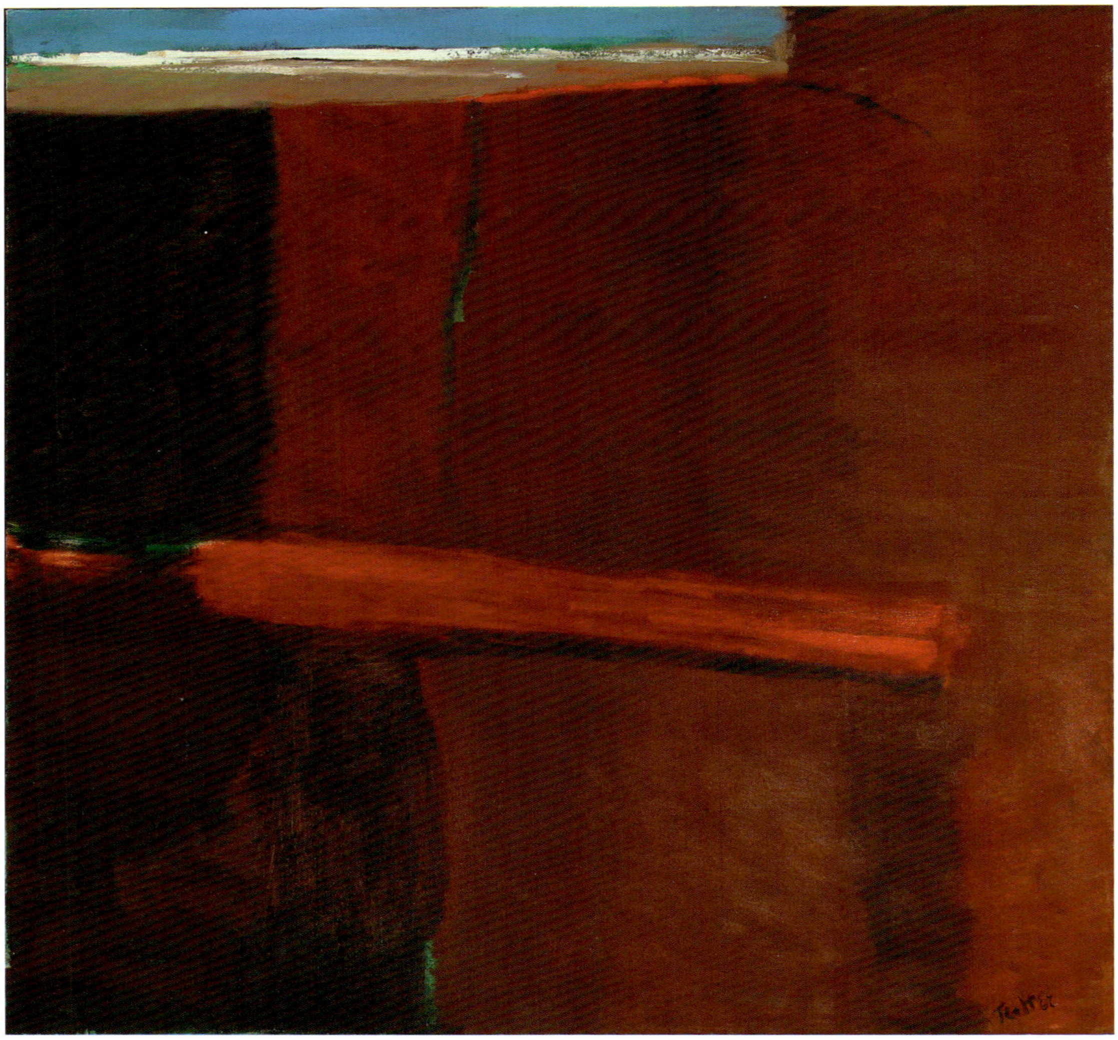

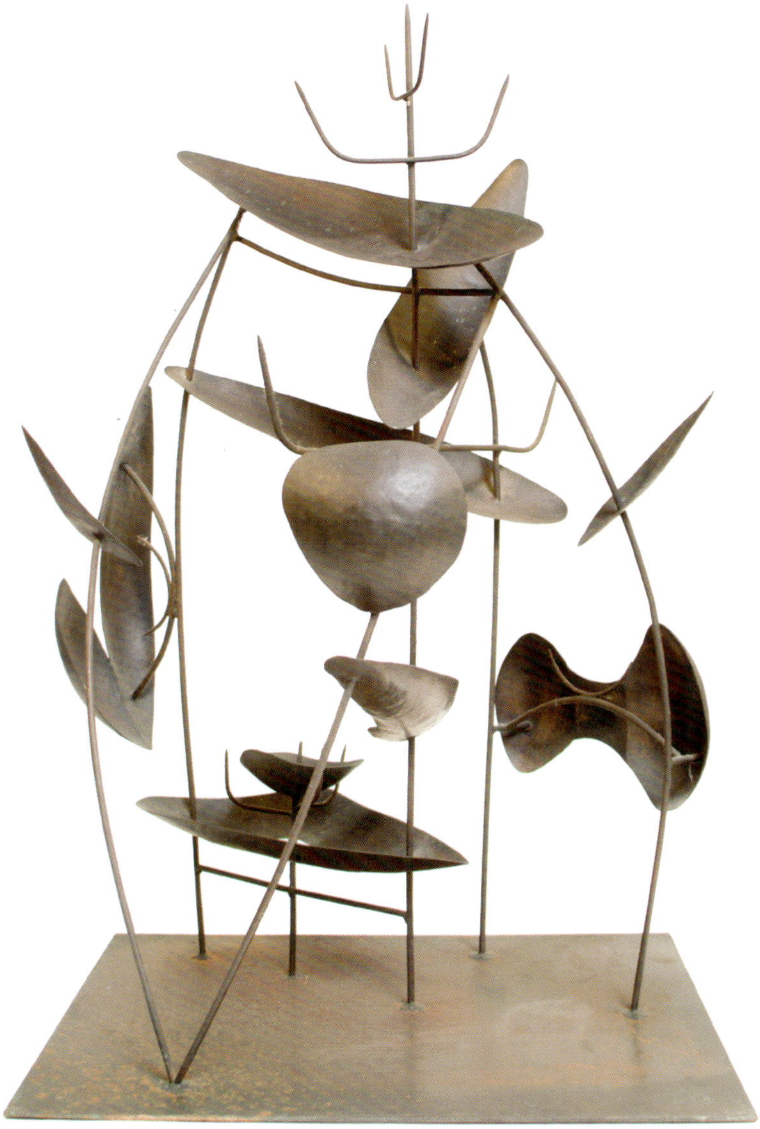

28 **Charles Truett Williams** (U.S., 1918–1966)

Maquette for the Weiner Fountain, 1955
bronze and sheet metal, 13 x 18 x 27 1/2 in.
Collection of Karl Williams; reproduction permission courtesy of Karl B. Williams.

Charles Williams was another vocal proponent for modernism in the Fort Worth area, and his studio often functioned as a gathering point for many of the local artists, including Boynton, as well as those outside Dallas–Fort Worth such as Oklahoma sculptor Duayne Hatchett. The biomorphic style of Williams's earlier pieces such as *Lava* persisted throughout the 1950s, although by the end of the decade he became increasingly interested in brazing, welding, and eventually assemblage as both a technical and formal approach. Just as the environment of northern New Mexico shaped *Lava*, the landscape continued to shape Williams's work. He often installed outdoor sculpture for important collectors in the area, such as Stanley Marcus, Raymond and Patsy Nasher, and Ted and Lucille Weiner, and their collections, which contained many of the foremost modern sculptors, exerted a powerful influence on Williams.[72] The Weiners also became patrons of Williams's work. In 1954, he completed a fountain for their gardens (fig. 28) constructed of a skeleton of bronze rods supporting a variety of biomorphic bronze sheets. Set atop a pool of water, the work drew allusions to both aquatic flora and the surrounding plants and trees of the gardens. Sunlight reflecting off the concave surfaces would have created a dialogue between the work and the sky above. Although the *Weiner Fountain* could not easily infer the vast spaces of the plains, as the paintings of Trotter and Boynton might, it engaged the surrounding landscape and sky by virtue of its site and materials. The fountain's open lattice framed perspectives and vistas of the landscape beyond.

Williams conceived of the form of the fountain in part through experimentation with Chinese calligraphy, as Thomas Motley has demonstrated.[73] Asian calligraphy in general had been associated with modern painting since 1950, when Franz Kline's large black-and-white paintings were first compared to calligraphy.[74] Williams used the technique as a kind of improvisational drawing in which the stylistic language of Zen calligraphy helped him to invent new forms.

29 **Charles Truett Williams** (U.S., 1918–1966)

Three Posts (Heritage of the Great Southwest Series), 1961
cedar and iron, 85 x 18 1/2 x 22 in.
Collection of Karl Williams; reproduction permission courtesy of Karl B. Williams.

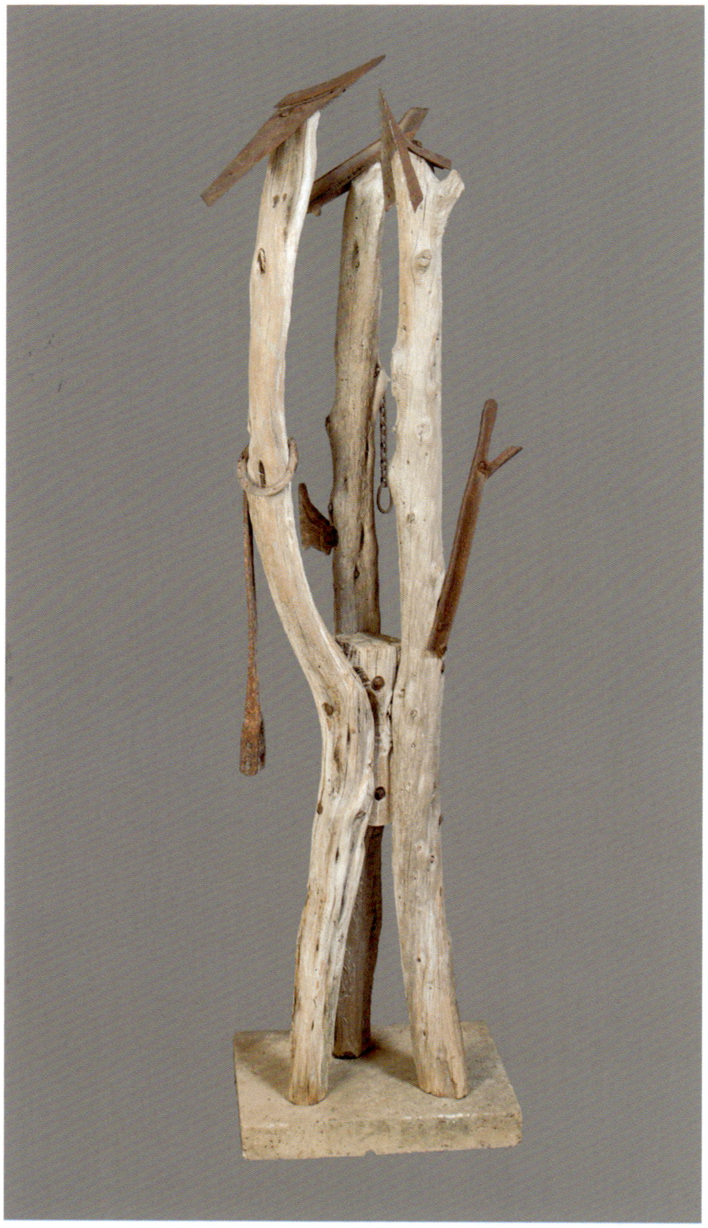

Site specificity continued to concern Williams into the 1960s, yet his formal and technical interests expanded to include assemblage, found objects, and junk, especially through the influence of his younger colleague Jim Love. Williams and many of his fellow sculptors frequented Gachman Metals in search of suitable scrap. Found objects contributed to the construction of monumental works in Williams's later career that spoke in some measure to the Southwestern landscape. *Three Posts* (1961; fig. 29), which belongs to Williams's *Heritage of the Great Southwest Series*, achieves that intent through an arrangement of cedar poles and rusted iron scavenged from the Texas prairies. Adorned with a lever, a chain, and other discarded tools, *Three Posts* recalls the agricultural and ranching history of Texas, and the native cedar may have served as fence posts at one time. Art historian Katie Robinson Edwards has interpreted the sculpture as a humorous meeting of three ranch hands, with tools at their sides and plowshares as hats.[75] Williams's humor aside, *Three Posts* also stands as a talisman of the relatively recent history of the land and its use. The rust and weathering of the materials evokes the passage of time, deterioration, and change.

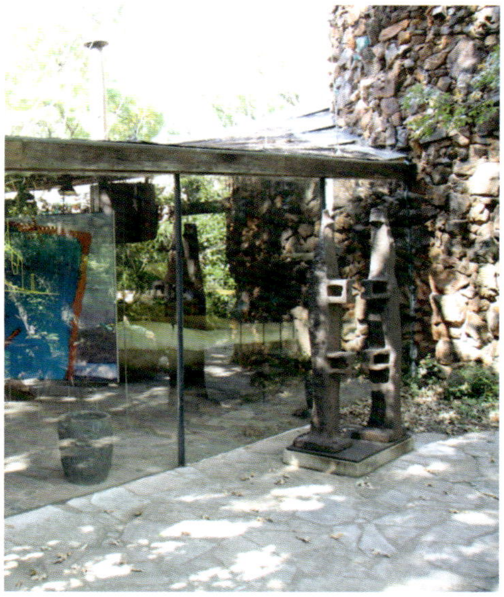

30 **Charles Truett Williams** (U.S., 1918–1966)

Ironcesters #2, 1962
cast iron
Collection of Karl Williams; reproduction permission courtesy of Karl B. Williams.

Those themes seem to have preoccupied Williams in the early 1960s. In 1962, Williams completed the first of multiple sculptures for the Norman home of his friend and colleague, artist and University of Oklahoma professor Eugene Bavinger. Bavinger and his wife Nancy had commissioned architect Bruce Goff to design the innovative structure in 1950–51 and, relying on themselves and volunteers for much of the construction, the home was finally completed in 1955. Based on a logarithmic spiral, the structure employed local sandstone, slag glass, and reclaimed petroleum drilling equipment as the primary materials. The Bavingers asked Williams to design a sculpture for the exterior entry in exchange for a painting, and the result was *Ironcesters #2* (1962; fig. 30). Although the pair of cast iron, vertical columns are intended to be figural, their origin in the industrial landscape of Texas and their relationship to the spaces surrounding the Bavinger House help to demonstrate Williams's interest in place. The two structures had served originally as supporting columns for a conveyor belt connected to an acid dip. Found discarded along the Houston Ship Channel, the pieces had suffered years of corrosion, making them suitable for Williams' artistic recontextualization. His title infers the cryptic personages are progenitors or forbearers, presumably defaced by the passage of time and ravaged by the elements. That suggestion of the long, slow course of decomposition and entropy certainly intrigued Bavinger, whose work dealt with similar themes, and later led Williams to a series of monumental granite sculptures placed around the grounds, which were jocosely titled *Stonehenge* (1965; fig. 31). Williams based the works on the post and lintel construction of its famous predecessor, but undoubtedly hoped to infer a similar degree of enigma and age in his decidedly modern adaptation. The deliberate archaicism of both form and concept imbued the landscape surrounding the Bavinger House with a supposed antiquity, not dissimilar from that the New Mexicans perceived in the geological formations of their state. Williams's monolithic Stonehenge also anticipates the work of Jesús Bautista Moroles, whose site-specific granite sculptures may be found readily across the Southwest.

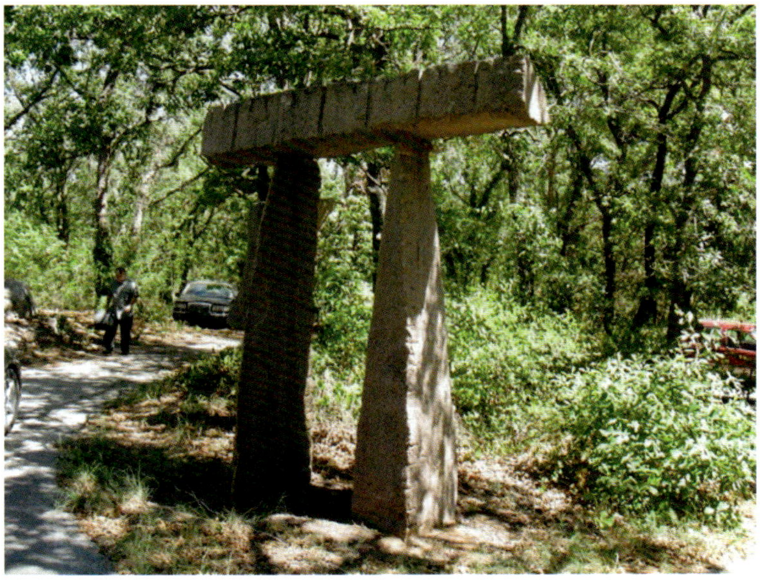

31 **Charles Truett Williams** (U.S., 1918–1966)

Stonehenge, 1965
granite
Collection of Karl Williams; reproduction permission courtesy of Karl B. Williams.

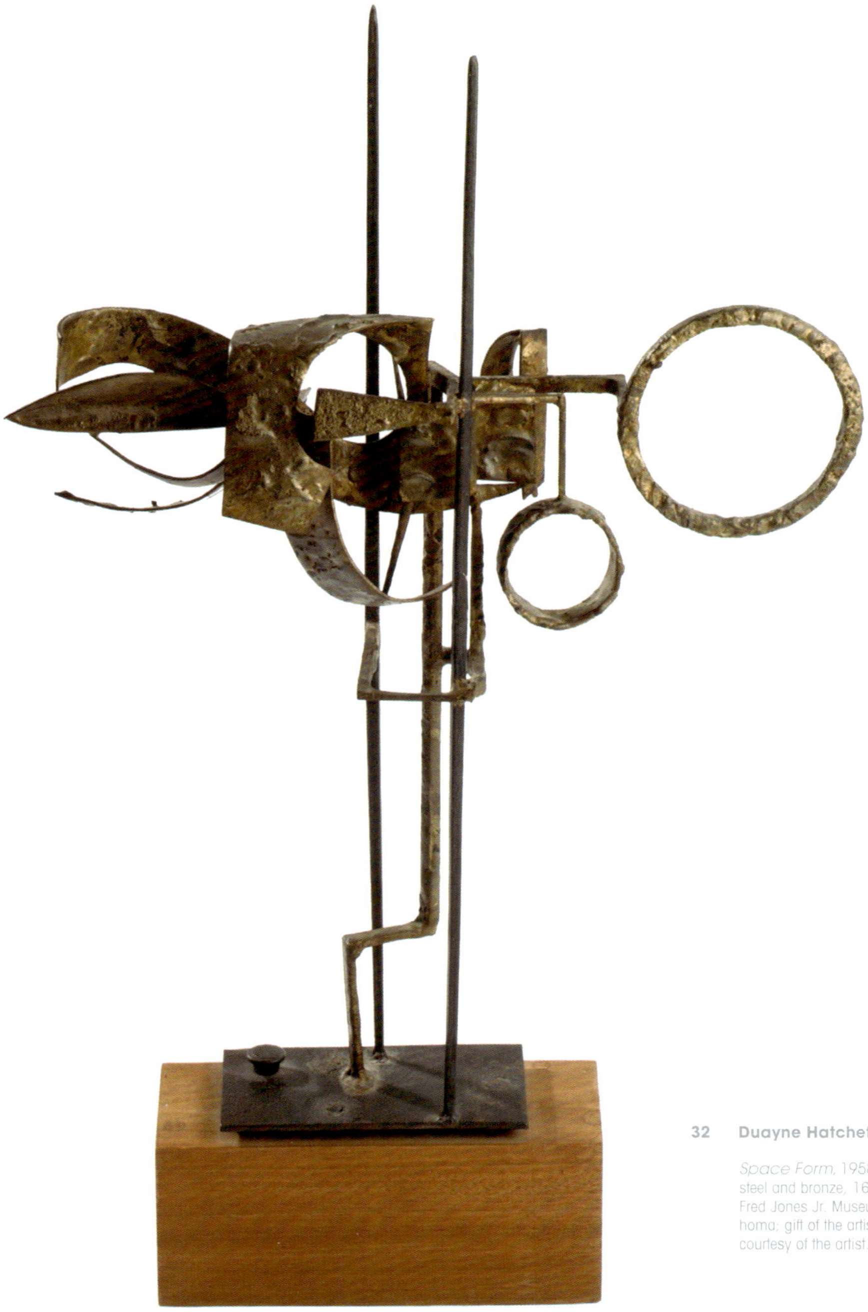

32 **Duayne Hatchett** (U.S., b. 1925)

Space Form, 1958
steel and bronze, 16 x 25 x 4 in.
Fred Jones Jr. Museum of Art, the University of Oklahoma; gift of the artist, 1959; reproduction permission courtesy of the artist.

Bavinger was not the only Oklahoman with whom Williams was in regular contact. Williams also befriended Bavinger's former student at OU, Duayne Hatchett, who had accepted a professorship at the University of Tulsa in 1954.[76] In the 1950s, Hatchett looked to sculptors among the New York School such as Ibram Lassaw, Seymour Lipton, and Theodore Roszak, who used brazed bronze to construct archetypal forms. Hatchett's *Space Form* (1958; fig. 32) compares favorably to similar works of the New York School with its ideographs and geometric shapes that offer varied articulations of space. The hoops and blades of *Space Form* not only shape space, generally speaking, but also seem to describe a blazing sun and orbital bodies. It is unknown whether Hatchett, like Kirkland, looked to the vast night sky over Oklahoma for inspiration or whether his subject is more universal; however, Hatchett depicted his surroundings in subsequent assemblages.

Williams's friendship with Hatchett demonstrates "the spell of companionship" that Douglas MacAgy observed upon his arrival in Texas in 1959 to assume the directorship of the Dallas Museum of Contemporary Art MacAgy recognized Williams's importance in promoting modernism in northern Texas and his camaraderie with artists across the region: "Williams was not an advertised attraction. While Charlie was exploring the countryside for choice litter, he himself had to be discovered on his beat in the bare lands outside Fort Worth. He was an unexpected bonus in whatever quest brought artists to reside in the region."[77] MacAgy acknowledged Williams's role in that respect through exhibition. When MoMA's *Art of Assemblage* visited Dallas in 1962, MacAgy included Williams and those of his circle in the exhibition, with the blessings of curator William Seitz.

After 1960, when Hatchett began visiting Williams in Fort Worth with some regularity, the two combed Gachman Metals for raw materials, and scrap became Hatchett's primary medium. The welded steel of *Landscape West* (1962; fig. 33) is clearly reclaimed scrap and used by Hatchett to represent the grasses of the Great Plains, a whimsical bird perched in a tree, and the ever-present sun. The dialogue between sun and horizon, a defining feature of the Southern Plains, is understated yet essential to Hatchett's conception of the environment in *Landscape West* and would appear in the work of many contemporaries, including Boynton, Bunnell, and Fitz.

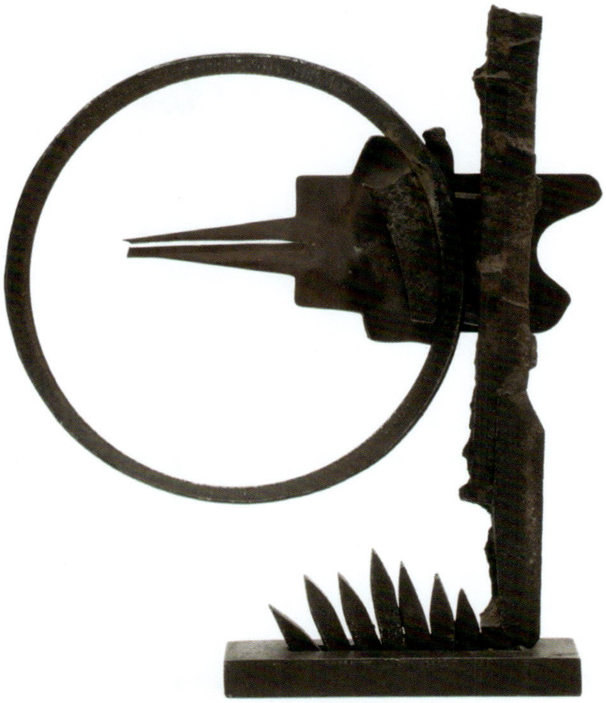

33 Duayne Hatchett (U.S., b. 1925)

Landscape West, 1962
steel, 17 x 15 x 2 in.
Collection of the artist; reproduction permission courtesy of the artist.

Hatchett also addressed the vast industrial development of the Southwest in *Railroad Mask* (1964; fig. 34). The totemic form acknowledges the work of both Williams and David Smith, whom Hatchett met and greatly admired.[78] The abstracted head and columnar body act as a talisman or emblem personifying the creative energies Hatchett had recently discovered in assemblage and the detritus of the railyards. *Railroad Mask* bridges a perceptible gap between a shamanistic investigation of the unknown and the decaying ruins of industrial America. Hatchett has reclaimed scrap considered useless and imbued it with magical significance. Despite its figural referent, *Railroad Mask* references the aging network of tracks that first bridged the great distances of the Southwest in the late nineteenth century and were used less frequently by the 1960s, as automotive and air travel supplanted locomotives.

That fascination with the built environment also found expression in the paintings of Ben Culwell. Following his inclusion in *Fourteen Americans*, Culwell worked intermittently for much of the 1950s and remained largely aloof from the rest of the Dallas–Fort Worth art community. He experimented freely with a

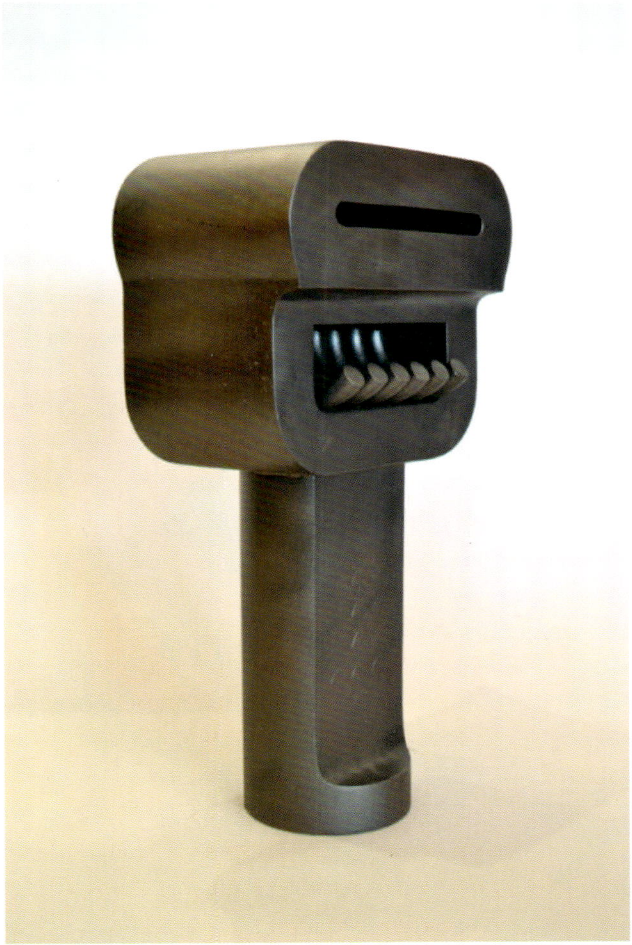

34 Duayne Hatchett (U.S., b. 1925)

Railroad Mask, 1965
steel, 27 x 14 x 9 in.
Collection of Randy and Sheila Ott; reproduction permission courtesy of the artist.

range of materials in addition to oil paint, including auto enamels, resins, sand, and glass shards. Culwell defined his approach as "purely Expressionistic" with materials and stylistic tendencies combined in unexpected juxtapositions to convey emotional intent.[79] While contemporaries such as Boynton and Trotter often looked to nature unadulterated in the 1950s, Culwell seemed more concerned with the domesticated. His depictions of the Texan urban and suburban landscape capture the diversity of color, form, and texture in the built environment through a network of improvisational and structural passages.

Culwell developed paintings like *Back Yard Sun Dance in Suburbia* (1954–75; fig. 35) over the course of twenty years, piling layers of oil and Duco lacquer laden with sediment onto his support as if in emulation of the stratification of the constructed landscape. Even though Culwell believed his paintings could be seen from any orientation, the section of blue at the top register and green at the bottom infer a suburban site for the exuberant play of stripes, streaks, and splotches that compose the ceremony of the title. Whether *Back Yard Sun Dance in Suburbia* refers to the ceremonial dance of the Plains Indians or some other rite is unclear, yet Culwell likely intended a sardonic contrast between pagan rituals and the backyard amusements of idyllic Texan suburbia. The diverse textures and materials invite close investigation, but Culwell's title also speaks to suburban sprawl and the expansive Texan sky. This is clarified by Culwell's *Texan* (1958–74; fig. 36), a dizzying vertical stretch of techniques, stylistic approaches, and materials. He carefully partitioned the composition into aesthetically cohesive components, linked by linear avenues and courses of smeared or scraped paint. For example, a dense brocade of enamel drips flanks an intersection of diagonals in the lower right, as though he deliberately contrasted gestural abstraction with the geometric in recognition of the modernist idioms of the day. The combination presents a kaleidoscope of patterns organized along a rough lattice of verticals and horizontals, similar in many respects to an aerial view of the urban landscape with its disparate components that compose a city.

35 **Ben Culwell** (U.S., 1918–1992)

Back Yard Sun Dance in Suburbia, 1954–75
oil, resin, sand, glass, pebbles, automotive paint on board,
20 1/8 x 30 1/4 in.
Collection of Jill and Stephen Wilkinson; reproduction permission courtesy of Elizabeth Culwell-Collins and the Ben L. Culwell Estate.

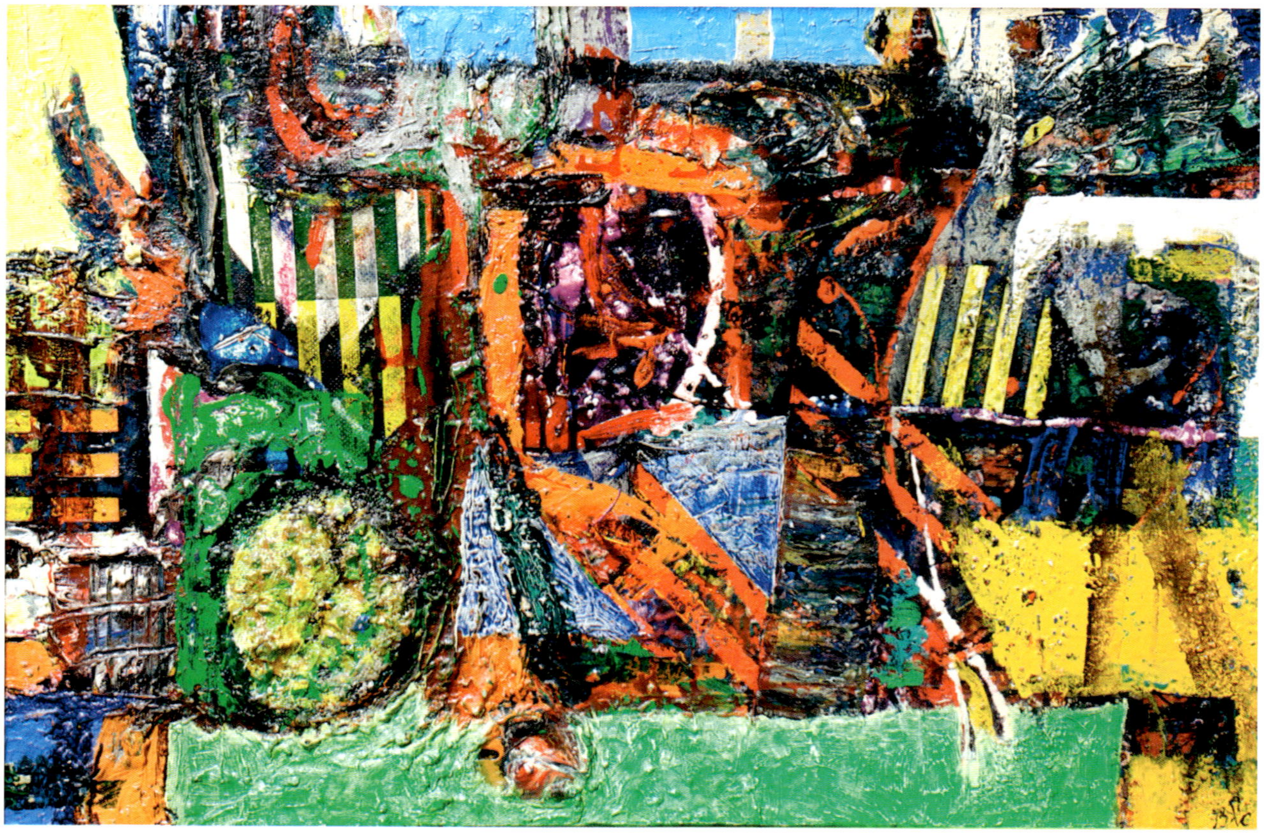

36 **Ben Culwell** (U.S., 1918–1992)

Texan, 1954–74
oil, resin, sand, glass, pebbles, automotive paint on board,
60 x 48 in.
The Summers Collection; reproduction permission courtesy of Elizabeth Culwell-Collins and the Ben L. Culwell Estate.

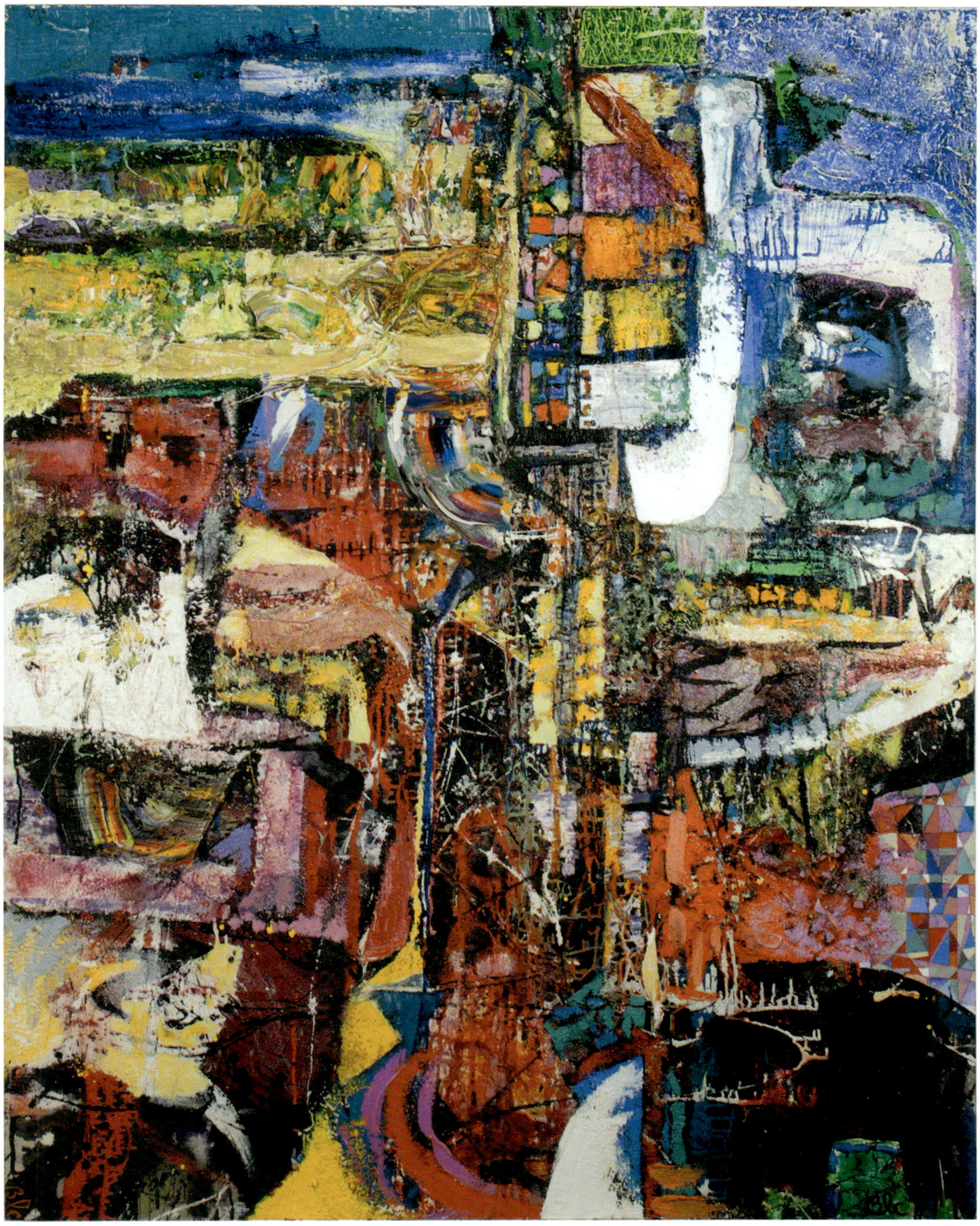

Culwell worked intermittently on *Texan* during a period of astounding growth in his home town of Dallas. According to the U.S. Census, the population doubled from 434,462 in 1950 to 844,401 in 1970. Dallas's footprint expanded even more dramatically during this time, from 112 square miles in 1950, to 279.9 in 1960, and finally 674.2 square miles in 1970. Much of the growth in the 1960s existed outside the official city limits. The Central Expressway was completed in the early 1950s, leading business and retail to move away from the center of the city and, by the 1970s, four major interstates, 20, 30, 35, and 45, passed through the city.[80] Culwell's working and reworking of the painting during that time mirrors in some respects the rapid development of Dallas as the city's population and infrastructure swelled and transformed at mid-century, although his title does not identify the city as his inspiration. Rather, Culwell uses a descriptive title as though the painting somehow captures the essence of Texas. The diversity of forms, the congestion of space, the dense strata of disparate layers, and the unrestrained growth must have seemed apropos of his home state. In many ways, Culwell's interest in the complexity of urban and suburban Texas offers a counterpoint to many of the artists included in this exhibition, save perhaps for Hatchett, yet his feeling for space, and its expanse, connects him with the broader intellectual program of Southwestern Abstract Expressionists.

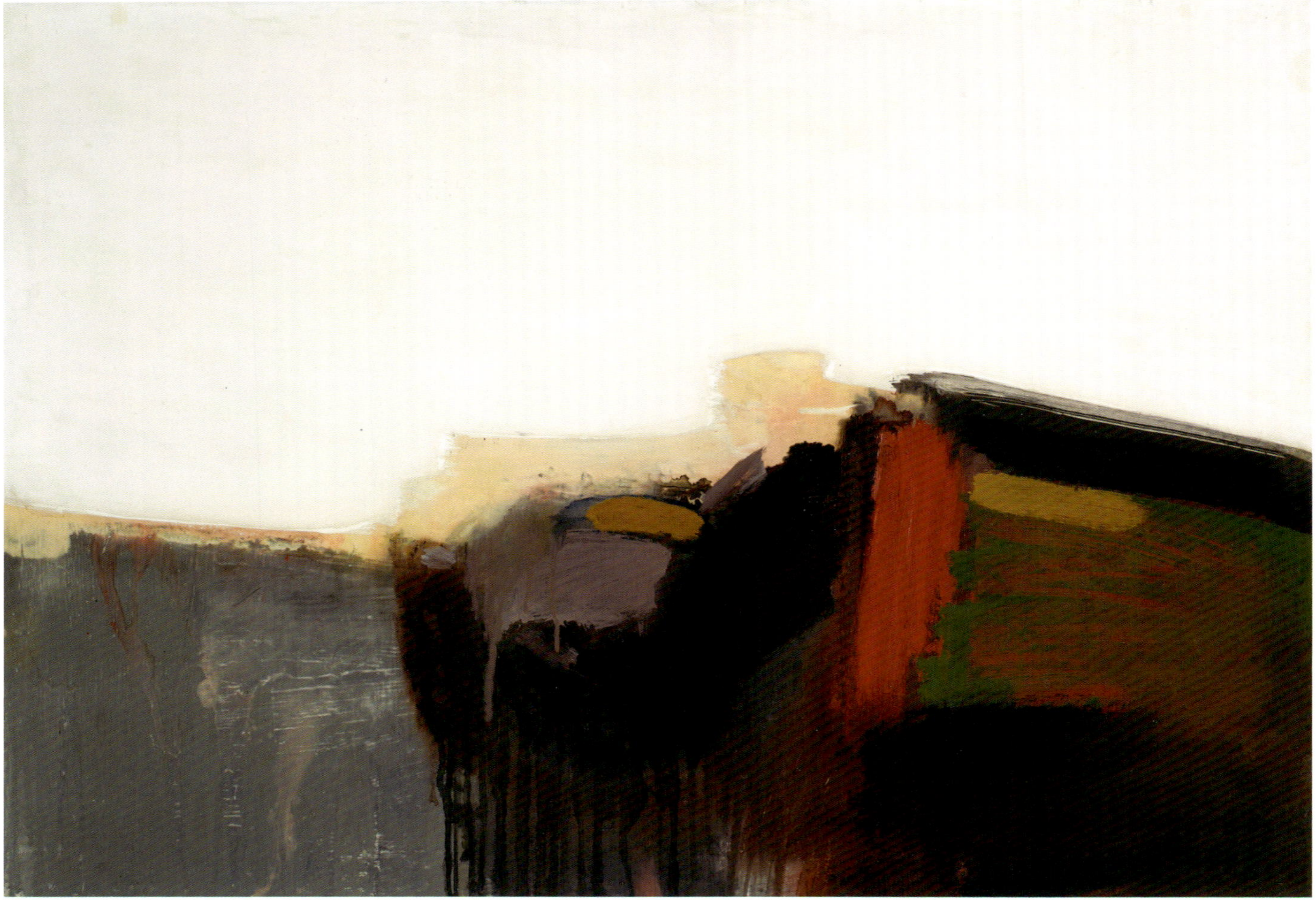

37 **Richard Stout** (U.S., b. 1934)

Landscape with White Sky, 1956
oil on Masonite, 23 1/2 x 34 7/8 in.
The Hallmark Art Collection, Kansas City, Missouri.

Despite the presence in Dallas–Fort Worth of Culwell, who took a hiatus for much of the 1960s, and Williams, who passed away prematurely in 1966, most of the artists sympathetic to Abstract Expressionism gravitated to Houston in the late 1950s and early 1960s, including Boynton, who relocated in 1955. There Boynton became closely connected to a group of young artists, including Richard Stout, Leila McConnell, and Dick Wray, who brought to Houston their experiences and influences from across the U.S. and abroad.

Stout, who was born in Beaumont, left Texas in 1953 for study at the School of the Art Institute of Chicago, where his instructors included Isobel Steele MacKinnon. A former student of Hans Hofmann's between 1925–29, MacKinnon still worked in a German Expressionist manner when Stout began his education. Hofmann's aesthetic influence filtered through MacKinnon to some degree, but the modern collections at the Art Institute had an equivalent impact on Stout. Both Willem de Kooning's *Excavation* (1950) and Jackson Pollock's *Greyed Rainbow* (1953) demonstrated the possibilities of non-objectivity to the young artist and encouraged him to experiment during his student career. *Landscape with White Sky* (1956; fig. 37), painted prior to his departure from Chicago, demonstrates Stout's appreciation and grasp of the lessons of the New York School. Emphatic, gestural strokes describe contours and a spare topography below a relatively undifferentiated white firmament. The streaks, splatters, and drips convey the immediacy with which Stout approached the painting. Vibrant colors and a heavier impasto at right project towards the viewer, while thinner washes and muted tones create recession at left. When paired with the strong horizon, this technical approach to the construction of space evokes both the near and the far, similar to that of Boynton's *Thunderstorm*. Thomas McEvilley has credited this spatial dynamic to the lessons of Hofmann, although Stout "carried the push-pull principle to extremes in his evocation of near and far distances."[81] That collapse of the middle ground must have been inspired, in some measure, by memories of the wide-open spaces of Texas, especially since Stout produced the painting in Chicago. Jermayne MacAgy, director of the Contemporary Arts Museum in Houston (and former spouse of Douglas MacAgy), regarded the painting as exemplary of the distinctive approach Texans had taken to Abstract Expressionism. *Landscape with White Sky* served as an introductory illustration to her important essay, "Texas—From Blue Bonnet to Blue Streak," published in *Art in America* in 1961. She observed, "As in other sections of the country, abstract expressionism has influenced other styles here; and a strong accent is the feeling for space." Texas modernists, MacAgy contended, captured the essence of Southwestern space in their works and used "for their starting point their reactions to nature's elements."[82] The vastness of the Southwestern landscape and its distinctive geography left an indelible mark on its artists.

MacAgy had become a critical champion of Texan modernists after she relocated to Houston in 1955 to serve as the director of the Contemporary Arts Association (CAA). By that time, she had already distinguished herself as one of the foremost curators in the country at the California Palace of the Legion of Honor, where she began as a temporary instructor in 1941 and eventually held the position of assistant director and of acting director by the time her tenure ended in 1955. MacAgy established relationships with many of the notable modernists working in the U.S. in part through her relationship to the CSFA, where Douglas served as director, but also through a prescient and innovative exhibition program. She curated major exhibitions on Hassel Smith and Clyfford Still in 1947 and organized the *Annual Exhibition of Contemporary American Paintings*, which began in May 1945 and continued for another three years. In Houston, she developed engaging, thematic shows, such as *Yard Art*, as well as major exhibitions on Mark Rothko and *The Magical Worlds of Redon, Klee, Baziotes*.[83]

MacAgy's "Texas—From Blue Bonnet to Blue Streak" demonstrated that art in Texas was not restricted to the Sunday painters of bluebonnets. The "blue streak" of her title referred to the work of Leila McConnell, who had recently embraced Color Field after a brief stint with Surrealism. McConnell studied at the CSFA in 1949, prior to the departure of Corbett, McChesney, and Spohn. She met Rothko during that time, but it was not until a trip to Italy in the late 1950s that she began her non-objective "sky paintings."[84] McConnell painted simple, reductive forms hovering in an atmospheric ether that encouraged a meditative experience. *The Time Between* (1959; Menil Collection, Houston), with its subtle horizontal of blue, helped inspire MacAgy's article title and resulted in an ongoing series for McConnell. A slightly later painting, *The First Bar of Peace* (1961; fig. 38), also captures the essence of space MacAgy perceived in the Texas variant of Abstract Expressionism. A blue bar indicative of the horizon bisects the subtly differentiated field, encouraging both scrutiny and introspection. In turn, the title promises peace or spiritual tranquility through absorption in the color and form (or formlessness).

38 Leila McConnell (U.S., b. 1927)

The First Bar of Peace, 1961
oil on canvas, 35 5/8 x 23 11/16 in.
Collection of Charles M. Peveto, Austin, Texas; reproduction permission courtesy of the artist.

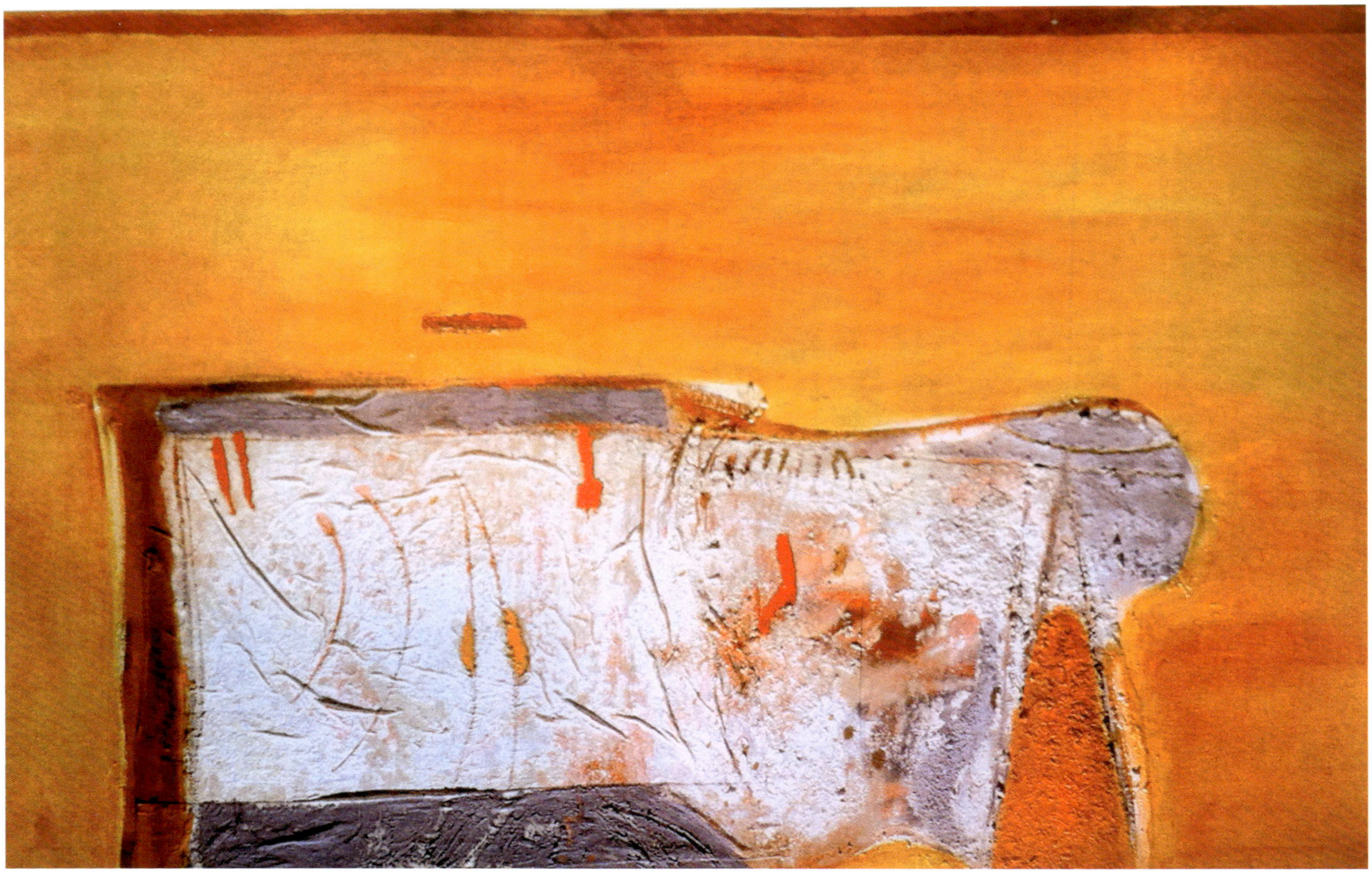

39 **Dick Wray** (U.S., 1933–2011)

The Bull, 1960
oil and sand on canvas,
43 1/2 x 66 in.
Collection of Richard Stout.

McConnell, Stout, Boynton, and others received critical attention from MacAgy, but she also facilitated patronage through her influence with Dominique and John de Menil. The de Menils brought MacAgy to rescue the flagging CAA. She became a close friend and advisor to Dominique and, when MacAgy's contract was not renewed at the CAA in 1958, the de Menils arranged for her to chair the art department at the University of St. Thomas, where she remained until her untimely death in 1964. Jermayne and Dominique worked jointly on numerous curatorial projects, taught art history together at St. Thomas, and generally encouraged appreciation for modern and contemporary art in Houston.[85]

In addition to MacAgy, the de Menils became close friends and supporters of James Johnson Sweeney during his directorship of the MFA. John sat on the search committee for Sweeney, and the three shared a similar perspective on art as a lens for investigating binary philosophical oppositions. As Marcia Brennan has noted, the three saw art as a means of fusing paradoxical propositions: "For Sweeney and the de Menils, this fusion not only encompassed a convergence of the seen and unseen worlds, but also signified the coexistence of the microcosmic and macrocosmic, presence and absence, creation and destruction, modernism and primitivism, historical temporality and archetypal timelessness."[86] This intellectual stance also informed their appreciation of local modernists, who were concerned with many of the same questions.

Like the de Menils and MacAgy, Sweeney took a vested interest in the Houston modernists, including Boynton, Stout, and Dick Wray. During Sweeney's tenure between 1961–67, Houstonian modernists were exhibited regularly, and he acquired their works for the collection, including Wray's *Klee Gone Mad, Almost Beserk* (1963). Wray recalled Sweeney's sympathy for his paintings and opined that "Nobody would deal with me up til Sweeney."[87] It was likely Wray's sympathy for the European avant-garde movement CoBrA, and especially the work of Asger Jorn, that attracted Sweeney, who had actively collected Art Informel and Art Brut at the Guggenheim.

Wray encountered the European avant-garde, as well as the paintings of the New York School, during a trip to Europe in 1958–59. Although he was drawn initially to Paris, he eventually wound up in Denmark, where he worked in the office of a local architect. He had developed an abiding interest in Danish architecture, art, and design while studying at the

School of Architecture of the University of Houston between 1955–58, and he developed a sympathy for the work of CoBrA, as well as Art Informel.[88] His paintings from the early 1960s demonstrate diverse influences from Jorn, Italian Alberto Burri, and Spaniard Antoni Tàpies. Tàpies clearly shaped Wray's approach in *The Bull* (1960; fig. 39), which depicts an abstracted white and gray carcass stained by blood from the corrida. An arena of yellow and orange, suffused with sand and other aggregates, surrounds the bull and evokes the earth itself through its textural surface. Materiality and tactility marked much of the work Wray produced upon his return to Houston, providing an important aesthetic link to European modernism.

The physicality and materiality of Wray's paintings would seem diametrically opposed to those of his contemporary, Dorothy Hood, if not for the sense of space. Born in Bryan, Texas, Hood studied initially at the Rhode Island School of Design and then at the Art Students League in 1940 and fell under the spell of Surrealism early in her career. She left for Mexico in 1941 and spent the next twenty years there, traveling to Central and South America with her husband, the Bolivian composer Velasco Maidana. She continued to exhibit in New York and at the Proteo Gallery in Mexico City, which also represented Mexican modernists such as Germán Cueto and Enrique Echeverría. In 1961, Hood relocated to Houston, where the environment induced in her thoughts of space, as she revealed in 1974: "I enjoy the Southwest terrain; the earth is benign. You're confronted with outer space and sky. You see from the heart upwards, out over the horizon. There are great distances that you can feel. A gravitational uprightness. Like a plant, the city grows toward the sun."[89]

If the limitless sky above the Texas horizon prompted Hood's early artistic ruminations on the cosmos, then it was the subsequent development of NASA and the release of Stanley Kubrick's *2001: A Space Odyssey* (1968) that encouraged her development of the theme. Following President John F. Kennedy's ambitious promise in May 1961 to land a man on the moon by the end of the decade, Houston became essential in the design of spacecraft and control of space exploration with the completion of the Manned Spacecraft Center (later the Lyndon B. Johnson Space Center) in September 1961, the same year Hood arrived. The decade culminated with the Apollo 11 moon landing in July 1969, as well as the release of *2001* the previous year, both of which have frequently been cited as influences on Hood's conception of space and human transcendence.[90]

Hood interpreted both light and space as fundamental in unifying the human spirit with the universe: "Light is the measure and the return of the gift of magnetic fields; space extends itself over and is the breadth of every essence. The eye is our own earthly right of possession of the cosmic orbs."[91] Painting became Hood's vehicle for exploring the expansion of human thought and spirituality into the astral plane, and she began pouring and staining large canvases in irregular passages, occasionally delineated by hard edges, as a representation of her communion with celestial phenomena. *On Untrodden Paths* (1972; fig. 40) invites an exploration of the unknown, where nebulous clouds of gray, blue, red, and orange drift and eddy. The contrast of cool and warm, like a meeting of two fronts, creates a tumultuous space, and a bolt cuts across the upper left foreshadowing a coming tempest. Hood's sensitive manipulation of the stains draws the eye to the surface of the painting, while the layering of the fields implies an infinite recession. She explores the collapse of the near and far in *On Untrodden Paths* not only through the spatial dynamics of the painting but also by encouraging a meditative response, in which contemplation of the formal elements serves as an avenue for emotional, philosophical, or spiritual exploration.

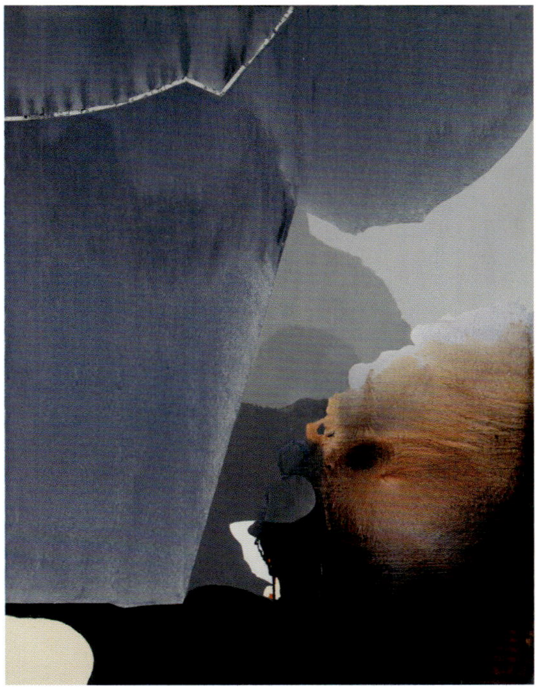

40 Dorothy Hood (U.S., 1918–2000)

On Untrodden Paths, 1972
oil on canvas, 90 x 70 in.
The McNay Art Museum; gift of C. Thomas Wright; reproduction permission courtesy of Dorothy Hood Foundation, Museum of South Texas.

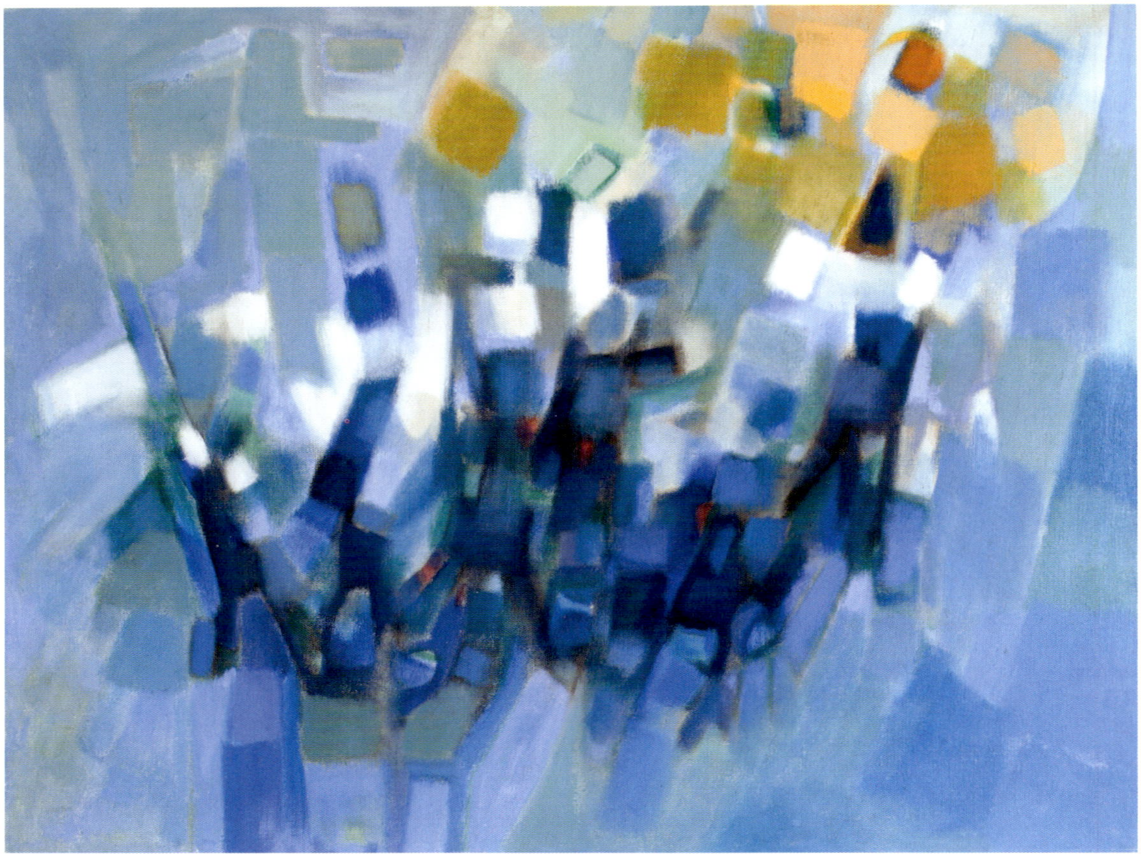

41 **John O'Neil** (U.S., 1915–2004)

Fragmented Landscape, 1957
oil on canvas, 36 x 48 in.
Fred Jones Jr. Museum of Art, the University of Oklahoma, Norman, Oklahoma; gift of the artist, 1960.

On Untrodden Paths encourages consideration of cosmic mysteries and the limitless reaches of outer space, yet Hood, like Kirkland a decade earlier, began her artistic investigation initially through an appreciation for the vast sky and horizon of the Southwest. The seemingly measureless Southwest prompted others to consider the infinite in similar ways. Oklahoma's broad, bright skies inspired John O'Neil to paint "distillations of light and color" using abbreviated patches of paint arranged like a mosaic.[92] He extracted the essential colors of nature in his *Fragmented Landscape* (1957; fig. 41) with an eye toward the sun, clouds, and sky, given the largely atmospheric palette of azure and yellow. The tonal variations of blue and gray are less a description of specific forms than the glitter and gleam of light reflecting off forms. O'Neil accorded light a metaphysical significance in his paintings, as he explained in 1963: "To be born is to experience light, and to die is to lack it, to lose it. What the artist makes, even ineptly, is a light-existence paralleling our own, but intensified and all absorbing."[93] By associating light with the quintessence of human existence, O'Neil valorizes his role as a painter, who immerses the viewer in that phenomenon.

O'Neil's comments are less mystical in tone than those of Hood, but they share a sensibility. Hood and O'Neil became acquainted in the late 1960s after he accepted a position as chair of the art department at Rice University in Houston in 1965. A student of Emil Bisttram in 1942 and a former convert to Surrealism, O'Neil had experimented with most modernist idioms before developing his mature style in the mid-1950s while serving as the chair of the art department at OU, a position he held between 1951–65. During his brief tenure at Rice, he helped to develop the fledgling program with the support of the de Menils, who began to shift their attention away from St. Thomas in 1967.[94]

The Rice administration and the de Menils hoped O'Neil would build a program similar in strength to that of OU. He reflected that in the postwar years, prior to his departure for Houston, the visual arts in Oklahoma were in "robust health, at least in the higher education centers in Tulsa, Stillwater and Norman, where creative activity among faculty and students was exuberant and often of excellent quality. Energy that fueled the New York School reached even the mid-America places."[95] The example of the New York School exercised some influence on O'Neil but, in the early 1960s, he became increasingly interested in European modernism, especially that of Italy and Denmark.[96]

Under O'Neil, the environment at OU's School of Art was formative for a number of artists, including his younger colleague Eugene Bavinger. The latter had been a student at OU before World War II and then returned as faculty in 1947. In the late 1950s, he joined O'Neil in the investigation of light and its abstract possibilities. Bavinger's painting *Atmospheric* (1960; fig. 42) compares stylistically to O'Neil's work from the period with its rippling, shortened brushstrokes that suggest a scintillating play of light against a loose strata of blue, yellow, and green. *Atmospheric* also recalls the late work of Bradley Walker Tomlin, who demonstrated an interest in fusing impressionist effects with Abstract Expressionism, as art historian Stephen Polcari has suggested.[97] The basis for *Atmospheric* was likely one of the forests or verdant fields surrounding his house east of Norman, but he was far more interested in the phenomena of light, energy, and change, as he explained: "I am working from nature. It could be landscape, seascape, skyscape. . . . What I try to capture is a feeling of what I have about this particular event—the energy, the gesture, the movement, the changing light during the day and all the kinds of transformation experiences that can take place when things move through the landscape with birds, animals, etc."[98] Change, as a constant in nature, informed Bavinger's stippled technique in *Atmospheric*, and the depiction of temporal changes in nature and the effects of Southwestern light links his work to that of O'Neil and numerous contemporaries, including de Kooning, Mandelman, and especially his close colleague, Charles Williams. Despite the visual flurry of Bavinger's stylistic approach, the evocation of dappled light falling across a greening landscape also conveys quiet and solitude.

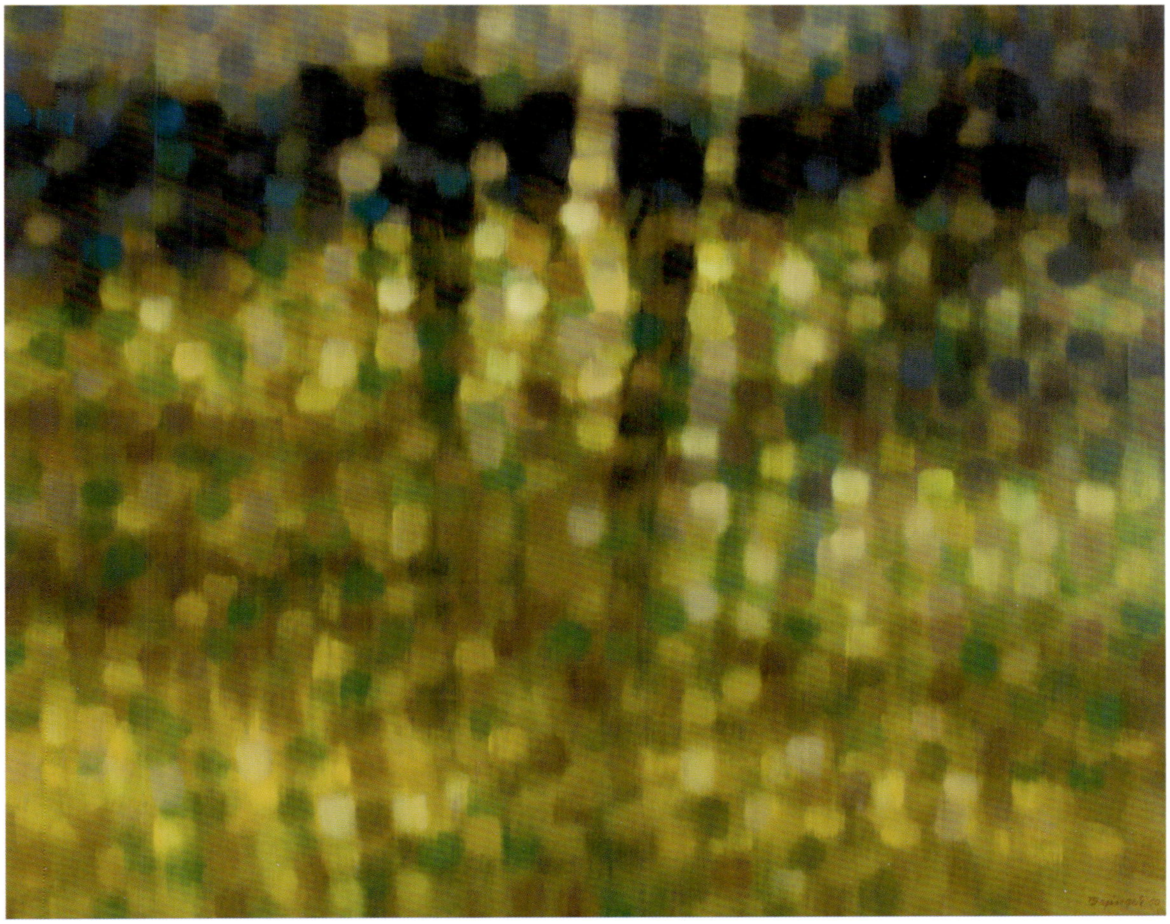

42 Eugene "Gene" Bavinger (U.S., 1919–1997)

Atmospheric, 1960
oil on linen, 47 x 60 in.
Fred Jones Jr. Museum of Art, the University of Oklahoma, Norman, Oklahoma; museum purchase, 1973.

The silence and remoteness of the Southwestern landscape informed the work of Bavinger and other Oklahomans, in ways comparable to their counterparts in Colorado, New Mexico, and Texas. Myron Dale McKinney, a professor at Oklahoma State University in Stillwater, explored similar themes in works such as *By-Product of Silence* (1954; fig. 43). An enthusiast of jazz and classical music, McKinney often attempted to integrate the aural into his paintings and created numerous sound and kinetic works in the 1960s. He painted *By-Product of Silence* following a 1953 sabbatical trip across the western U.S., Mexico, and Canada, where he visited national landmarks in addition to countless galleries and museums. The dominance of red and orange in his palette certainly speaks to the colors of the Southwest, and the translucent white pinnacles and points of the composition approximate mountains and the trunks and branches of trees shrouded in snow (fig. 44), although McKinney would have resisted a representational interpretation of the forms. Silent contemplation of a quiet winter landscape led McKinney to see past the trees to the microcosmic spaces of the earth. Between and beneath his abstract forest, a startlingly complicated and nuanced surface built through the meticulous accumulation and removal of paint implies a seemingly infinite detail. McKinney produced the dazzling minutiae of color splotches and cryptic forms through a collage of materials and techniques. He used a combination of oil paint, gouache, fine aggregates, and possibly enamels to produce splatters, stains, and stenciled forms. At times, he scraped the surface or removed a layer of paint with a solvent to reveal forms and colors otherwise hidden in deeper layers. Thin superficial layers of paint were likely designed to crack and flake, giving the painting a weathered or aged appearance. *By-Product of Silence* is a veritable strata of fields, veins, and bands of paint that evoke geological diversity of the Southwest, built and eroded over centuries by water, wind, and other natural forces.

McKinney's obvious facility with abstraction notwithstanding, he paid little attention to national trends in the visual arts, yet *By-Product of Silence* approximates the work of Richard Pousette-Dart in its complicated layering of ideographic forms.[99] By contrast, J. Jay McVicker, McKinney's colleague at OSU, followed developments closely through frequent trips to New York City and by reading periodicals such as *Art in America*.[100] For instance, McVicker, who showed with Fitz regularly, accompanied his dealer to New York in 1958, where they met with Alfonso Ossorio, the de Koonings, Ibram Lassaw, and others.[101]

44 Myron Dale McKinney (U.S., 1911–1994)

Landscape, 1952
serigraph, 29 1/8 x 35 in.
Fred Jones Jr. Museum of Art, the University of Oklahoma; gift of Sam Olkinetzky, 1960.

43 **Myron Dale McKinney** (U.S. 1911-1994)

By-Product of Silence, 1954
oil on board, 21 x 25 1/8 in.
Fred Jones Jr. Museum of Art, the University of Oklahoma,
Norman, Oklahoma; gift of Roger Corsaw.

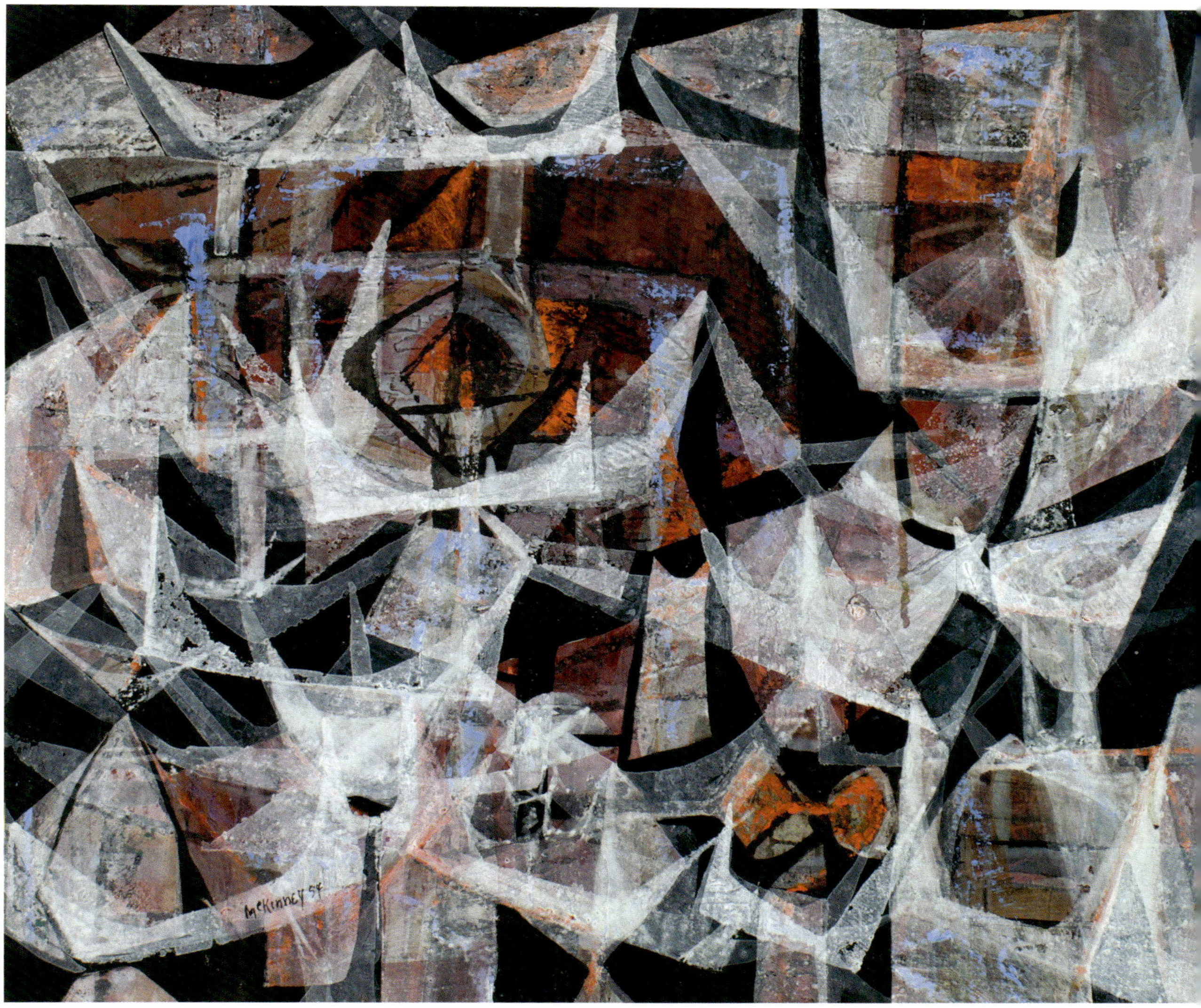

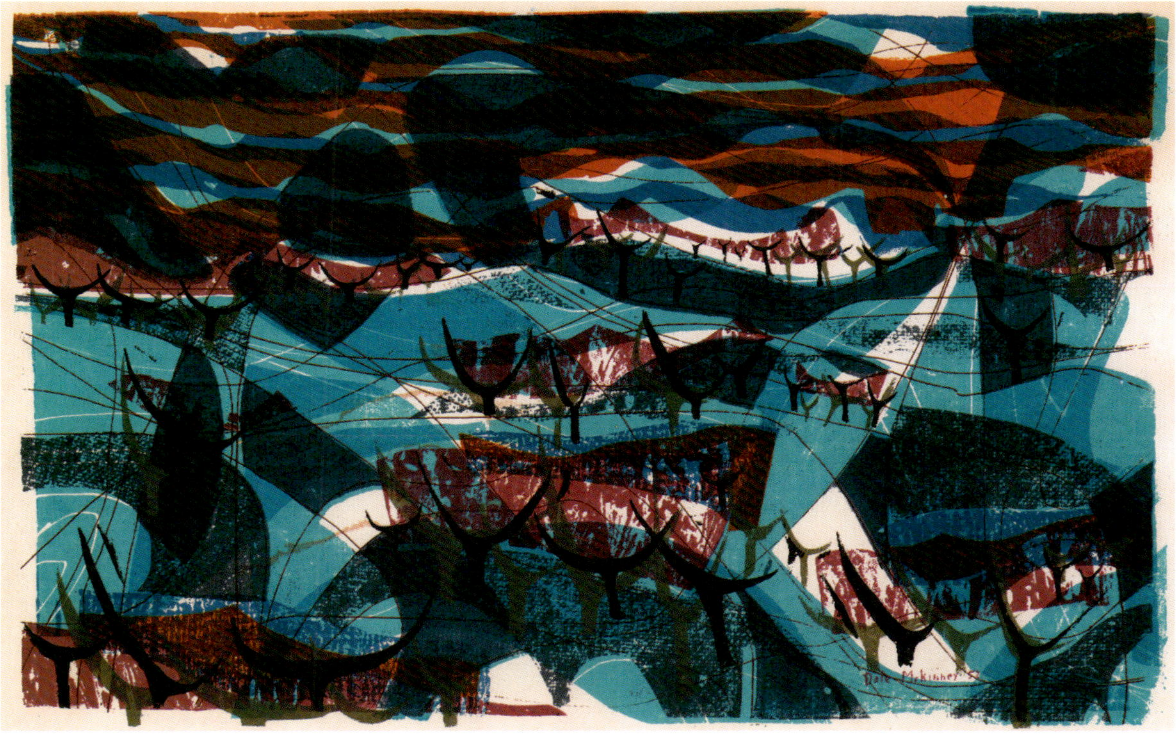

45 **J. Jay McVicker** (U.S., 1911–2004)

Painting No. 5, 1960
oil on canvas, 34 x 34 in.
Fred Jones Jr. Museum of Art, the University of Oklahoma, Norman, Oklahoma; gift of the artist, 1971.

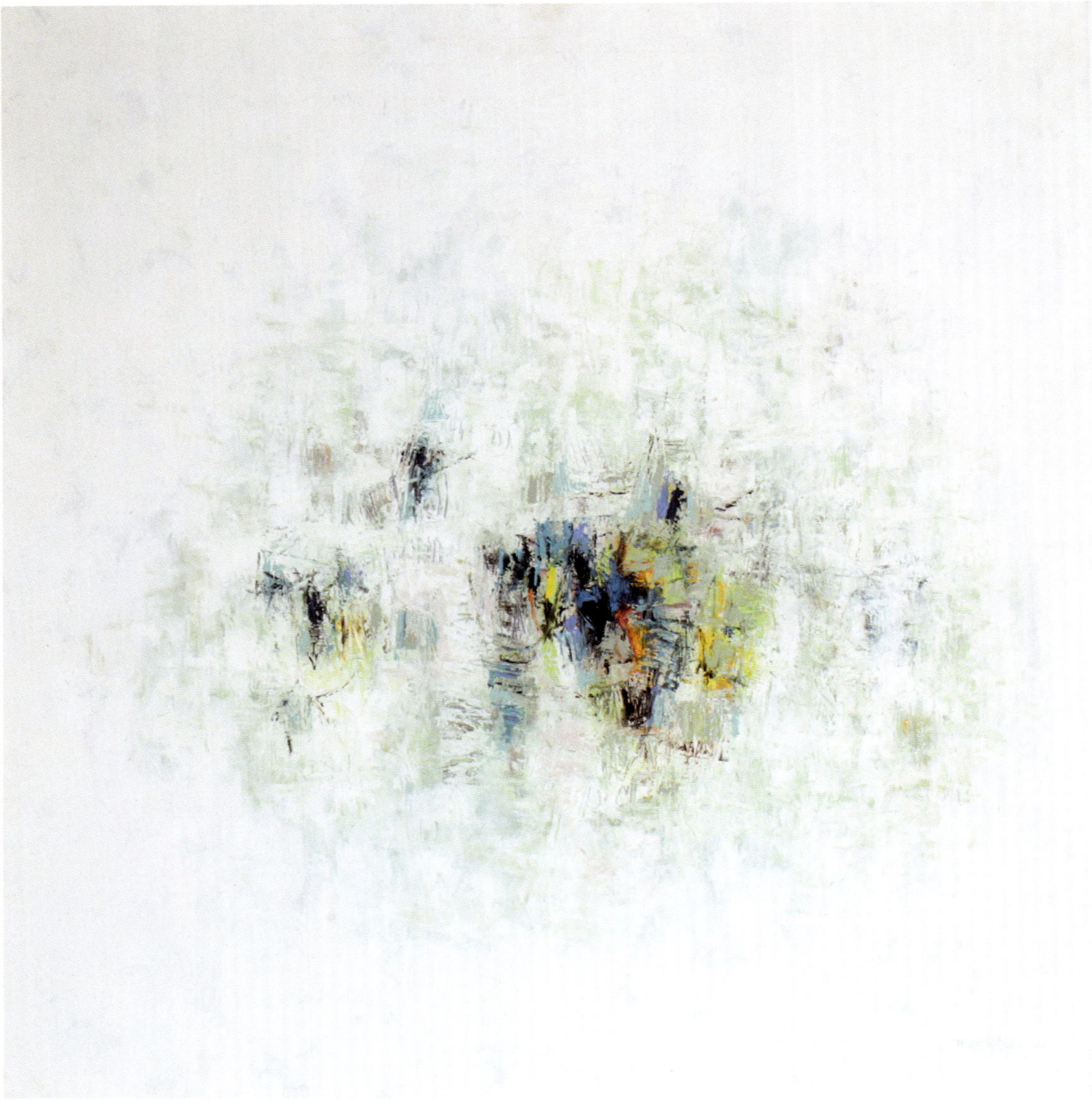

McVicker's knowledge of the New York School is evident in *Painting No. 5* (1960; fig. 45), which compares in style to that of Philip Guston. McVicker painted a lattice of short vertical and horizontal strokes in the center of the board using variations on the range of primary and secondary colors. He then used a palette knife to cover much of the surface in a layer of white, with the exception of scattered, isolated patches around the center of the painting. He occasionally scraped the surface revealing tints of blue and yellow beneath the blanket of white. Although McVicker often avoided overly descriptive titles during this period to encourage a formal appreciation of his paintings, his inspiration may have been a winter setting, with a glimpse of flora and soil beneath the snow. McVicker grew up on a farm near the rural community of Vici, located in the high plains of western Oklahoma, and landscape dominated his early prints such as *Before Winter* (1942; fig. 46). The graphic marks describing the diverse prairie terrain of grasses, soil, and planted crops informed McVicker's later approach in *Painting No. 5*, which relies on a similar juxtaposition of linear elements.

Those methodical brushstrokes, when combined with a surrounding placid white, convey a meditative stillness, similar to McKinney's *By-Product of Silence*. McVicker intended his works to foster a contemplative experience as a means toward expanded awareness. He practiced yoga for much of his life and found inspiration in Richard Maurice Bucke's *Cosmic Consciousness: A Study in the Evolution of the Human Mind* (1901).[102] Bucke proposed a hierarchy of consciousness culminating in cosmic consciousness or a total awareness of the cosmic order. Evolution of mind and soul, Bucke believed, was imminent for humanity, and McVicker, in turn, saw meditation, not to mention artistic practice, as a means towards enlightenment. As such, McVicker likely intended the expansive white field in *Painting No. 5* as metaphorically unbounded, encouraging contemplation of the immediate environment as well as the greater cosmos.

McVicker shared this concomitant interest in limitless space and palpable silence with colleagues such as McKinney, Fitz, and Bunnell, as well as contemporaries Dorothy Hood and Edward Corbett, but all artists included in this volume engaged these themes to some extent. As Elaine de Kooning recognized, these essential characteristics of the Southwest pervaded the work of the region's artists, although their styles were not as distinct from Abstract Expressionists on the East and West Coasts as she supposed. Influence from the CSFA through Diebenkorn, Corbett, and Spohn clearly affected artists working in New Mexico, and de Kooning's presence had a similar effect in both Albuquerque and Texas.

Despite the great distances between artists in New Mexico, Colorado, Texas, and Oklahoma, a network of communication did exist between them, and key figures like de Kooning, Boynton, and Williams helped to establish connections between the different communities. Art historians, gallery owners, and collectors such as Douglas and Jermayne MacAgy, James Johnson Sweeney, Eulalia Emetaz, Dord Fitz, and the de Menils helped to promote Southwestern Abstract Expressionists in exhibitions and publications across the region. Jermayne MacAgy and others recognized that Southwestern artists adapted aesthetic approaches in use on the coasts, such as Action painting, Color Field, and staining, to express the distinctive traits of their region.

The Southwest prompted considerations of vastness in its sprawling, seemingly vacant spaces and often led the artists to collapse the background and foreground as reference to the odd optical dissonance, which drew together the faraway and the nearby. In turn, many of the artists were drawn to the horizon as an omnipresent feature of the region and as a compositional axis by which they could explore the dialogue between the expansive land below and the limitless sky above. Many reacted to the perceived seclusion of the Southwest by instilling in their paintings a suggestive silence that encouraged introspection, meditation, and contemplation in artist and viewer alike.

The contemplative mood induced by Southwestern space frequently led artists to paradoxical considerations of the macro and micro, as well as the timelessness of the region's geological antiquity versus a persistent mutability visible through the traces of volcanic activity, tectonic uplift, and erosion. Time and change, as conveyed through natural processes, became a recurring theme among Abstract Expressionists in the Southwest, as evident in McKinney's *By-Product of Silence* or McVicker's *Painting No. 5*. However, neither artist was alone in finding metaphysical significance in natural cycles.

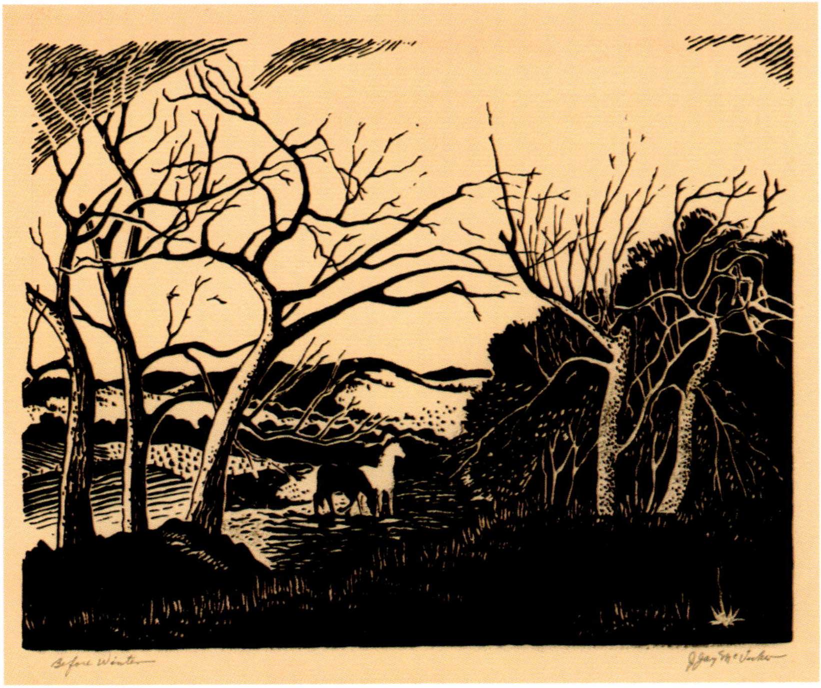

46 J. Jay McVicker (U.S., 1911–2004)

Before Winter (from the Graphic Oklahoma portfolio), 1942
serigraph, 11 x 13 in.
Fred Jones Jr. Museum of Art, the University of Oklahoma, Norman, Oklahoma; gift of William Harold Smith, 1965.

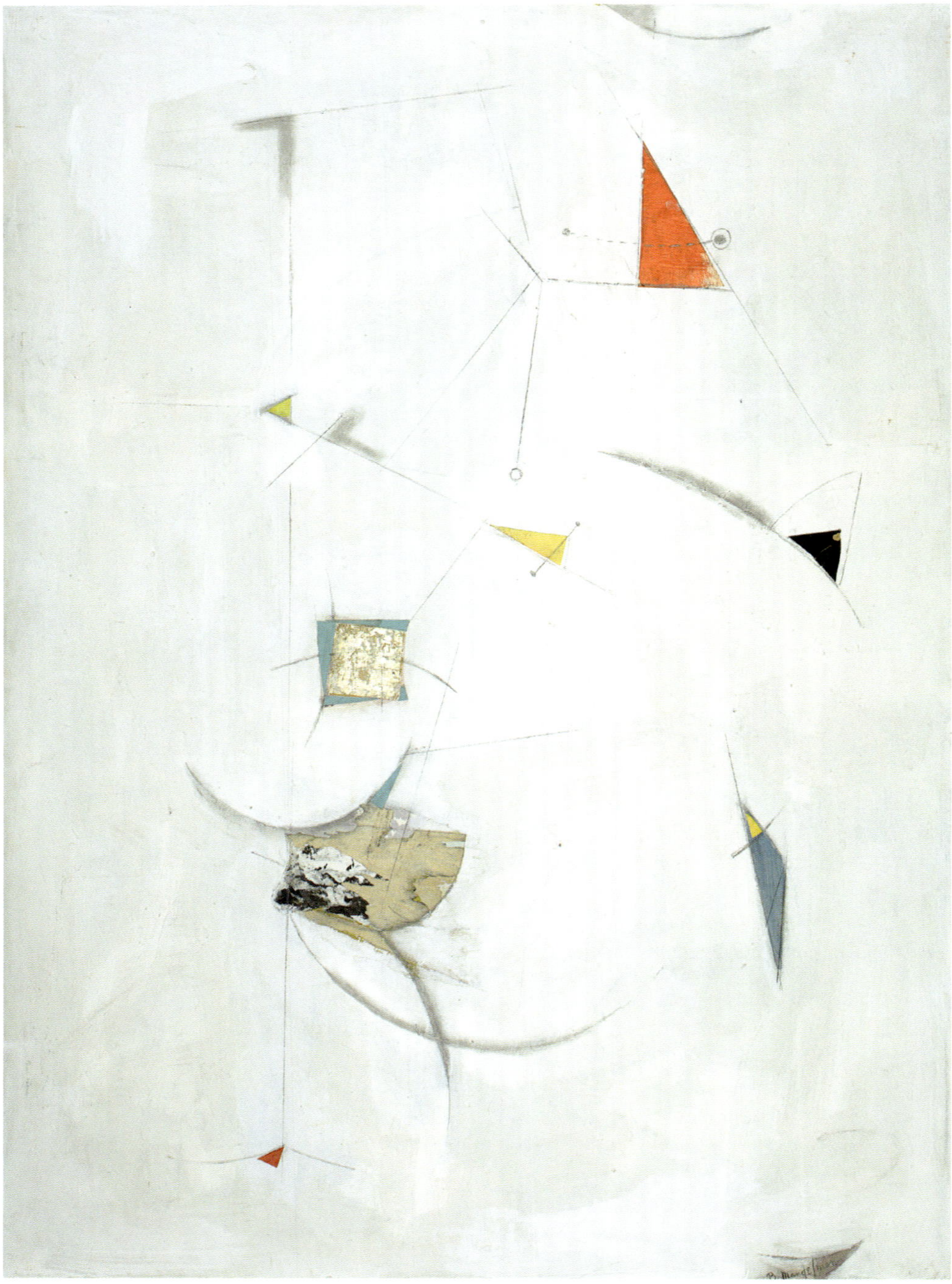

47 **Beatrice Mandelman** (U.S., 1912–1998)

Winter, 1954
oil on Mascnite, 48 x 36 in.
The Harwocd Museum of Art, Taos.

48 **Robert Donald Ray** (U.S., 1924–2002)

Snow I, 1956
oil on linen, 26 x 38 in.
The Harwood Museum of Art, Taos.

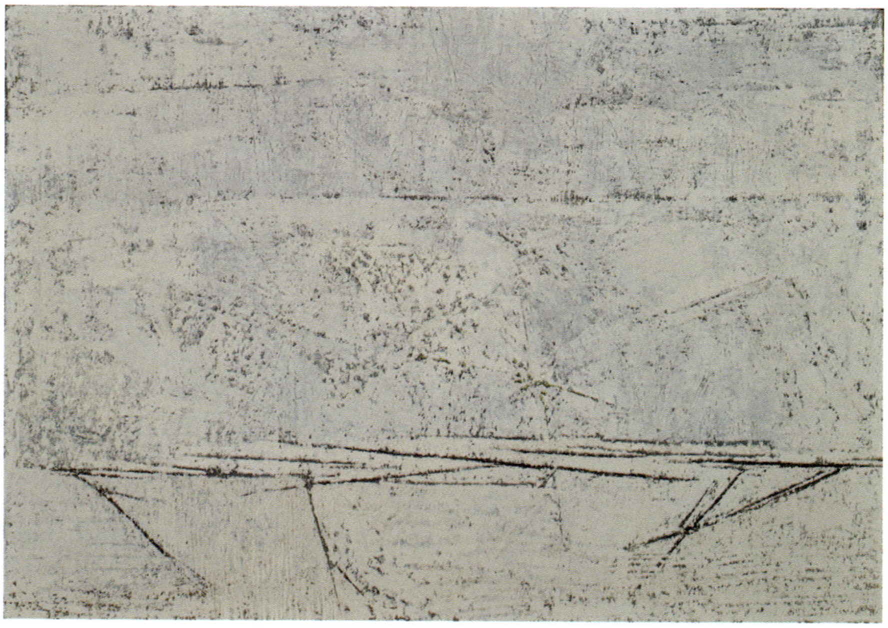

Time Changes All

Given the importance of nature in the works by Southwestern Abstract Expressionists, it is of little surprise that a concern for the seasons and the vicissitudes of the region would manifest in their work. These concerns helped to link the Southwesterners with a broader community of artistic thought, particularly their colleagues in New York. Polcari has argued that the New York School viewed life as "a continuity of self-sustaining action, an eternal mutability, forever operating on the same principles and forces. It was a continual generation, a constant energy, a change in time."[103] That eternal mutability and change in time seemed particularly appropriate for subject matter in the Southwest, where seasonal shifts produced dramatic variations in the landscape and geological processes were abundantly evident.

The contrast of the seasons as an expression of change engaged most of the Southwestern Abstract Expressionists at some point in their career. In Taos, modernists reacted to a series of long winters and heavy snowfalls. Beatrice Mandelman addresses the spell of winter throughout the 1950s and '60s with a severity similar to that of *Moonlight*. A stark white dominates her *Winter* (1954; fig. 47), save for a constellation of triangular forms, intersecting lines, and rough passages of pigment. Mandelman used geometric form, as well as a compass and straight edge, to bring a semblance of order to the bewildering experience of northern New Mexico blanketed by heavy snow. The points, arcs, and even textures offer points of reference, courses, and markers to lead the viewer through the undifferentiated white, in a manner akin to that of Martin's 1954 *Untitled* or Robert Ray's *Snow I* (1956; fig. 48). Ray moved to Taos from Denver in 1954 and began exhibiting with La Galeria Escondida shortly thereafter. His uneven application of paint emulates the pack of snow, but it is the representation of a whiteout that most closely approximates Mandelman's approach in *Winter*. Incised lines sketch a rough topography in *Snow I*, yet any clear sense of the lay of the land seems futile, given the veritable blizzard Ray depicted.

Similarly, Mandelman's plotting of the composition offers an aesthetic solution to the astounding vacancy she perceived in the region: "How does one relate to this vast, vast emptiness of the landscape? One can only feel very humble. How does one dare to take that experience and put it into an expression. That's really the mystery of it."[104] Mandelman's contemplation of this vacuity undoubtedly produced the sparse composition of *Winter* and suggests a metaphysical interpretation of space. Attempting to find form in the void, Mandelman constructed *Winter* as a speculative investigation of such contrasts.[105]

Winter in the Southwest prompted in Mandelman and others quiet contemplation of the vastness of space, with white serving as both a reference to the season and a vehicle for philosophical ruminations. Corbett, too, found white a compelling tool for exploring space and silence. In 1953, he accepted a position at Mount Holyoke College but spent summers in Taos between 1953–56 and, thereafter, in Provincetown between 1957–61. Memories of winters in Taos, paired with his experiences in Massachusetts, led to a series of white canvases wittily titled *Paintings for Puritans*. In what seems to be a deliberate rejection of Action painting, Corbett eliminated color and gesture from the series save for trace hues visible in the sculpted cracks or fissures that offer the only deviation from the uniform surface.[106] By suppressing the sensual, Corbett took an introspective path. In his *White Painting* (1957; fig. 49), an irregular cleft in the white surface runs from the left center to a point near the lower right corner. Areas of greater separation reveal a range of subtle reds, blues, and grays. Corbett's space may be seen as both limitless and limited depending on whether the viewer chooses to read the cleft as a crevasse or a mere crack. Gerald Nordland has associated the series with a stark winter in Taos in which Corbett experienced "whiteness for seventy miles," the result of which was *Journey to the Gorge* (1957; destroyed). Susan Landauer, by contrast, associates the series with Corbett's time in New England, since he began *Paintings for Puritans* during his tenure at Mount Holyoke.[107]

In all probability, the heavy winters in both locations inspired the series, but it is less the specific place than Corbett's approach to space that evokes his time in the Southwest. *White Painting* and the other *Paintings for Puritans* also possess a serenity that critic Emily Genauer described as "significant silence" and associated with Zen Buddhism.[108] The meager composition prompts meditation on both the greater expanse of white and the nuances of the fissure, resulting ideally in expanded awareness of an emotional, intellectual, or spiritual nature.

Whereas the seclusion of winter inspired Corbett, the monotony of the season troubled Clay Spohn and probably influenced *Gray Tones* (1958; fig. 50). Spohn painted the work either in Mount Holyoke, where he taught in Corbett's stead that spring while the latter was in New Orleans at Tulane University, or in New York City, where he settled later that year. Nevertheless, the atmospheric qualities, angular brushstrokes, and vertical reach of *Gray Tones* owe a debt to earlier Taos paintings such as *Blue Abstraction*. Spohn's balance of warm and cool grays creates

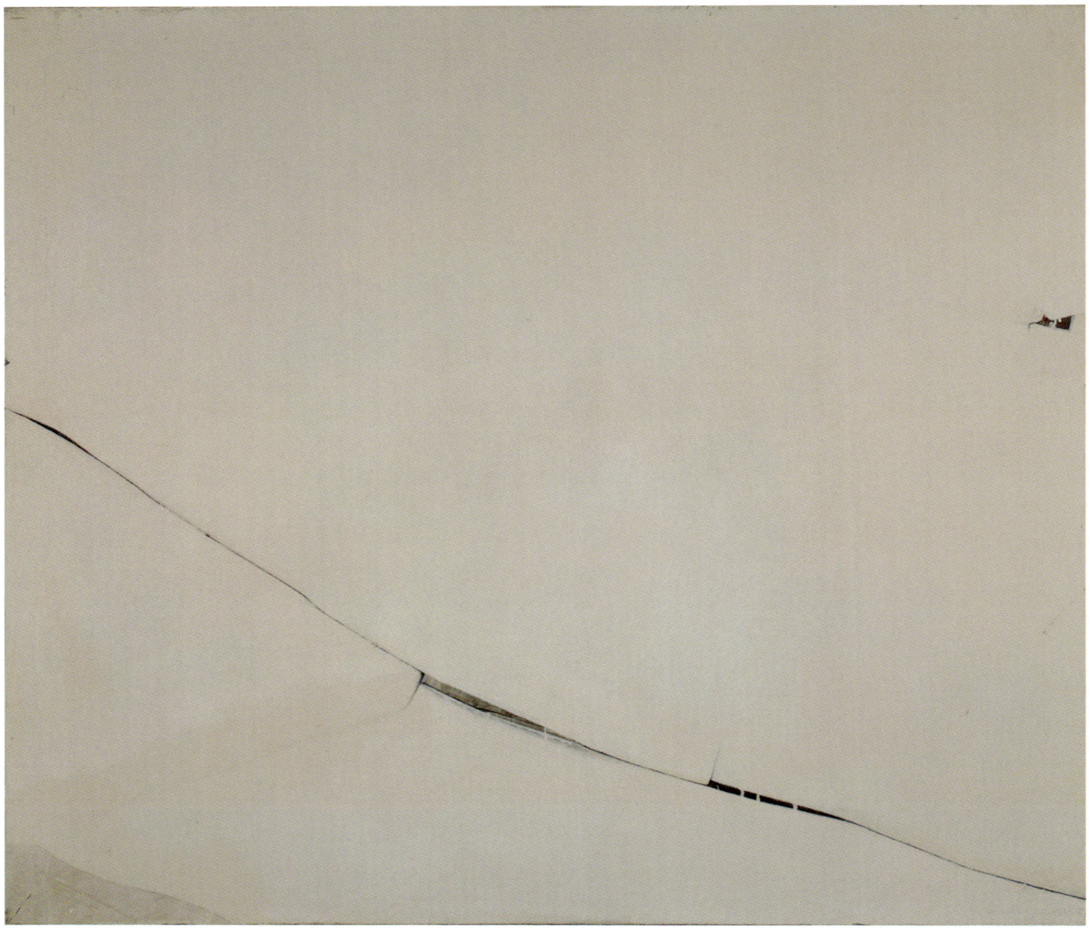

49 **Edward Corbett** (U.S., 1919–1971)

White Painting, 1957
oil on canvas, 35 3/4 x 43 1/16 in.
The Harwood Museum of Art, Taos.

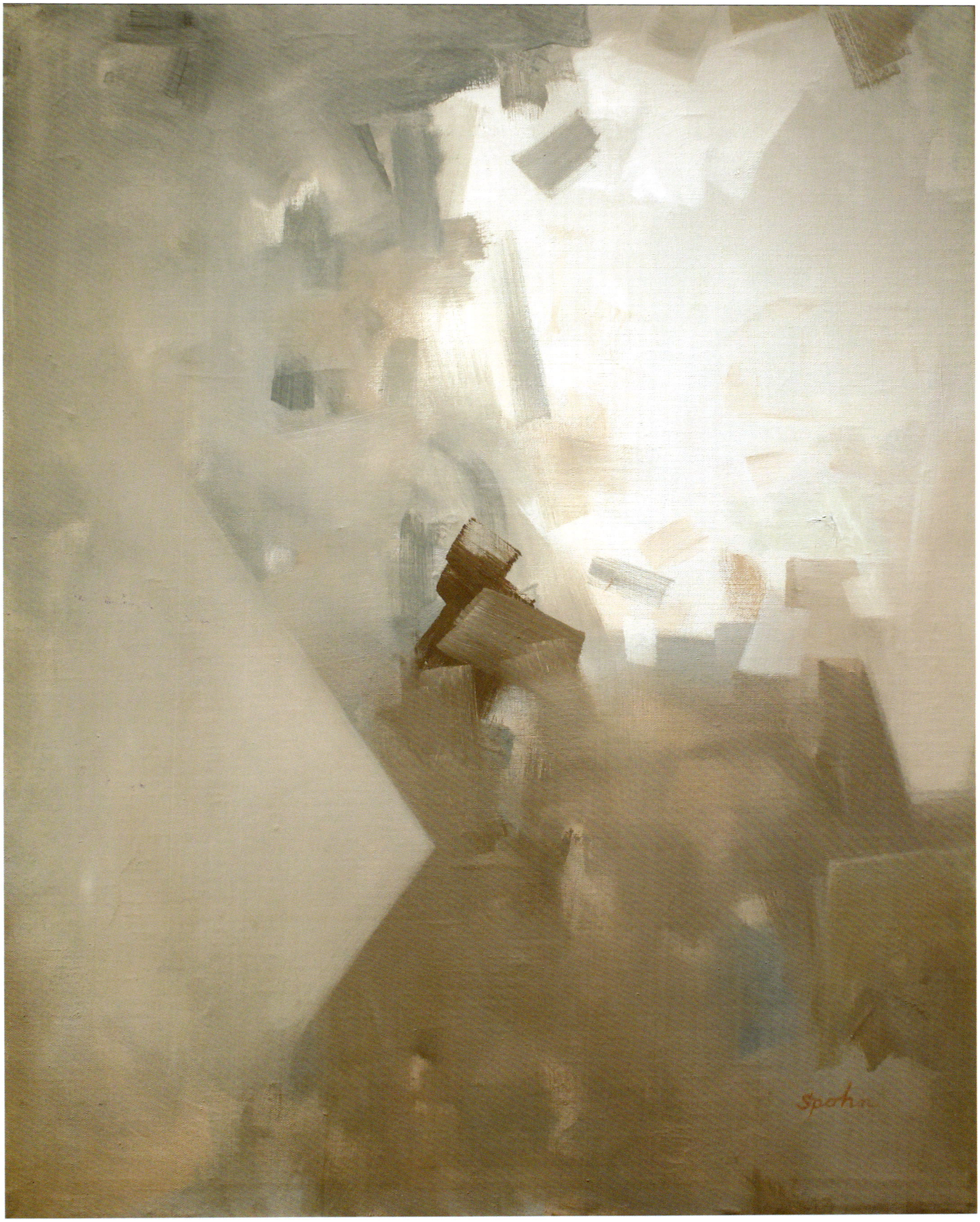

50 **Clay Spohn** (U.S., 1898–1977)

Gray Tones, 1958
oil on canvas, 42 x 34 in.
The Albuquerque Museum of Art and History.

passages of light and dark reminiscent of Hood's tempestuous *On Untrodden Paths*. The somber winter sky of New England, with a building or some other angular impediment intruding at lower left, likely shaped Spohn's approach. His arrangement of tones creates the impression of an upward spiral culminating with the brightest passage in the upper right as though Spohn is leading the viewer ever higher.

Gray Tones may have been painted outside the Southwest, but the sense of infinite space, an inexhaustible vertical reach, certainly has roots in Spohn's experiences in New Mexico. The perceived uniformity of the winter landscape allowed Spohn, Corbett, Mandelman, and McVicker to address familiar issues of expansive space and its metaphysical implications. That space was not merely terrestrial, as questions of boundlessness encouraged Abstract Expressionists to think beyond the earth's surface.

John O'Neil explored such considerations with his painting *In Winter* (1962; fig. 51), completed during a summer residency at the Huntington Hartford Foundation in the Pacific Palisades. His approach to winter was unquestionably informed by his visit to Scandinavia in 1960, and winter light would serve as inspiration for his *Scandia and Norway* series during the next several years. *In Winter* employs the same distillations of light and color found in his *Fragmented Landscape*, but with recollections of the evanescent greens, reds, and blues of the

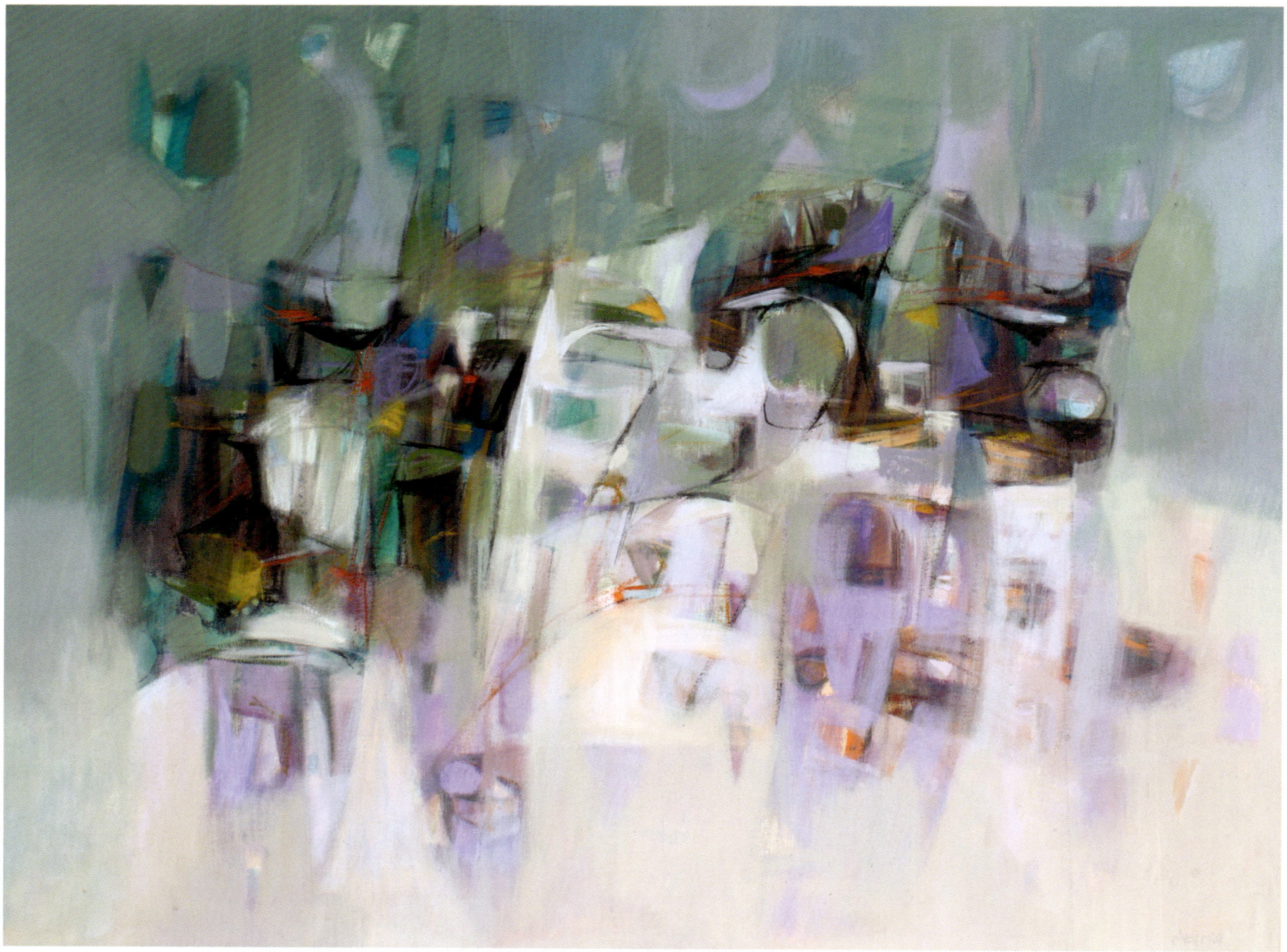

51 John O'Neil (U.S., 1915–2004)

In Winter, 1962
acrylic on canvas, 34 x 46 in.
Fred Jones Jr. Museum of Art, the University of Oklahoma, Norman, Oklahoma; gift of Eleonore Gunning, 1977.

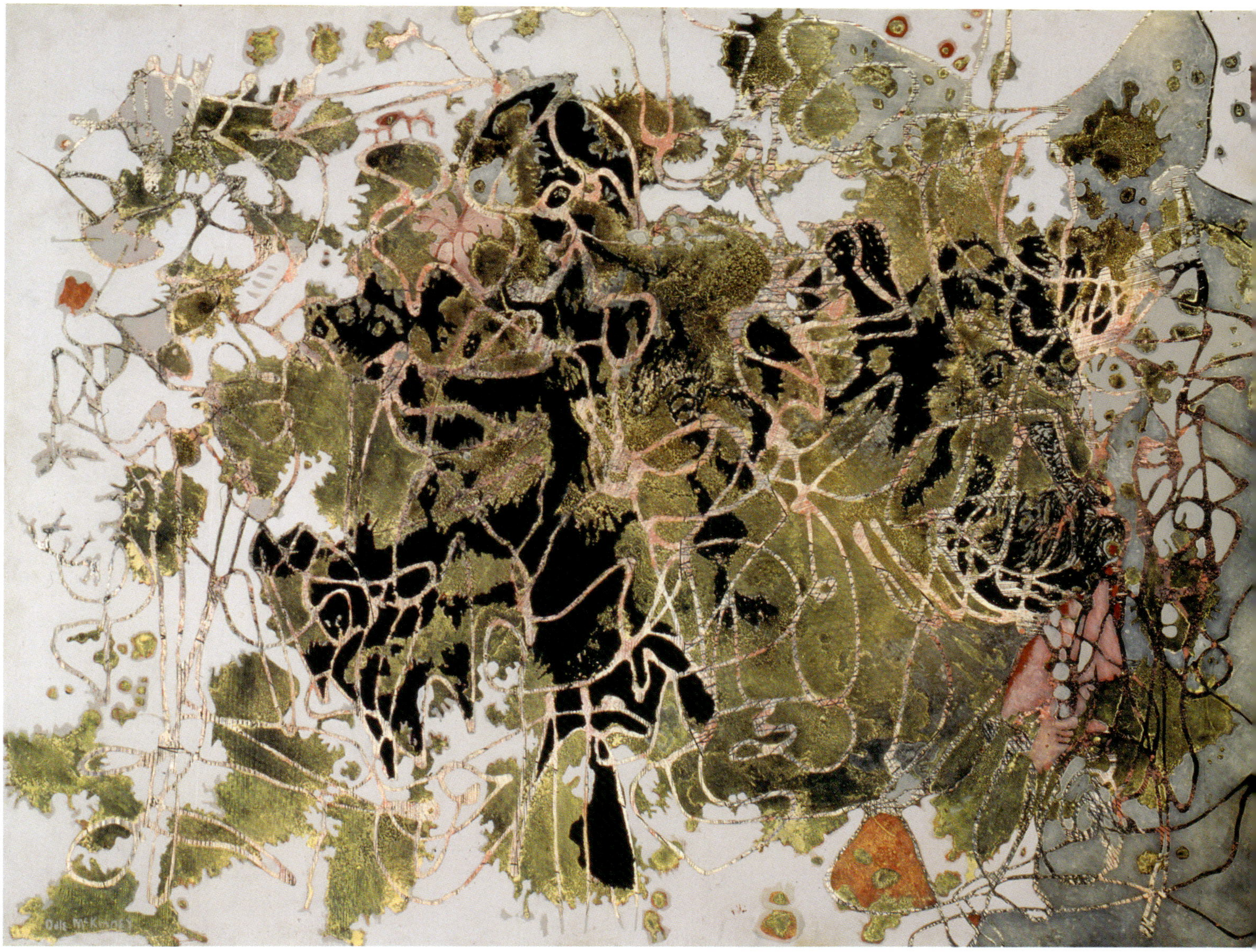

52 **Myron Dale McKinney** (U.S., 1911–1994)

Spring, ca. 1960
oil and paper mounted on plywood, 36 x 48 in.
Oklahoma Arts Council. Photo credit: John Jernigan.

aurora borealis. O'Neil organized the composition along a rough snow-laden horizon with the shimmering northern lights above represented by fragmentary passages of color and lyrical lines. *In Winter* takes as its subject the distinctive atmospheric conditions of the season, as well as electromagnetic phenomenon. In 1962, scientists still debated the causes of the aurora borealis although most agreed with Norwegian physicist Kristian Birkeland, who theorized in 1902–03 that the effect was caused by solar electrons flowing through the upper atmosphere of the poles. Whether O'Neil was familiar with the scientific theories is unclear, but *In Winter* makes implicit reference to space beyond.

Even when O'Neil and others worked outside the Southwest, the expansiveness of the region left an indelible mark on their aesthetic and conceptual approach to nature. The stark simplicity and evocative silence of winter instilled in them a contemplative mood often resulting in speculation on the infinite. By contrast, the arrival of spring sparked a reverie in the renewal of the land and an unbridled fecundity. McKinney, who had demonstrated an interest in nature dormant with *By-Product of Silence*, looked to the Eros in his *Spring* (ca. 1960; fig. 52).[109] Amorphous passages of blues, greens, oranges, and pinks bleed and seep across the panel, an effect McKinney achieved through a resist technique and judicious application of solvents. Sinuous lines weave throughout the composition, and close inspection reveals that the lines are not dripped paint but the result of some resist, perhaps wax, that the artist poured across the surface to conceal a lower layer of the painting. McKinney then removed that substance to make visible the lower layer, which includes translucent areas of scraped paint and a dizzying

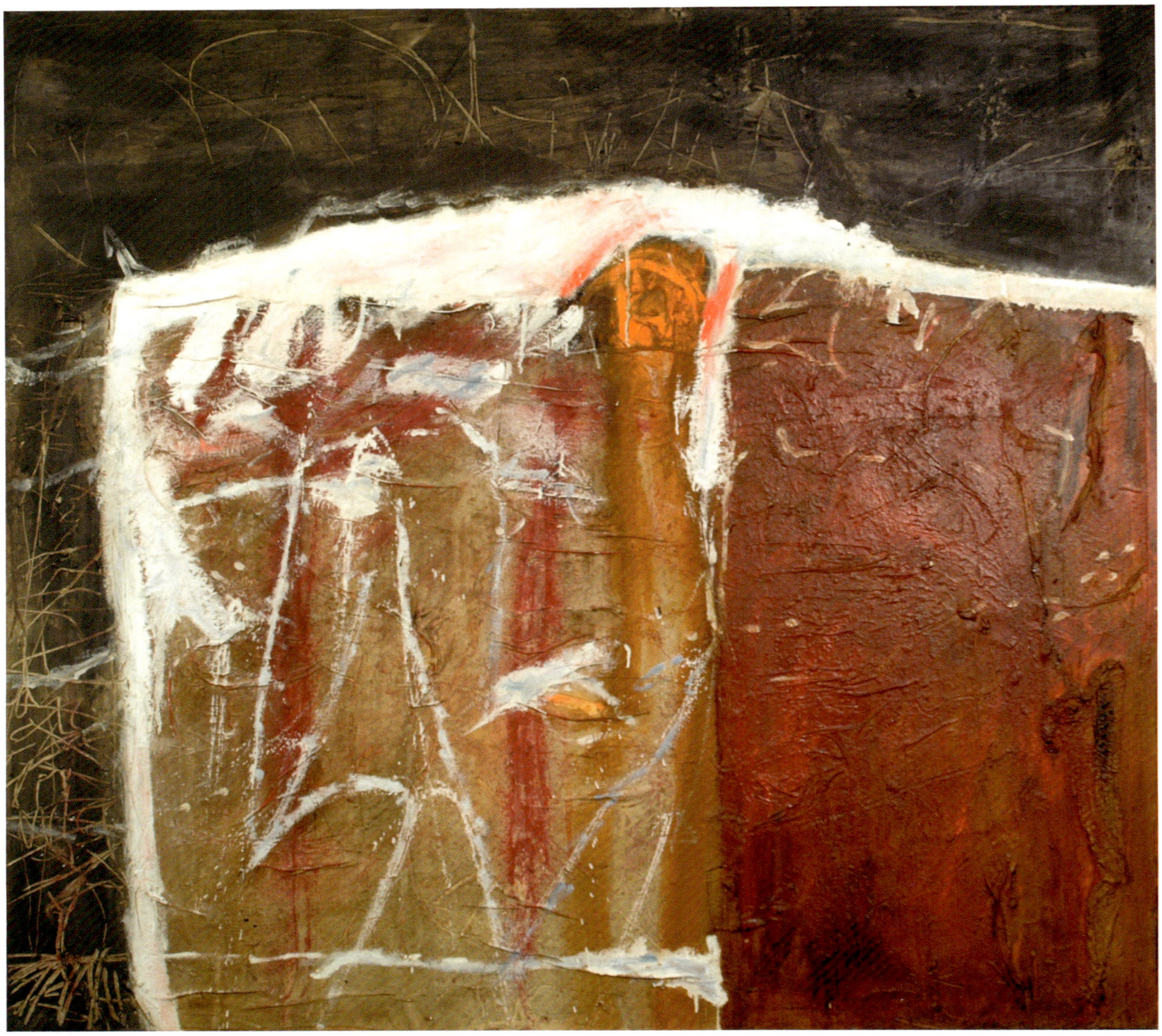

53 **Dick Wray** (U.S., 1933-2011)

Green Grass Man, 1961
oil on canvas, 51 3/4 x 58 in.
The Summers Collection.

network of intersecting lines. The tumultuous imagery and exuberant palette of *Spring* recalls the growth of trees, grasses, and vines, as well as winds, storms, and other climatic events associated with the season. McKinney most likely found inspiration in the cumulative vitality of Oklahoma springs, which are notable not only for their greening, but also for their high winds and unbridled, sometimes tornadic, storms.

Comparisons to the work of Janet Sobel, Hans Hofmann, and especially Jackson Pollock notwithstanding, McKinney's *Spring* stands apart with its distinctive layering that infers activity above and beneath the soil, namely the spring winds and rain and the germination of new life. Phenomenal changes in the landscape find metaphorical form in *Spring* through McKinney's aesthetic layering of color and texture, but especially through the frenetic energy of the lines and scuffs of the composition. In a similar manner, Wray used gestural brushwork and frenzied scrawls to capture the energy of nature in *Green Grass Man* (1961; fig. 53). A border of grayish green serves as a field for an energetic scribble that educes patches of turf. The green flanks a pair of monolithic, creased forms in light buff and deep red, suggestive of uneven patches of terrain. He created the forms by affixing another canvas to his primary support, creating textural possibilities akin to Burri's *Sacchi* paintings. Heavy swaths of white, red, and orange add further energy to the composition and help to convey the artist's empathetic engagement with his subject. Wray may not have intended the painting to be a depiction of spring, but he certainly envisioned an invocation to nature, with a title indicative of mid-century vernacular: "Green grass, man."

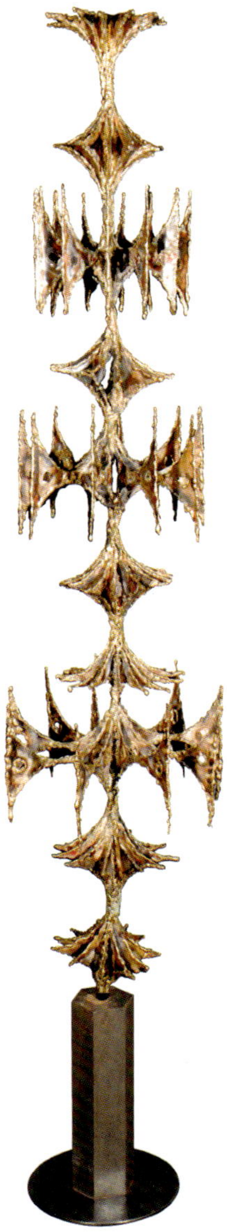

55 **Wilbert "Bill" Verhelst** (U.S.)

Construction # 4, 1960s
bronze, 37 x 8 3/4 in.
Collection Kirkland Museum of Fine and Decorative Art, Denver.

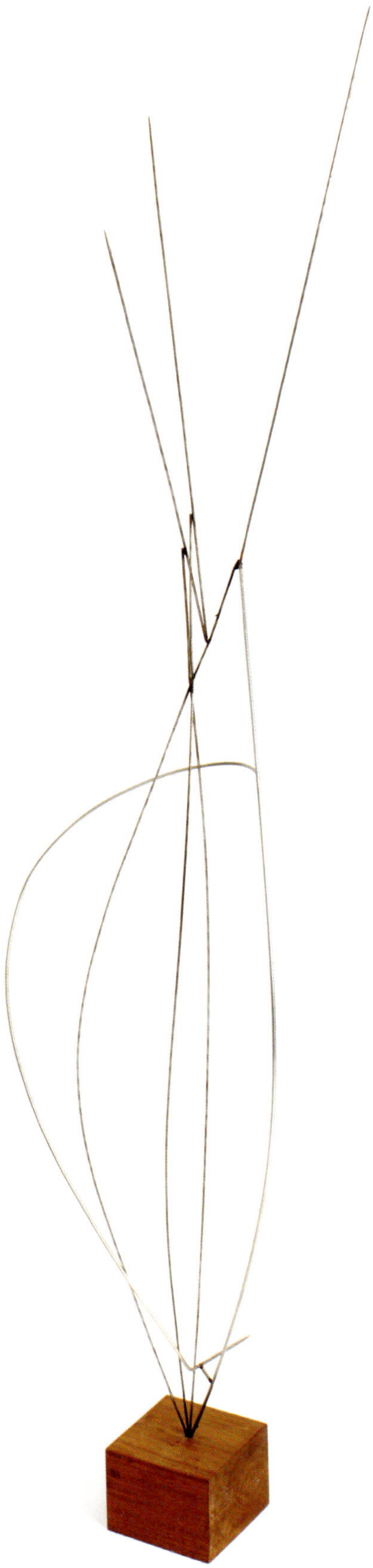

The *joie de vivre* expressed in Wray and McKinney often manifested in the works of other artists as a celebration of growth. Oklahoman James Henkle represented the germination of plant life through an economical arrangement of pliable steel rods in his *Growth* (1952; fig. 54). Henkle joined the faculty of OU in 1951 as an instructor in design and, although he worked actively in product and industrial design, he continued to paint and sculpt for much of his career.[110] Using industrial materials, Henkle drew in space, constructing a form similar to that of a budding plant. In a similar fashion, Wilbert "Bill" Verhelst's *Construction # 4* (1960s; fig. 55) depicts the blossom of an abstracted plant, its stalk ringed with leaves. Verhelst studied at the University of Denver receiving his MA in 1956, while teaching and working at the Denver Art Museum between 1948–57. He then joined the faculty of Southern Methodist University in Dallas in 1963.[111] His *Construction # 4* uses a sequence of copper and zinc blades on a vertical axis to suggest upward movement. Growth and seasonal change were Verhelst's primary themes, and his *Construction # 4*, in this respect, compares to similar works by Hatchett, Seymour Lipton, and Herbert Ferber, all of whom dealt with growth and change in nature in similar ways.[112]

54 **James Henkle** (U.S., b. 1927)

Growth, 1952
stainless steel and wood, 53 x 13 1/4 x 13 1/4 in.
Fred Jones Jr. Museum of Art, the University of Oklahoma, Norman, Oklahoma; gift of Professor Emeritus Roger Corsaw; reproduction permission courtesy of the artist.

The renewal of spring spoke to the timeless cycles of nature, even as the blossoming of flora suggested a transitory existence. Southwestern Abstract Expressionists applied such archetypal themes to the local. Stout painted *Flowers* in the spring of 1957 (fig. 56) with memories of Texas wildflowers in mind. The painting seemingly combines an intimate view of blooms and grasses in the large sweeping gestures of green, yellow, and pink at center with that of a more expansive field near the upper left, painted with abbreviated strokes. The diagonal emphasis of Flowers implies a gentle hill, fertile with spring growth, and Stout's compression of space offers a perspective of both the near and far.[113]

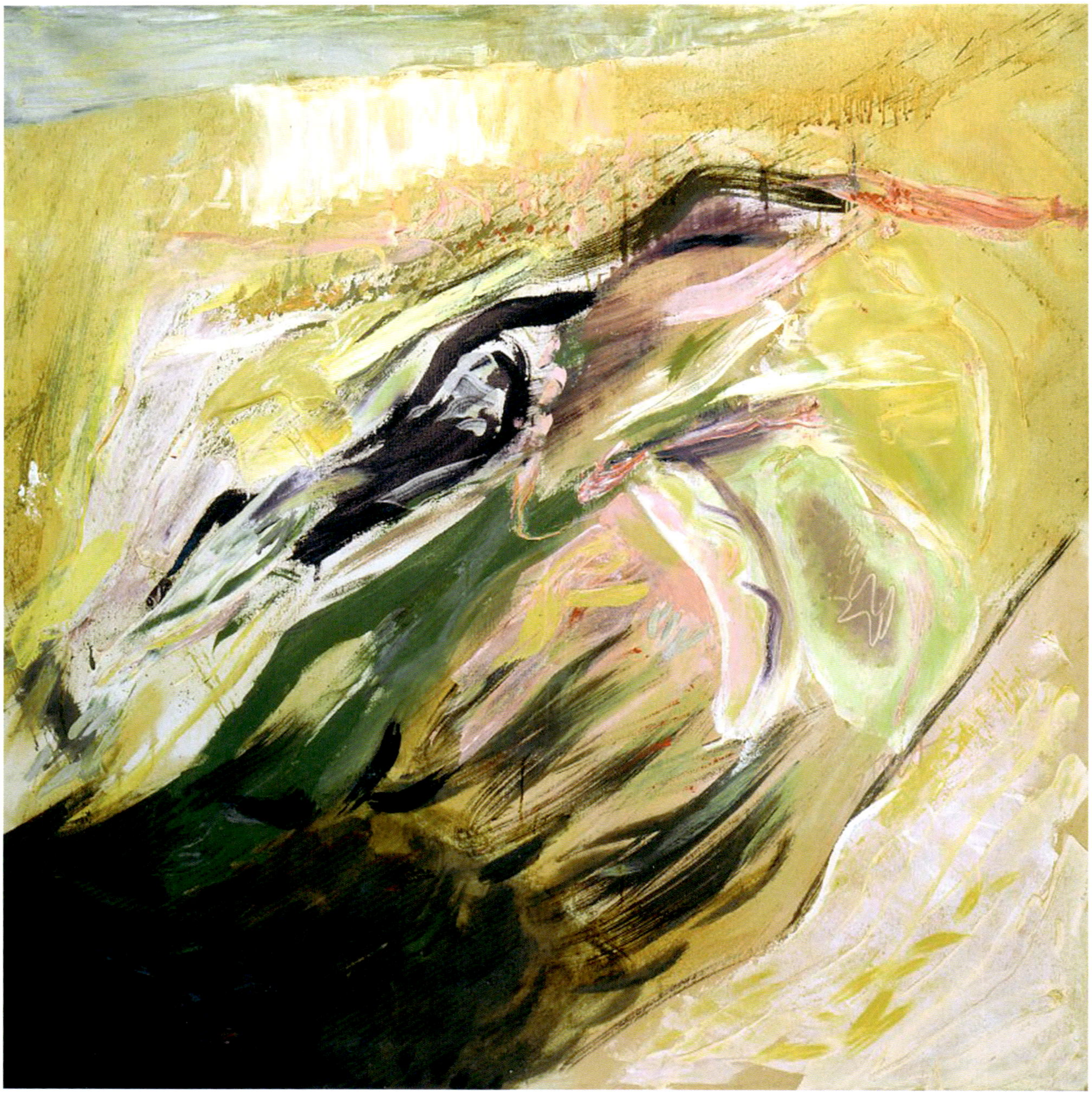

56 Richard Stout (U.S., b. 1934)

Flowers, 1957
oil on canvas, 50 x 50 in.
Collection of Linda and William Reaves;
reproduction ccurtesy of the artist.

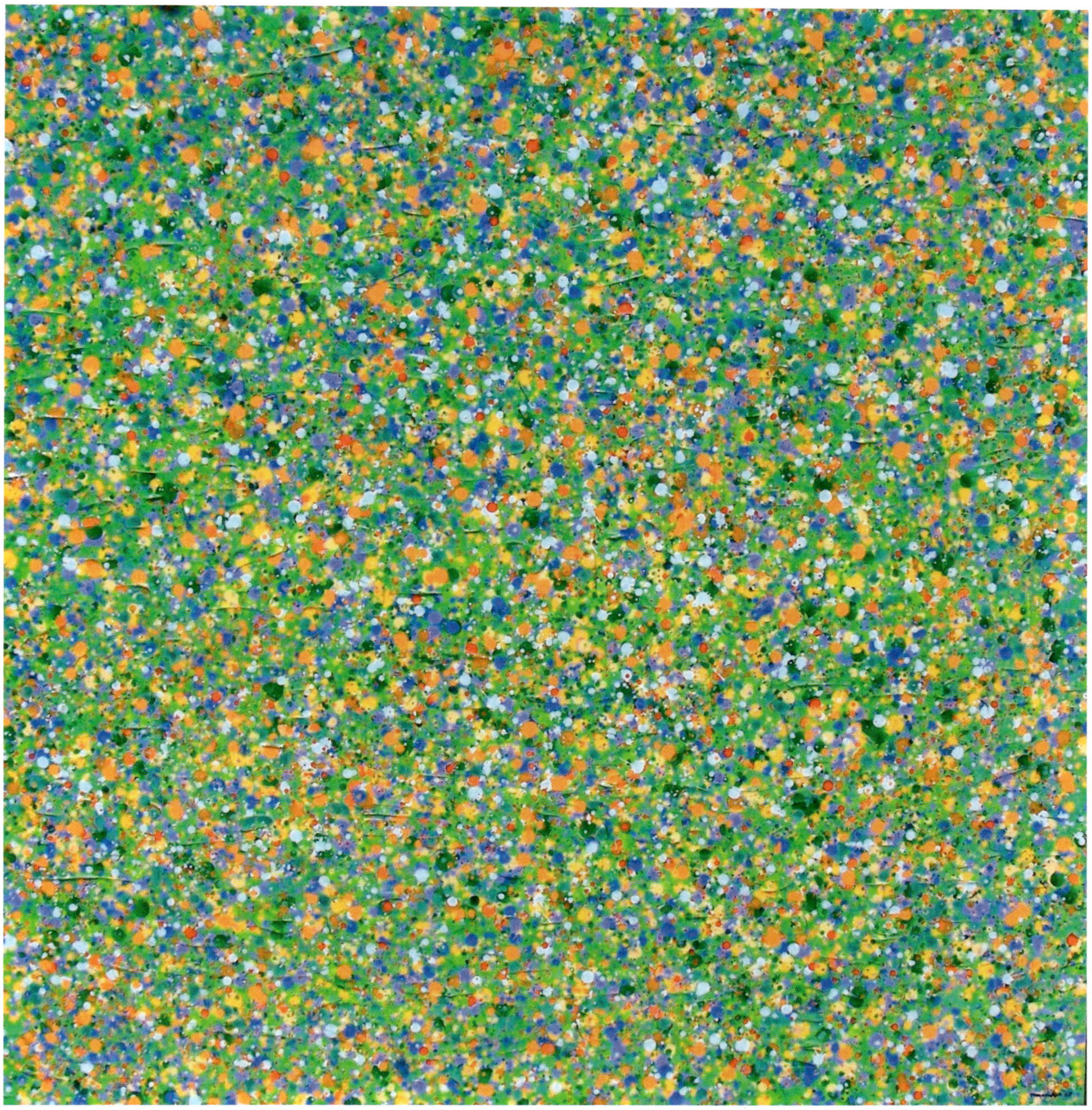

57 **J. Jay McVicker** (U.S., 1911–2004)

Yellow Green, 1967
acrylic on canvas, 48 x 48 in.
Collection of Jonathan and Talitha Nichols.

Flowers possesses a painterly immediacy expressive of the anima of nature. McVicker explored a similar approach with *Yellow Green* (1967; fig. 57) but relied on innumerable drips of yellow and green, as well as every other primary and secondary color, to convey the vivacity of springtime. The stippled effect recalls a pasture abounding with wildflowers; however, McVicker's title focuses on color and its seemingly chaotic arrangement, which emphasizes both visual energy and randomness. The absence of focal points in *Yellow Green* impels the viewer to find order or structure in the repetition of certain colors or size of the drips. Wandering through the composition, the viewer is immersed in patterns of his or her own making, effectively getting lost in the exuberance of the drips.

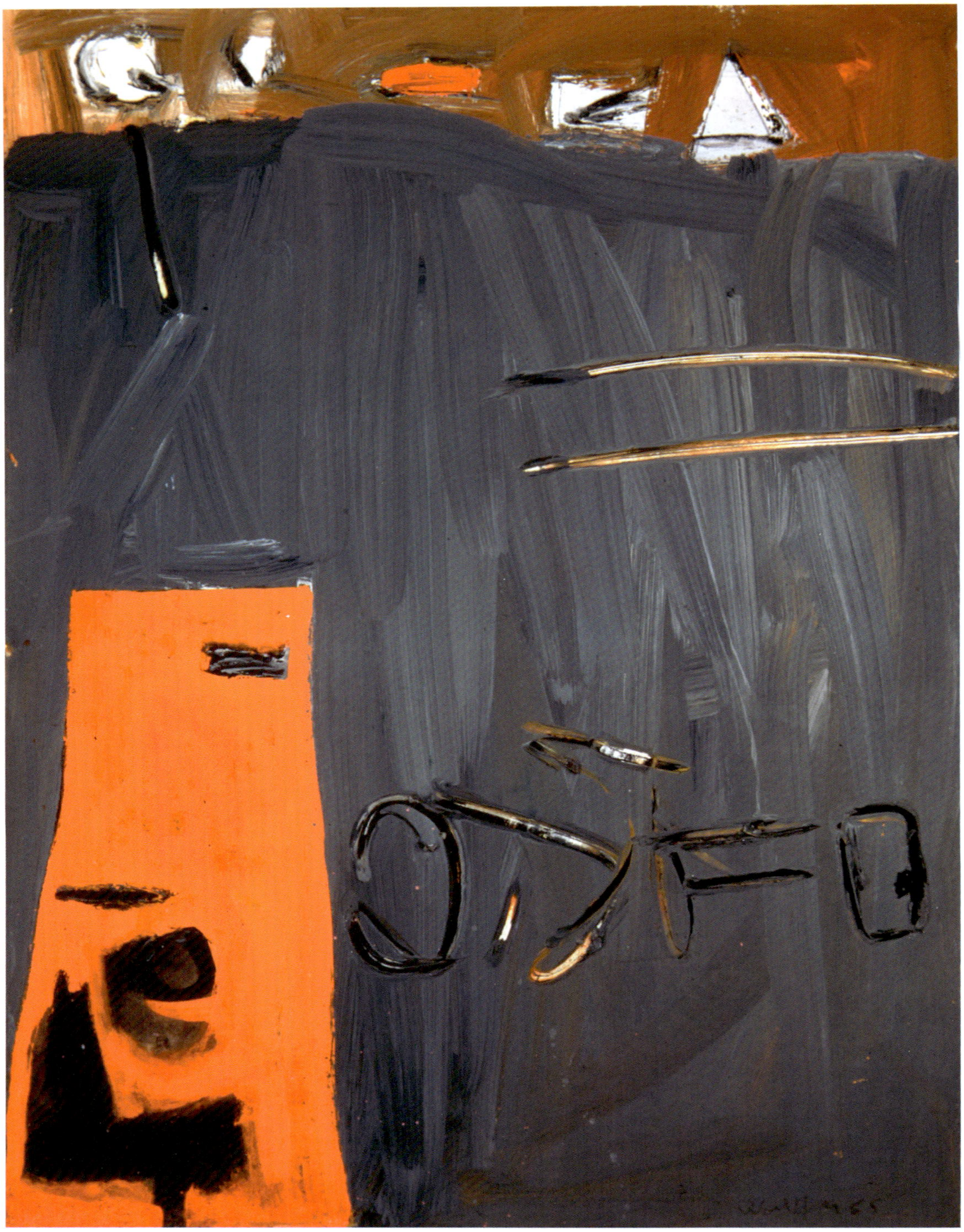

58 **Emerson Woelffer** (U.S., 1914–2003)

Morning Earth, 1955
oil and collage on canvas, 36 x 28 in.
Manny Silverman Gallery, Los Angeles, CA; Artwork Courtesy of the Otis College of Art and Design Emerson Woelffer Collection.

The glorification of nature's renewal extended beyond the fertility of spring. Dawn prompted a similar aesthetic salutation among many of the Southwestern Abstract Expressionists. Given the insistent horizon of the stark Southwest, the interaction between sun and earth, and especially the brilliance of sunrise, is a mainstay of daily existence and particularly suitable for artistic treatment. Woelffer's *Morning Earth* (1955; fig. 58) seems to capture the moments before dawn as the sky, still a burnt orange, has yet to illumine the gray terrestrial mass below. Ambiguous ideographs, perhaps foliage, line the horizon above and cryptic signs below flank an orange monolith that contains a possible personnage. The title may be read as both a description of the specific conditions Woelffer witnessed as the sun rose over the rurals outside Colorado Springs, and also as a greeting addressed to nature at the beginning of a new day.

Like his contemporary, Bunnell also was inclined to capture the radiant daybreak in his *Texas Dawn* (1958; fig. 59) during one of his frequent trips to visit Fitz in Amarillo.[114] An indistinct yellow sun at the upper left illuminates the sky resulting in a range of subtle gradations of red, orange, and yellow. A single amorphous passage in the lower right, perhaps some vegetative form, is the only deviation from an atmosphere ablaze with incendiary color. *Texas Dawn* lacks Bunnell's customary impasto and planar forms, creating an unfettered experience of color. Given his metaphysical tendencies, *Texas Dawn* was likely intended as a transcendental experience, in which materiality dissipates, leaving only light and an exultant spirituality.

59 **Charles Ragland Bunnell** (U.S., 1897–1968)

Texas Dawn, 1958
oil on canvas, 38 x 38 in.
Private collection

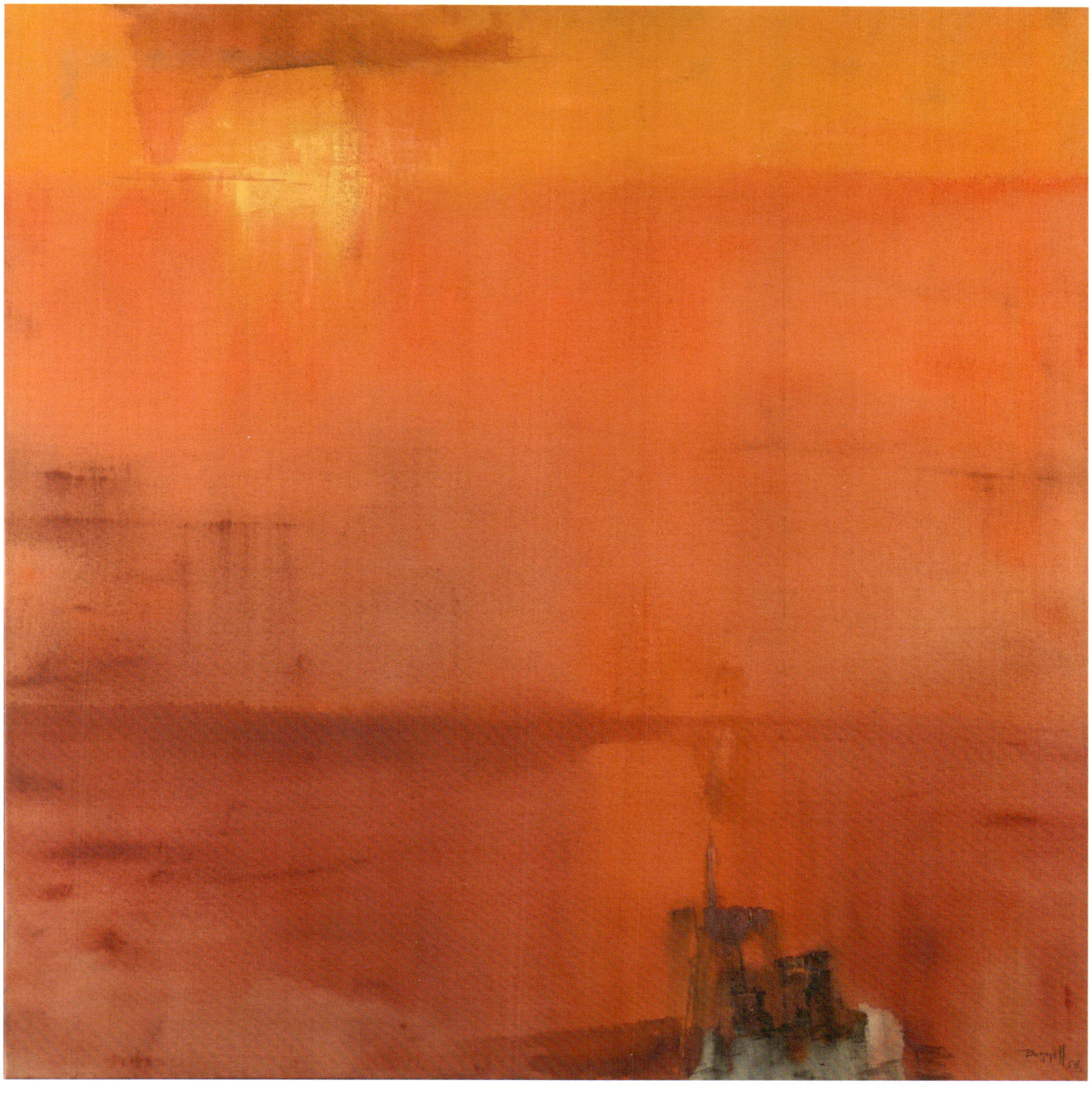

Fitz also associated the dialogue between a blazing sun and earthly plain with a spiritual experience. *Gathering One* (1957; fig. 60) depicts a series of bursts or pulses in black and white, each tinged with red, above an accumulation of black, gray, and blue strokes that suggest a rough ground plane. While the inspiration was likely the big sky of the High Plains, the imagery goes beyond a transcription of the environment. Fitz believed in the transmission of energy between the celestial and terrestrial and an omnipresent and omniscient "Life Force," or the "Gathering One" of the title, that collects and transmits those forces. As he commented, "The cosmic broadcast is always on and available to all aware beings."[115] Those willing to "tune in" could be assured profound insight. The bursts of *Gathering One*, in this respect, may represent points of interaction or discourse between the cosmic and earthbound.

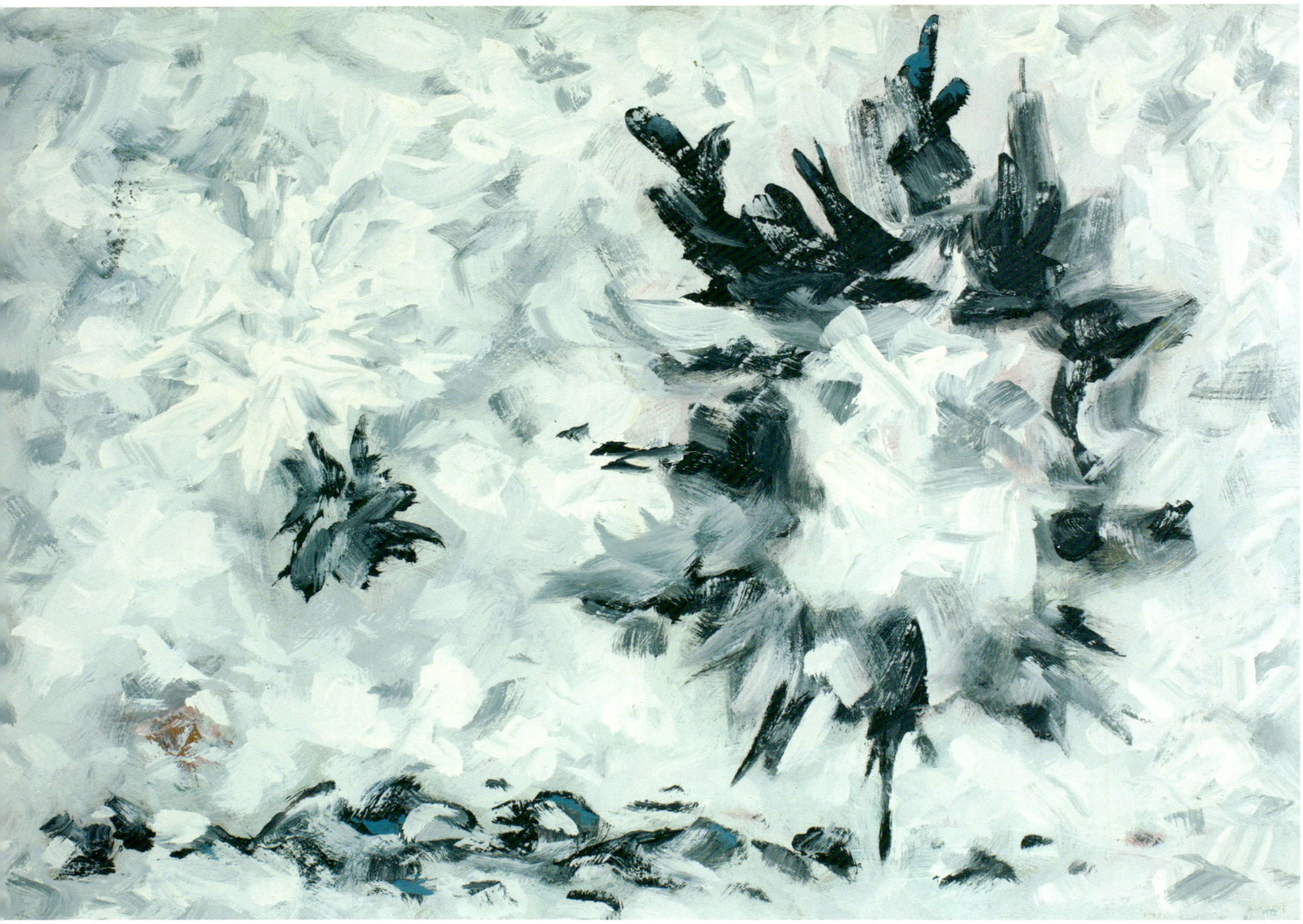

60 **George Edward "Dord" Fitz** (U.S., 1914-1989)

Gathering One, 1957
oil on Masonite, 33 x 48 in.
Fred Jones Jr. Museum of Art, the University of Oklahoma; Gift of Caroline E. Fitz; Dale E. Fitz; Brewster Fitz and Carol Moder, 2011

Fitz's depiction of cosmic communion in *Gathering One* had a clear basis in the unadulterated landscape of northern Texas. The distinctive qualities of the Southwest provided Fitz, and so many others, with intellectual, psychological, or spiritual transport. The prospect that a work of art offered passage to another state guided Boynton's *Outpost* (1957; fig. 61). The rolling plain, pinkish sun, ruddy soil, and panoramic breadth imply a Southwestern inspiration for Boynton's otherwise fantastical and remote settlement. Edwards has interpreted the painting as "a psychological outpost of the mind," and Boynton's setting seems unworldly, despite its obvious debt to geography of the Southwest.[116] Nature in *Outpost* is intentionally enigmatic and evocative, particularly in its contrasts of the resolute sun and the vacillating terrain below, which seems a combination of soil, plant, and even musculature and sinew. Boynton's mysterious composition invites metaphysical exploration of the dichotomy of sky and land, the relationship of flora and fauna, and the unfamiliar spaces of the mind.

Boynton's enigmatic study of such contrasts emphasizes that his relationship to the Southwest, or that of any of the Southwestern Abstract Expressionists, was never merely a representation of natural phenomena, whether inspired by winter, spring, or the dawn. Space in the work of these artists is always a portent for a thoughtful investigation of complicated philosophical questions. These questions were made all the more complicated at mid-century by scientific and technological advances that expanded human knowledge of the infinitely small and large spaces of the atom and the universe, respectively.

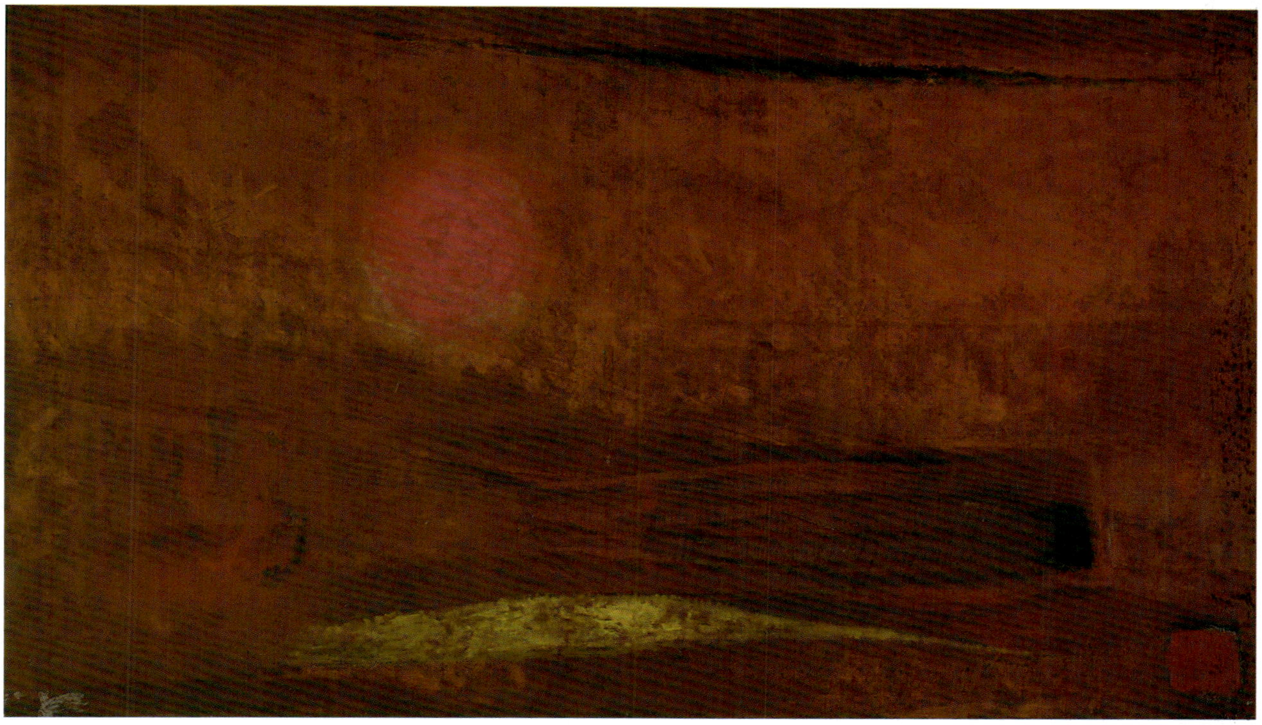

61 James Wesley "Jack" Boynton (U.S., 1928–2010)

Outpost, 1957
oil on Masonite, 49 x 85 in.
The Blanton Museum of Art, the University of Texas at Austin, Gift of D. D. Feldman, 1964; reproduction courtesy of Blanton and Sharon Boynton. Photo credit: Rick Hall.

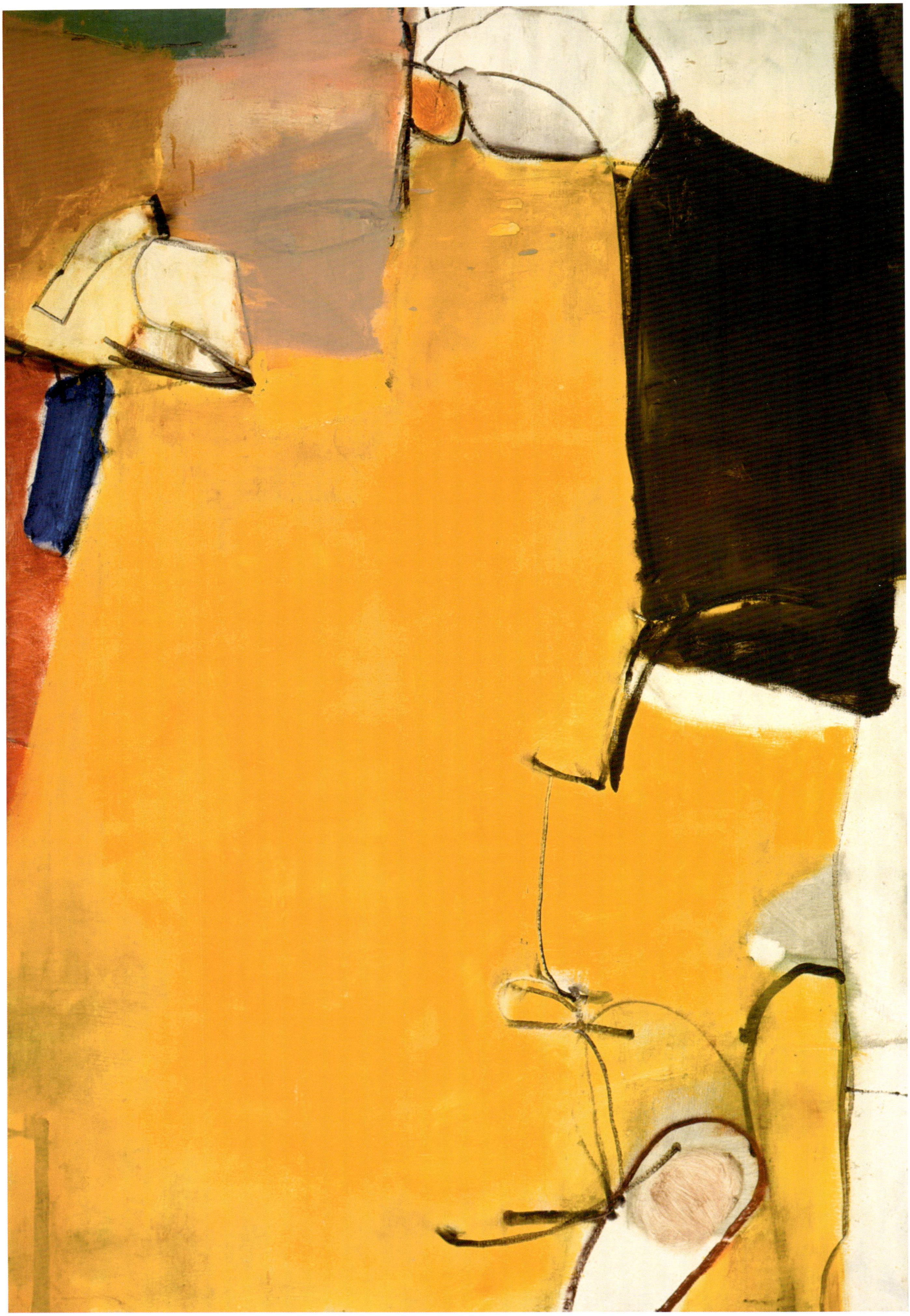

Macrocosm/Microcosm

In the 1950s and '60s, the Southwest became an important region in scientific and technological innovation, and the work of Southwestern Abstract Expressionists frequently acknowledged the changes that theory and invention played in changing human perception. One of the most important and accessible of those changes was air travel. To be sure, flight by aircraft was nothing new in the U.S. but, following World War II, increasing numbers of Americans traveled by air. A dramatic increase in transcontinental flights and the creation of coach fares by the major airlines made air travel more popular. By 1951, passenger traffic on the airlines reached approximately 26 billion miles, exceeding that of locomotives for the first time.[117] Diebenkorn was one of those passengers.

Following the completion of his MFA exhibition in the summer of 1951, Diebenkorn flew to San Francisco to see the Arshile Gorky exhibition at the San Francisco Museum of Art. He recalled, "I'd never taken a plane trip like that before. Flew fairly low over just all sorts of country which just absolutely blew my mind. It wasn't that I went right to the canvas and said I'm going to paint this but it just went right into the mill and started coming out strong." The flight, along with the influence of Gorky, produced a visible change in Diebenkorn's style, evident in *Untitled* (1951; fig. 62).[118] His aerial view of the varied geography resulted in areas of bright color, bounded by irregular borders. Diebenkorn's calligraphic approach to line remains, though deferential to the masses of color drawn from the Southwest and regions north. Color, line, and form allude to a patchwork of terrain, from which he extracted the essential colors and the characteristics of the natural contours. Rather than the carefully platted land of the Midwest, nature in Diebenkorn's *Untitled* is irregular, unpredictable, and somewhat disorienting. Fixed points and orderly rhythms seem absent.

That perspective was increasingly common among Americans, as they gazed out airplane windows at the changing scenery below. Author Bernard de Voto touted the advantages of carrying a map on transcontinental flights in order to make sense of the geography.[119] The novelty of the aerial perspective was hardly lost on Trans World Airlines (TWA), which marketed that experience to fliers in the 1950s. In a poster advertising their direct flight to the Grand Canyon, TWA promised a window view of the geological wonders below (fig. 63). While Diebenkorn had been moved by a similar experience, he was unconcerned with either mapping the country or representing major landmarks, but sought to express his sublime amazement.

That aerial view of the landscape was no less influential on Bavinger, although he was more familiar with the perspective. He served as an aviation instructor in the U.S. Air Force during World War II and continued to fly periodically thereafter. Like other amateur pilots, Bavinger took advantage of the expansion of municipal airports following the war in an established network of skyways,

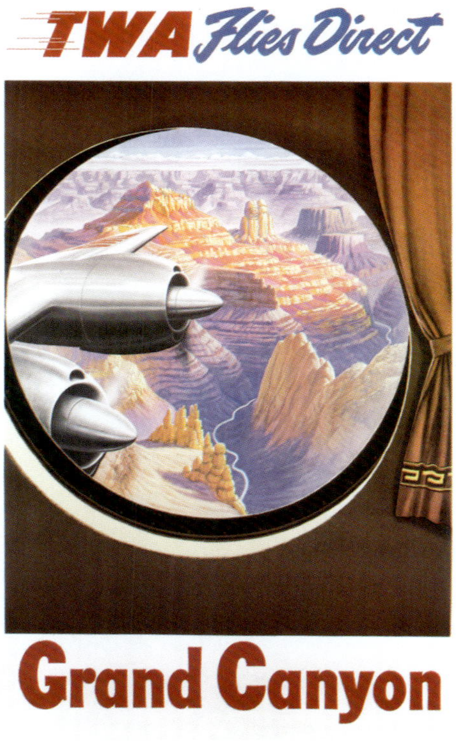

62 **Richard Diebenkorn** (U.S., 1922–1993)

Untitled, 1951
oil on canvas, 54 3/4 x 37 3/4 in.
University of New Mexico Art Museum, Albuquerque, 51.11; © The Richard Diebenkorn Foundation.

63 **David Klein** (U.S., 1918-2005)

TWA Flies Direct—Grand Canyon, 1950s

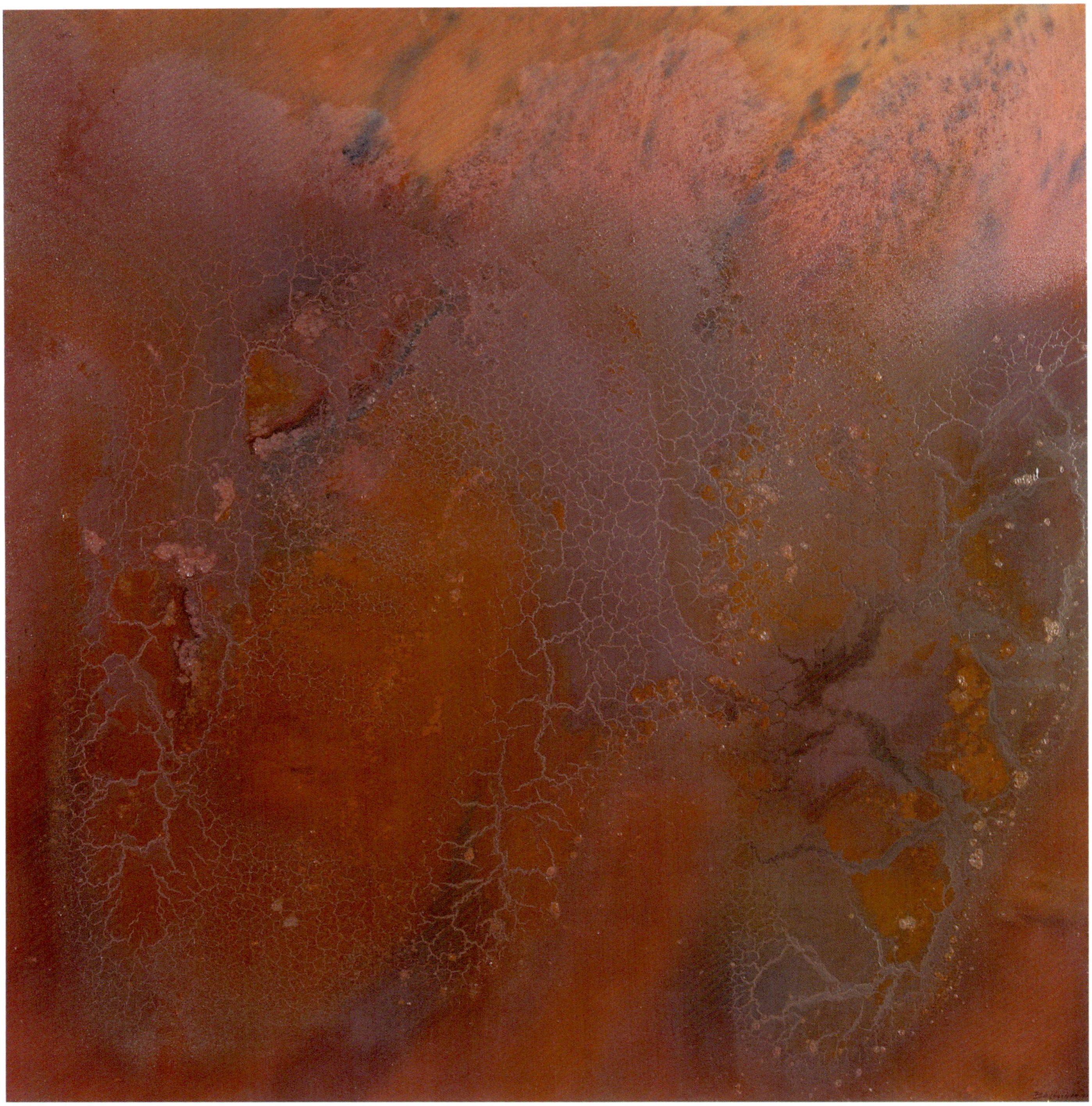

65 **Eugene "Gene" Bavinger** (U.S., 1919–1997)

Red Earth, 1971
oil on canvas, 69 x 69 in.
Philbrook Museum of Art, Tulsa, Oklahoma

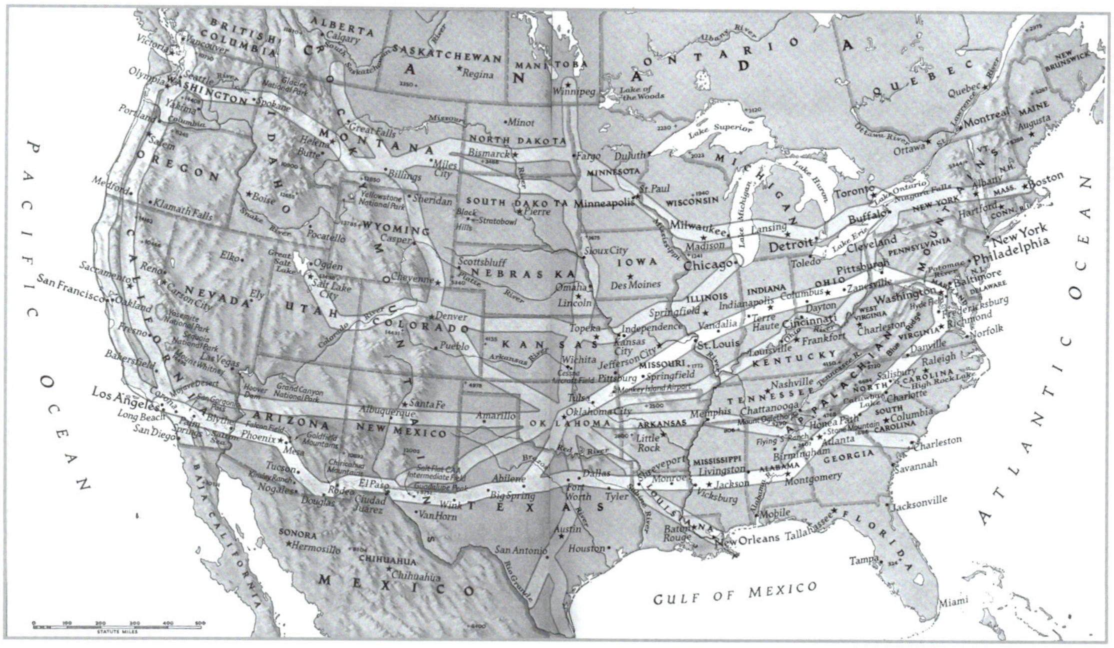

64 **Unknown artist**

"Nine Other Skyways Weave a Network of 'Highways' Below the Clouds,"
National Geographic, 1949
Courtesy of Nat'L Geographic Cartographic Division/National Geographic Creative.

the major intersection of which was located in Oklahoma City (fig. 64).[120] His experiences in the air ultimately influenced *Red Earth* (1971; fig. 65). The painting reads at once as a sprawling range of rubicund, eroded earth and as a small patch of soil cracked by water's passage and subsequent evaporation. Bavinger's title probably originated from the common term for the iron-rich soil dominant in Oklahoma but found across the Southwest. By pouring solvents onto a canvas stretched out on the floor, he emulated on the painted surface the effects of water on the naked ground, creating a startling geography of ridges, gullies, and sandy beds that seems as erratic as Diebenkorn's *Untitled*.

Bavinger's interest in natural processes developed in 1960–61, during his study at the Instituto Allende in San Miguel de Allende, Mexico. He visited Mayan and Aztec ruins repeatedly and found meaning in their deterioration and slow atrophy: "Something existed at one time and it existed in a certain form and has since changed through the process of erosion, deterioration, the jungle growth that covers these Mayan ruins and the final image is never constant—it is constant—it is constantly changing, if anything, so I tried to express that feeling that here is a form that is transforming—altering through time and through elements that are affecting it and the expression of it then becomes a sort of undefined image that having some kind of forceful feeling about the elements that have affected this change."[121] Change, as a fundamental trait of nature, is the primary subject of *Red Earth*, not only in terms of Bavinger's chemical alteration of the media, but also in the patterns of paint, which still seem viscous and unsettled. As such, *Red Earth* compares formally and conceptually to Robert Smithson's *Asphalt on Eroded Cliff* (1969; fig. 66). Smithson poured hot asphalt down an eroded cliff outside Rome, Italy, in a process analogous to Pollock's drip paintings but on a massive scale. *Asphalt on Eroded Cliff* was motivated, in part, by Smithson's interest in entropy and the second law of thermodynamics.[122] He hoped to mark aesthetically the disorder of the slope, making that process more visible while adding yet another element, the asphalt, to a system of slow change.

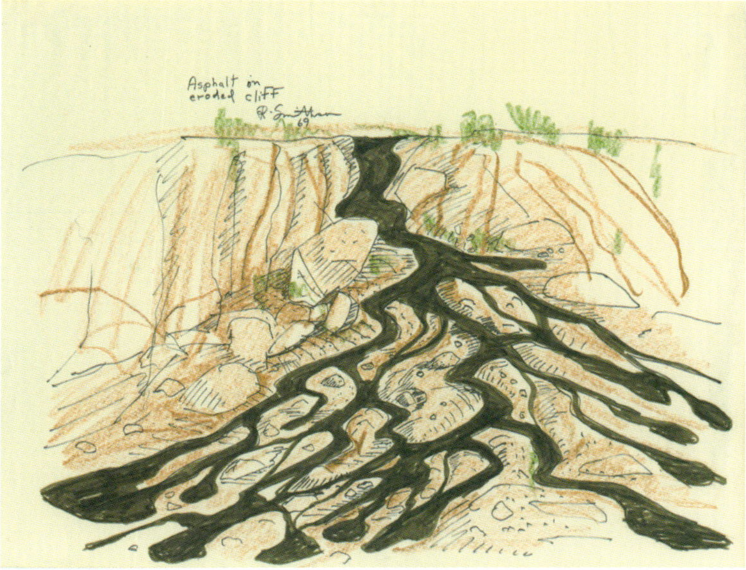

66 **Robert Smithson** (U.S.)

Asphalt on Eroded Cliff, 1969
ink and colored chalk on paper, 18 x 24 in.
Fred Jones Jr. Museum of Art, the University of Oklahoma, Norman, Oklahoma.
Art © Estate of Robert Smithson/Licensed by VAGA, New York."

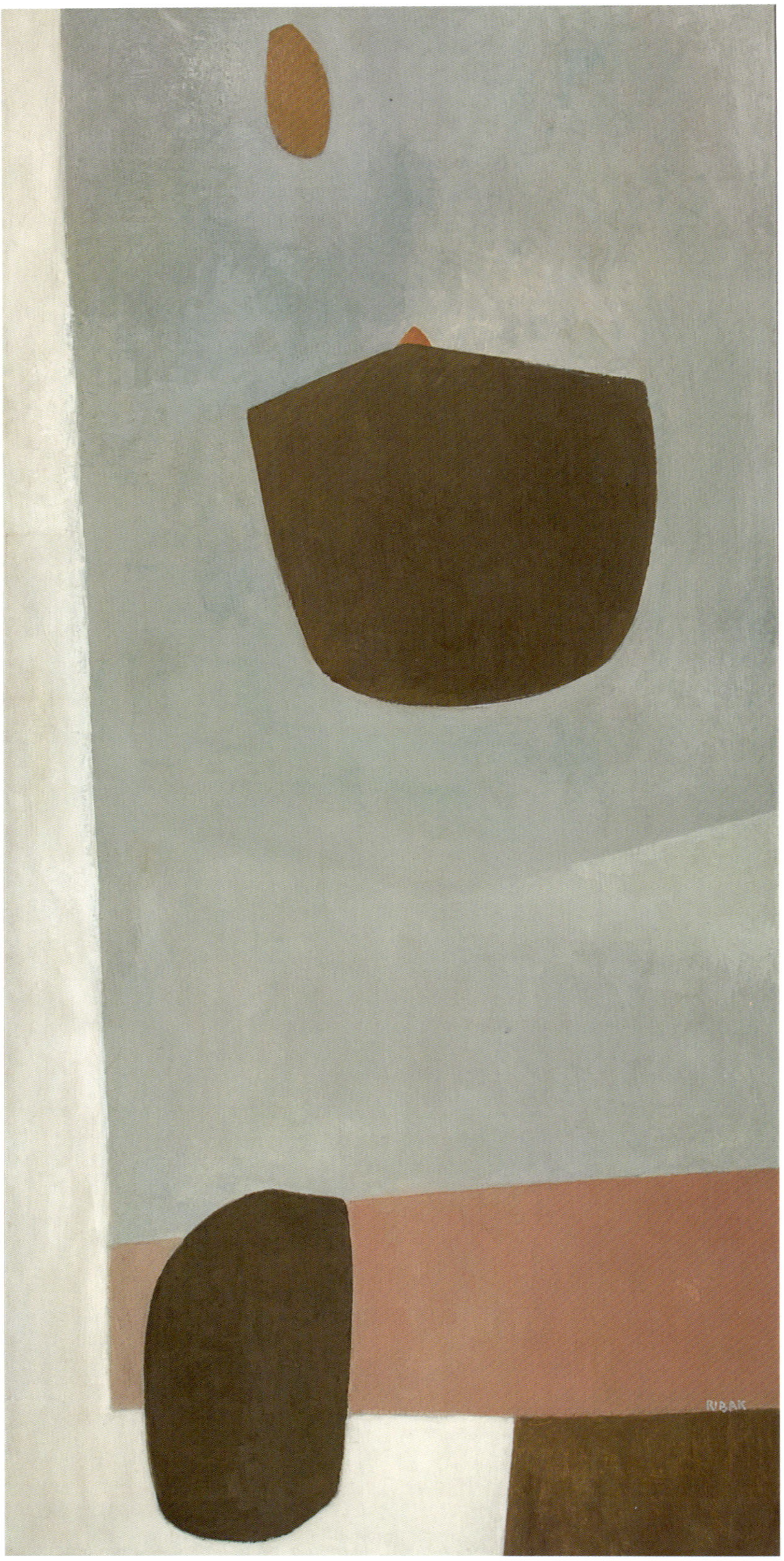

Mutability was a constant theme among the Southwestern Abstract Expressionists and is certainly primary in *Red Earth*, yet it is the aerial view, the local color, and the shifting perspective between the macro and micro that associates the painting with the Southwest. Access to aviation provided new and alternative means for both Bavinger and Diebenkorn to interpret Southwestern space. Flight ostensibly influenced Ribak's *Suspension* (late 1950s; fig. 67), with its hovering bodies and sectioned composition, but the painting may be read in a variety of ways. Three orbs float within an ambiguous space defined by geometric divisions in white, livid, rose, and dark brown. Given Ribak's title, the indeterminate masses may be interpreted either as clouds moving above a platted landscape or as more substantial bodies that are arrested or interrupted in the act of rising or falling against a graying sky, flanked at left by a precipice. Alternatively, the dark masses may actually be voids in a stratified surface, not unlike the eroded pockets in tuff formations. Light, shadow, and various minerals often tint the petrified ash in pastel hues, and Ribak undoubtedly found some inspiration in the tuff cliffs around Los Alamos.

67 **Louis Ribak** (U.S., born Lithuania, 1902–1979)

Suspension, late 1950s
oil on Masonite, 72 x 36 in.
The Harwood Museum of Art, Taos.

Archaeologist and writer Reginald Fisher certainly thought there was a connection, when discussing the relationship between the Los Alamos National Laboratory (LANL; formerly Los Alamos Scientific Laboratory) and contemporary art for the 1963 exhibition, *Art and the Atom: An Exhibition of Contemporary Art Used in Scientific Advertisements*. The exhibition was organized through a partnership between the Stables Art Gallery, the Taos Art Association, Inc., and LANL and included paintings by Taos artists that had been used in promotion of the laboratory by Ward Hicks Advertising. Fisher noted that the artists of Taos "live and work in a contemporary intellectual climate emanating in part from a scientific laboratory at Los Alamos, across the valley, where the atom bomb was born. The art of these painters wells from the profound dialogic relationship with environment—intellectual, technological, ethnic, geographic."[123] In this view, *Suspension*, and the other works in the exhibition, drew inspiration from the local landscape as well as the broader culture of northern New Mexico. Ward Hicks Advertising began using *Suspension* to advertise employment at LANL in 1961 with the header, "Contemporary education, like contemporary art, continues to find expression in new areas" (fig. 68). The ads ran in a variety of publications, including *Scientific American* and *Chemical and Engineering News*.[124] Just as LANL advanced the frontiers of science into the microcosmic, contemporary artists like Ribak explored new artistic territory. The ambiguity of *Suspension* lent itself to the promotion of nuclear science with its floating bodies that could be seen variously as microcosmic molecules, nuclei, or electrons bounded by fields of energy.

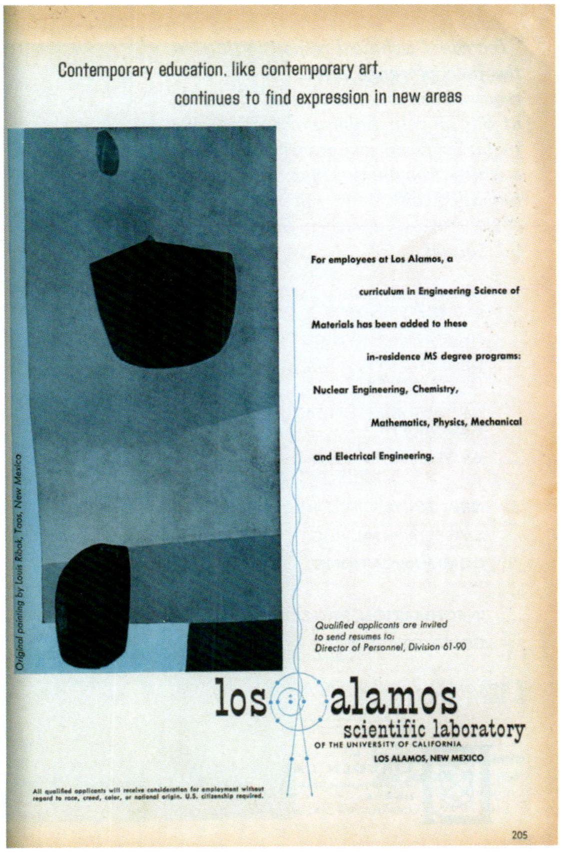

68 Ward Hicks Advertising

"Contemporary Education, like contemporary art, continues to find expression in new areas," 1961

That Ribak would have lent his painting to the support of LANL, chiefly associated with the Manhattan Project and the creation of the atomic bomb, is surprising, considering his leftist politics, but by the mid-1950s, various sectors in science and entertainment hoped to convince the American public that the atom was a useful tool in medicine, industry, and agriculture, and a new power source.[125] Popular periodicals such as *National Geographic* touted its applications in the 1954 article, "Man's New Servant, the Friendly Atom," and the *Disneyland* television program aired "Our Friend the Atom" in 1957.[126] Despite the horrors of Hiroshima and Nagasaki, interested parties heralded both the atom and radioactivity as a positive force in American life.

The ubiquity of all things atomic in the 1950s doubtlessly influenced Ribak and other artists living in the Southwest, who likely saw the landscape with different eyes at the advent of the Atomic Age.[127] The geological features of the region had attracted prospectors in search of uranium and other elements useful to nuclear science, prompting the U.S. Atomic Energy Commission and U.S Geological Survey to publish *Prospecting for Uranium* in 1949, with reissues in 1951 and 1957. The publication began with a classification of uranium and thorium minerals and their colors, which included black, brown, green, yellow, orange, gray, and red. The

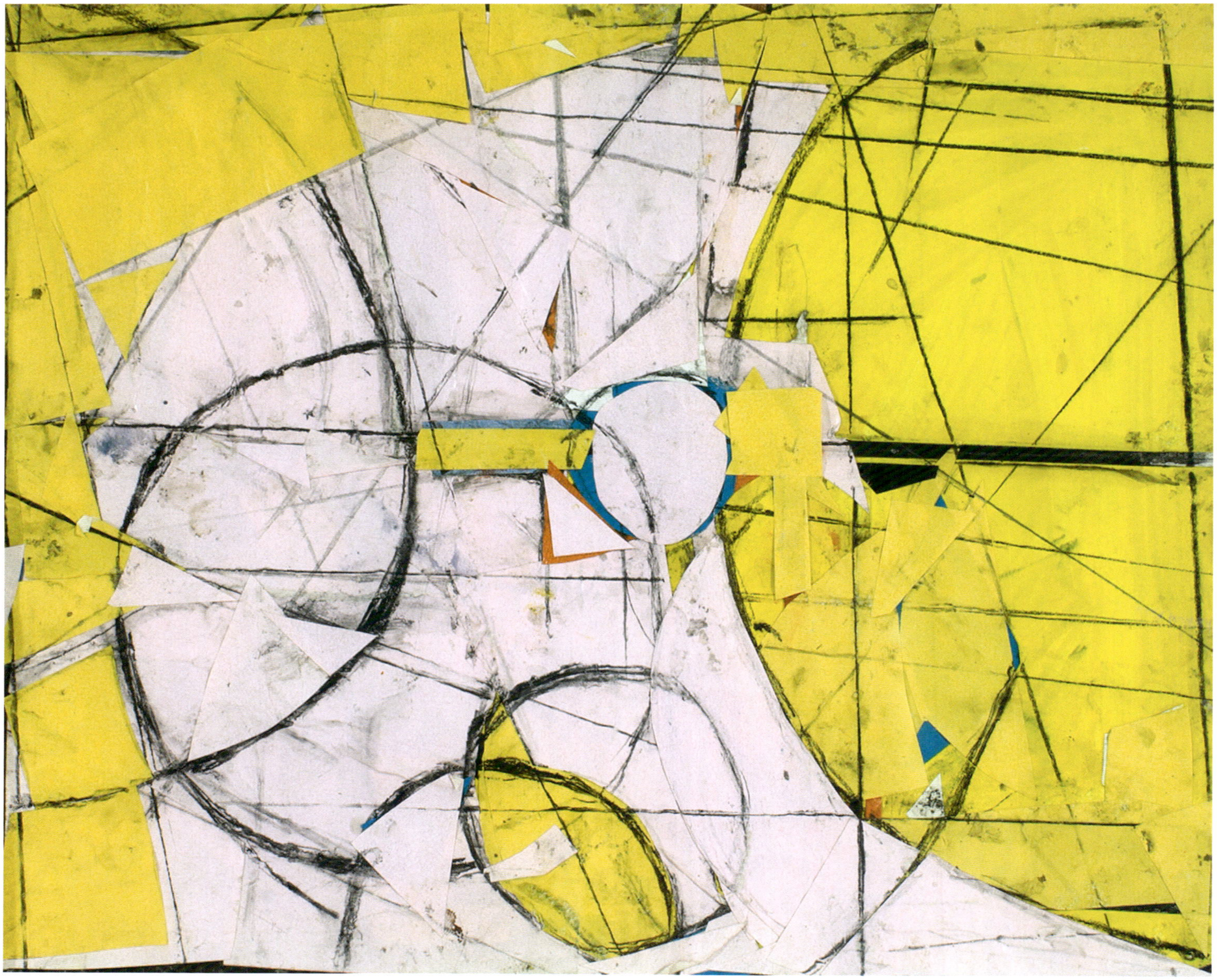

69 **Beatrice Mandelman** (U.S., 1912–1998)

Untitled (60.SP4.39), ca. 1960
mixed media collage on paper, 10 x 12 in.
Fred Jones Jr. Museum of Art, the University of Oklahoma, Norman, Oklahoma; gift of the Mandelman-Ribak Foundation, 2014.

booklet encouraged prospectors to look for deposits of favorable minerals in the Rockies, the Colorado Plateau, and in sandstone formations, and countless hopefuls wandered the region armed with Geiger counters, scintillation counters, and nucliometers in search of the mother lode. The colorful rocks of the Southwest were not merely inert but possible energy sources with considerable market value. In this respect, the paintings of the Southwestern Abstract Expressionists with their radiant geological references, painted during the height of atomic mania, may be understood in a new context. The glowing hues and telluric vim of Ribak's *Red Canyon Rising*, McChesney's *Arena No. 35*, Spohn's *Blue Abstraction*, and Mandelman's *Moonlight* suggests a landscape alive not only with the centuries of geological change, but also with atomic forces and radioactivity. McVicker's *Yellow Green* hums with varied bodies that may be read as wildflowers, as well as nucleonic particles, and the painting's dense conglomeration of colored dots bears some similarity to models of nuclei and molecules in which the component parts are colored to indicate different charges or elements.

The unseen forces of the atomic microcosm, with its attractions, repulsions, and orbits, likely provided some of the inspiration for Beatrice Mandelman's *Untitled (60.SP.4.39)* (ca. 1960; fig. 69). The collage belongs to the *Space Series*, begun around 1960 with a clear debt to the late *gouaches découpés* of Henri Matisse. Considerations of space motivated Mandelman for most of the 1950s and '60s, and she experimented continually with formal means to express vast, vacant spaces. In contrast to the utterly minimal compositions of *Moonlight* and *Winter*, *Untitled (60.SP.4.39)* teems with activity. Mandelman overlapped pieces of pink, yellow, red, and blue painted paper, cut in a variety of shapes, and drew a complicated network of intersecting lines and arcs, some of which are interrupted by additional pieces. Much of the composition is dominated by circular forms and arcs that, when considered together, evoke orbiting bodies and trajectories. Ribak's association with Los Alamos in the early 1960s may have encouraged Mandelman to ponder the orbs, magnetic forces, and spatial dynamics of the microcosmic world. Conversely, she may have also reflected on the parallels between the structure of atoms and the orbiting bodies of the solar system. The circular forms and arcs of *Untitled (60.SP.4.39)* may be inspired equally by planets, comets, meteorites, constellations, and especially by recent Soviet and American satellites that heralded the dawn of the Space Race.

By 1960, the Soviet Union and the U.S. were engaged in active competition for supremacy of outer space. The Soviet launch of Sputnik 1 on October 4, 1957, and the subsequent launch of Sputnik 2 on November 3 shocked the U.S., which responded on January 31, 1958, with its first satellite, Explorer 1. Over the next two years, the Soviet Luna satellites would successfully orbit the sun, and photograph the surface of the moon and impact its surface. The U.S. would initiate two other satellite programs prior to 1960, Vanguard and Pioneer, and establish NASA on October 1, 1958, which replaced the National Advisory Committee on Aeronautics.

With nearly twenty satellites shot into space between 1957–60, each of which were spherical in shape, it would not be surprising if Mandelman responded to the widespread interest in space exploration in a collage concerned with spatial dynamics and loaded with circular forms. The American fascination with Sputnik certainly impressed Hatchett, who constructed an homage to the original polished metallic sphere with *Sputnik I* (1960; fig. 70). He had served as a pilot in the U.S. Air Force during WWII and trained on a Lockheed P-38 Lightning. Hatchett's enthusiasm for flight must have led him to follow the Space Race closely, as he named his first found object sculptures after Sputnik. Scrap from Gachman Metals likely contributed the fins, hull, and other structural components of the sculpture, but the fact that *Sputnik I* resembles an airplane or a rocket ship from *Flash Gordon* more than the Soviet satellite seems to have troubled Hatchett little.[128] Obsolete junk serves as a technological tribute to space exploration, a theme that also seems to have motivated his earlier *Space Form*. Pointed aloft, *Sputnik I* soars through space.

The extraterrestrial held greater allure for Fitz, who sought a close encounter. *Gathering One*, as well as *The Way*, includes gestural celestial bursts that may also represent Unidentified Flying Objects. Fitz followed sightings of UFOs for much of his life and hoped for an alien visitation. Multiples sightings occurred in Texas and Oklahoma during 1956–57, most of which included hovering, intense lights of white, red, or orange.[129] *Gathering One* includes four such lights, suggesting a loose formation of alien craft. Fitz was interested in UFOs on a personal level, but it would have been difficult to escape the craze over extraterrestrial visitation in the late 1950s. Apart from the numerous science fiction movies released during the late 1950s, serious debate erupted over the legitimacy of alien life. Most notably, aviator Donald Keyhoe attempted to convince the American public of the reality of extraterrestrials with his popular book *The Flying Saucers Are Real* (1950) and even Carl Jung examined the topic in *Flying Saucers; A Modern Myth of Things Seen in the Skies* (1959), a book that Fitz surely read considering his admiration for Jung.[130]

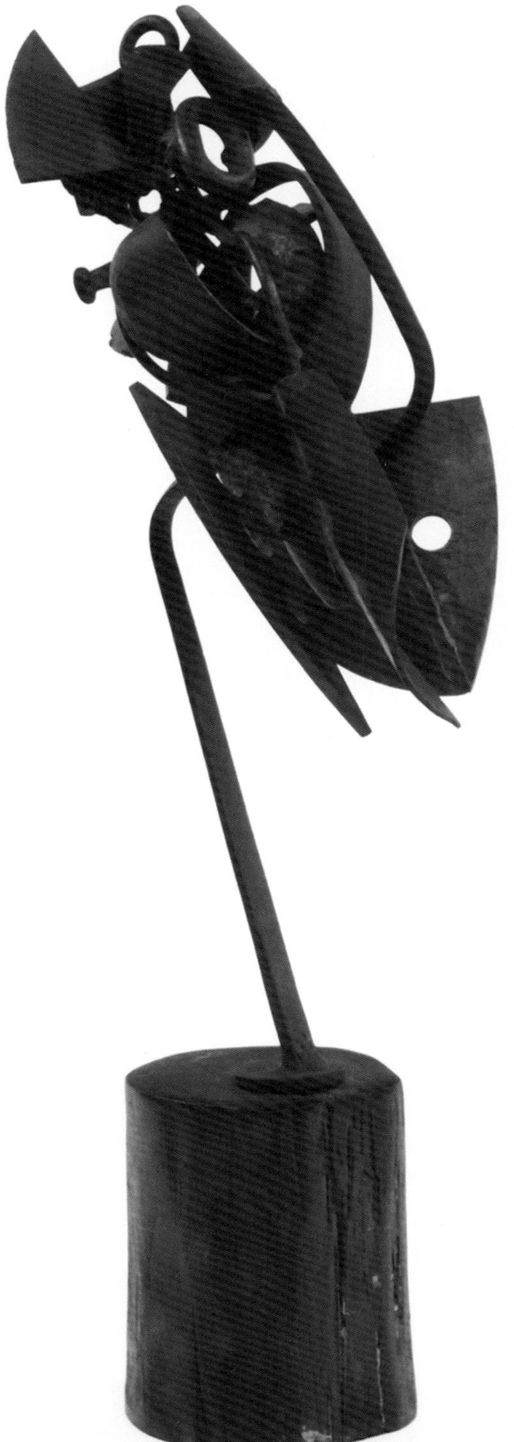

70 **Duayne Hatchett** (U.S., b. 1925)

Sputnik I, 1960
steel, 21 x 9 x 6 1/2 in.
Collection of the artist; reproduction permission courtesy of the artist.

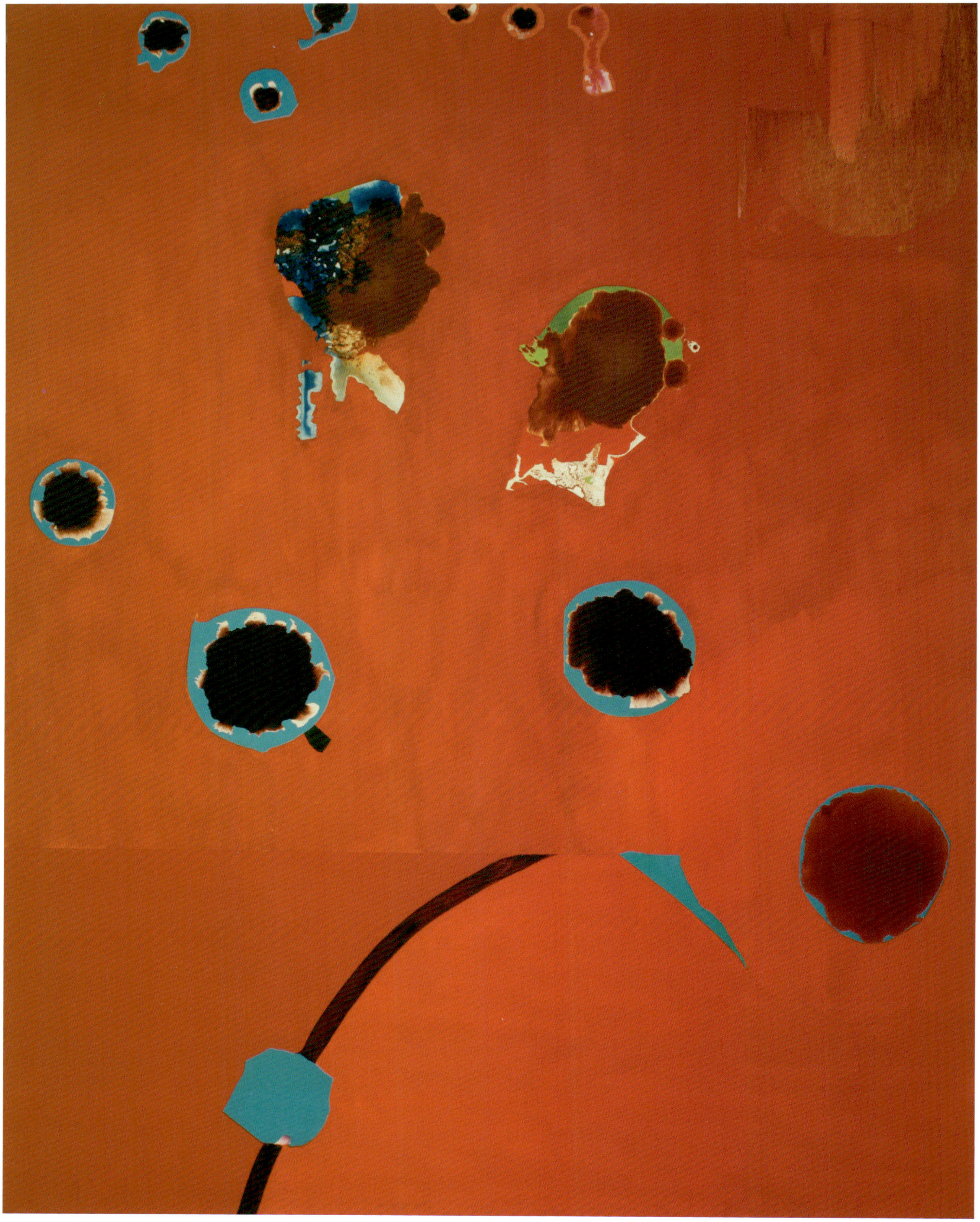

71 **Dorothy Hood** (U.S., 1918–2000)

The Blessings of Gravity, 1970s
oil on canvas, 120 x 96 in.
The Art Museum of South Texas, Corpus Christi; reproduction permission courtesy of Dorothy Hood Foundation, Museum of South Texas.

Fitz regarded communion with alien intelligence as a potential path to greater enlightenment and a profoundly important spiritual experience. He was hardly alone in associating spirituality with either the extraterrestrial or outer space. In the 1960s, Americans held a variety of opinions on the relationship between religious ideas and the otherworldly. Historian Kendrick Oliver has demonstrated that much of the space program during the 1960s was cloaked in questions of faith and Christian piety, as though space exploration might bring humanity closer to God. "The journeys they would make between the realms of earth and heaven seemed almost shamanistic," Oliver has concluded.[131] Culture also examined the conjunction of religion and spaceflight in a myriad of ways. Robert Heinlein's *Stranger in a Strange Land* (New York: G. P. Putnam's Sons,1961) addressed the ideas of alternative spirituality through its central character Valentine Michael Smith, the human boy raised by Martians after the death of his astronaut parents. Erich von Däniken's controversial book *Chariots of the Gods? Unsolved Mysteries of the Past* (New York: G. P. Putnam's Sons, 1968) posited that the technology and religion of ancient civilizations was the product of alien visitation. Arguably, Kubrick's film *2001: A Space Odyssey* was the most influential in this respect for its enigmatic ending, which may be interpreted as the promise of physical and spiritual evolution through space exploration or a deeply numinous experience achieved through technological means.

That cultural fascination with the spiritual import of space exploration had an unquestionable impact on Hood's paintings of the late 1960s and early 1970s. The stars, nebulae, and galaxies of her paintings have some basis in astronomical realities but were shaped by her own imaginative and psychic visions of the astral. She drew open analogies between outer space and the spaces of the mind and argued that a dialogue between the two might be established, resulting in communion with the universe: "There exist spaces of the mind's eye. If this kind of space meets cosmic space, then it is as though the mind's eye belongs to the orbs of the galaxies."[132] Hood's speculation of direct association between the psyche and celestial bodies resulted in paintings such as *The Blessings of Gravity* (1970s; fig. 71). Her title infers that the artist took some solace in the restrictive powers of gravity, which allowed her to gaze upon celestial wonders from afar. That physical limitation or barrier between Hood and the astronomical fantasies of her imagination is constructed in the subtle line that severs the pronounced arc in the lower third of the painting. A single galactic orb straddles that line and offers access to the constellation of more colorful, amorphous bodies above, which drift and expand. Whereas the arc initially offers a trajectory, the aborted path leaves the viewer adrift in an unbounded space of poured paint representing the void and volatile cosmic bodies. Hood purposely severed the arc, in contrast to Mandelman's *Untitled*, to prevent the plotting of space. Critic Ann Holmes rightly observed that Hood's cosmic paintings were "concerned with the limitlessness of space."[133]

Boundlessness implied unexplored intellectual and spiritual frontiers for Hood, yet *The Blessings of Gravity* acknowledges the importance of a firm footing on Earth, a platform by which she could investigate the cosmos. For Kirkland, that platform was the Rockies, where he had an unobstructed view of the ether. *Nebula Near Mars* and other works of the period are complicated abstractions derived from observation and imagination, but the NASA space launches of the early 1960s actually prompted a conceptual change in his work. He concluded the *Nebulae* or *Space Mysteries* series of the 1950s when popular periodicals began including photographs of outer space taken during Projects Mercury and Gemini. As he explained: "The paintings I had thought of being just abstractions on outer space all of a sudden had a very realistic look to them. I felt I should abandon it and not go any further; I didn't want to do what the photographer was going to do with space."[134] Kirkland began using less descriptive titles to disassociate his paintings from the constraints of realism, but his imagery maintained its tie to cosmic forms.

Painting No. 3 (1961; fig. 72) relies on a juxtaposition of clouds of atmospheric colors. Veils of red, orange, and yellow billow and expand, while cooler passages seem to contract, providing an unfathomable depth and complexity to the painting. Kirkland's oil and water resist technique led to chance occurrences, granting *Painting No. 3* a sense of flux, as though the formations will soon change shape and gain greater solidity or dissipate altogether. Each vaporous passage seems at a moment of transition and resolution in keeping with Kirkland's fascination with cosmic evolution. The tremendous, panoramic size of the painting encourages a perception of limitlessness, as though the nebulae, galaxies, or other cosmic formations that inspired Kirkland are not only distant but infinite in scope. The extent of the known universe expanded in the years surrounding Kirkland's *Painting No. 3*. In 1958, astronomer Allan Sandage gained notoriety for using Edwin Hubble's Constant to determine the reasonably accurate age and extent of the universe. Whether Kirkland followed these discoveries is unknown, although the findings were widely reported in the popular press.[135] Art historian Dianne Perry Vanderlip has suggested that Kirkland adopted "an explorer's look at the heavens" as though the artist, like an astronomer, engaged in an act of discovery.[136] *Painting No. 3* offers an imagined investigation of those undiscovered spaces, whether at the edges of the universe or in the recesses of the mind.

72 **Vance Kirkland** (U.S., 1904–1981)

Painting No. 3, 1961
oil and water on linen, 75 x 108 in.
Collection Kirkland Museum of Fine and Decorative Art, Denver; reproduction permission courtesy of the Kirkland.

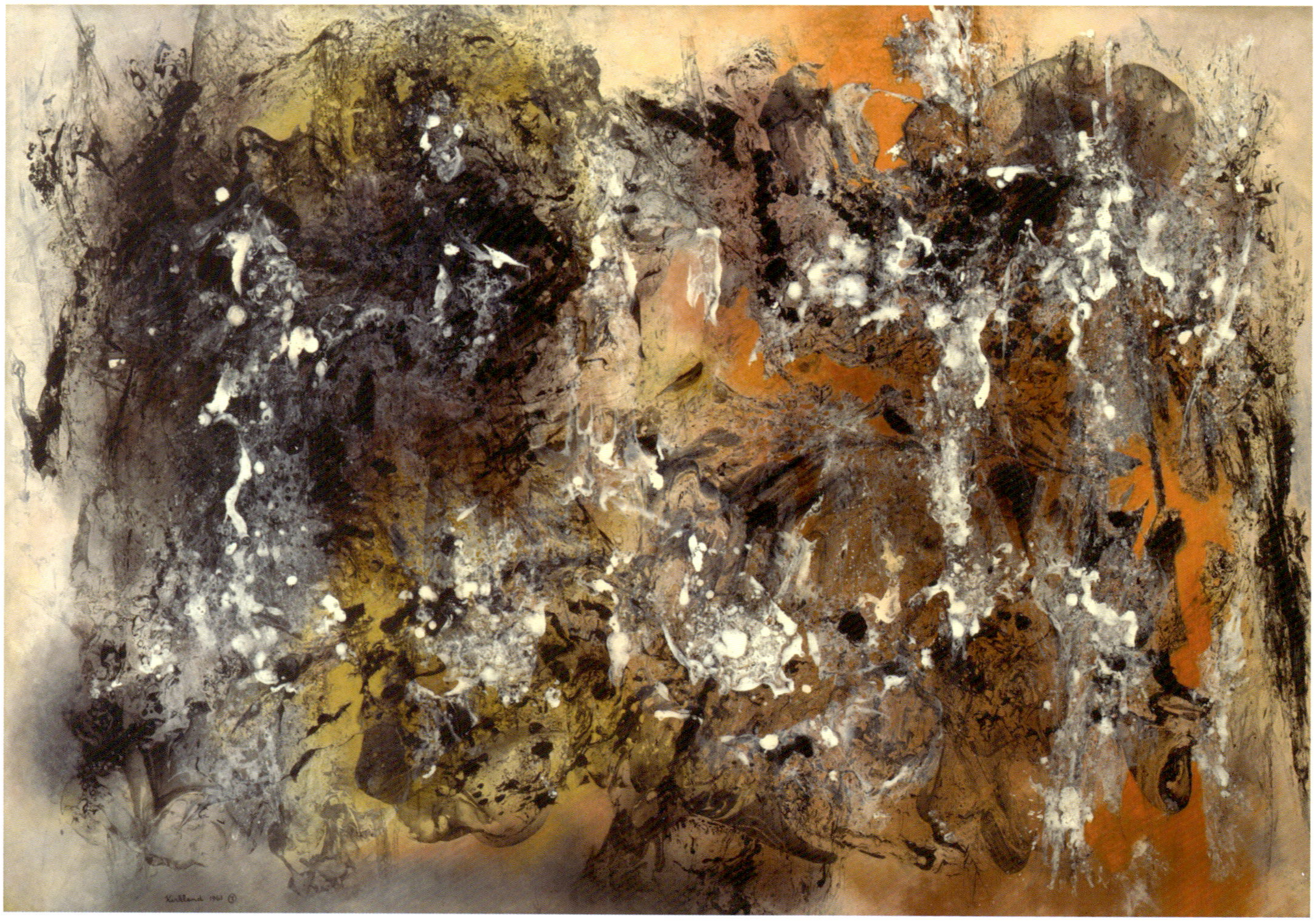

Kirkland's exploration of cosmic mysteries, no matter how distant, was rooted in the vast spaces of the Southwest, where he gazed upward in search of inspiration. The expansive spaces of the region provided the impetus for his ruminations on the infinite and the eons of cosmic evolution. Questions of space, and its limitations or lack thereof, united Kirkland in thought with his contemporaries across the region, who employed the techniques and aesthetic motivations of Abstract Expressionism to consider both their locale and beyond. Technological and scientific advances broadened the boundaries of space in the 1950s and '60s, and many of those developments and discoveries were closely linked with the Southwest. Aeronautics, nuclear science, and space travel informed how Southwestern Abstract Expressionists thought about space and its aesthetic expression.

But in many respects, Southwestern Abstract Expressionists were sympathetic to many of the same ideas that motivated earlier generations of artists in the region, whether Ansel Adams or Ernest Blumenschein, even though their respective aesthetic approaches differed dramatically. The Southwest prompted considerations of the macrocosm and microcosm, the slow course of geological change, and timeless cycles. Contemplation of these phenomena often resulted in questions of infinity and the mutability of creation. The salient characteristics of the region had a profound influence on the style of those at mid-century, yet their formal language and conceptual interests also demonstrated an awareness and understanding of national and international trends. Gestural abstraction, Color Field, Tachisme, and other aesthetic approaches offered technical means to express the physical and metaphysical character of the Southwest, and the Southwestern Abstract Expressionists were clearly conversant in the idioms of the day and recognized as such by the important critics and curators of the time.

Although it would be erroneous to consider them a cohesive unit, there were numerous connections between Abstract Expressionists in Arizona, Colorado, New Mexico, Oklahoma, and Texas, and lines of influence and communication did develop between distant points such as Taos and Colorado Springs or Norman and Houston. Connections with both San Francisco and New York helped to enrich the work these artists produced at mid-century, but without provinciality. Modernism thrived in the Southwest during the 1950s and '60s, not only through an influx of artists from the coasts, but also through the insights of homegrown artists cognizant of the concerns of their day. Abstract Expressionism was hardly limited to Manhattan or even to San Francisco, but had a strong presence in the Southwest, due in part to Elaine de Kooning's influence and that of others.

Macrocosm/Microcosm: Abstract Expressionism and the American Southwest reveals that modernists in the region not only kept pace with aesthetic innovations on national and international levels but avoided mere imitation by addressing the essential qualities of the local and regional. In this respect, this volume also provides a new perspective on art in the Southwest. These artists all sought new means of exploring a region that had fascinated artists for over fifty years, but with results strikingly different from the Taos Society of Artists, the Santa Fe colonists, or even Georgia O'Keeffe. Although Elaine de Kooning may not have been entirely correct that the Southwest had developed a style all its own, her perceptions of the vitality of the region and its artists was unquestionably accurate.

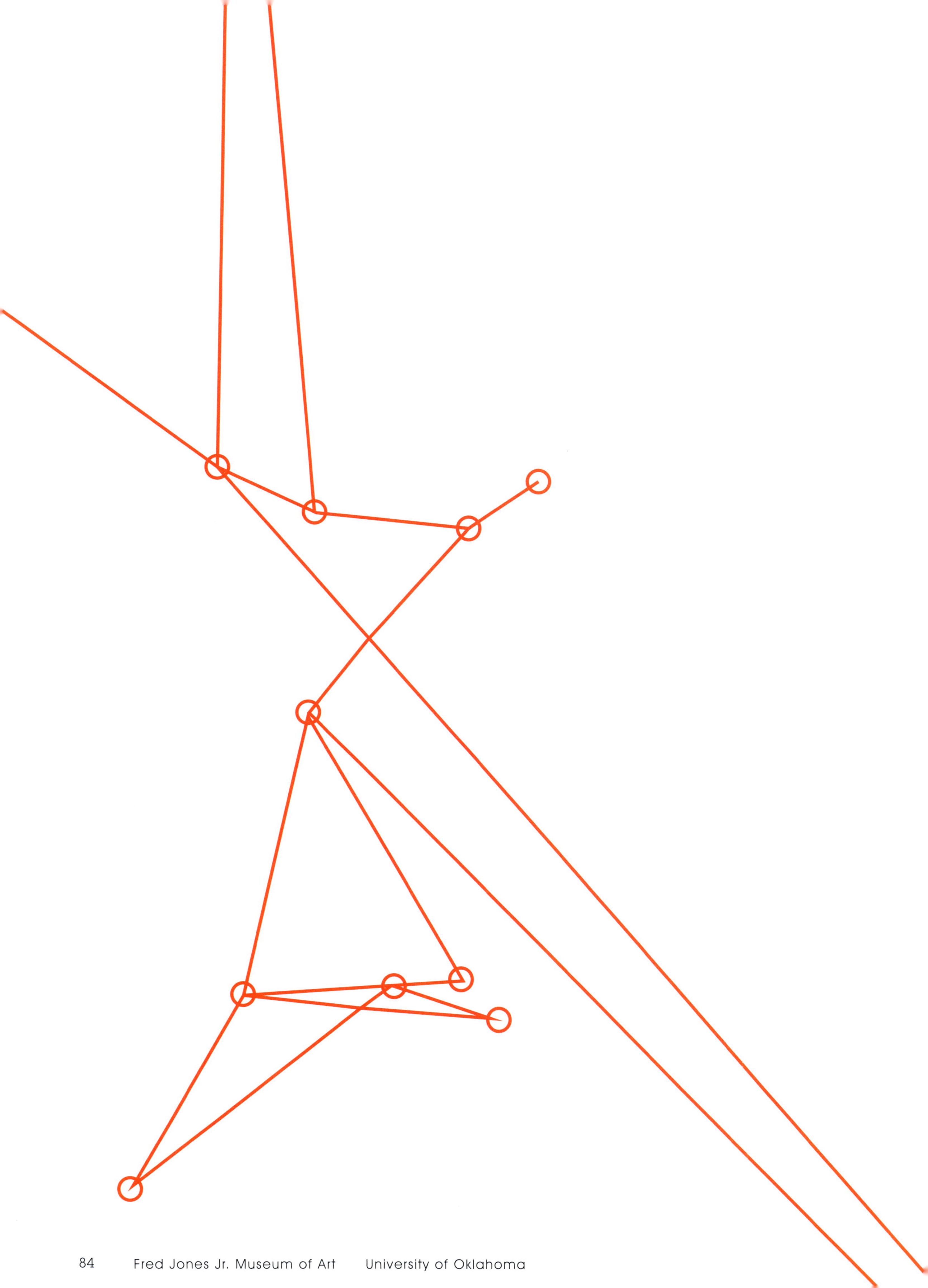

Notes

1 Elaine de Kooning quoted in Sally Bivins, "Visiting Artist Sees Southwest as Area of Distinctive Expression," *Amarillo Globe-Times*, October 25, 1962, 12.

2 Elaine de Kooning to Dord Fitz, 1959, Dord Fitz Papers, box 1, folder "Elaine de Kooning Correspondence and Sales," Western History Collection, University of Oklahoma, Norman. Hereafter cited as WHC.

The Southwest, as a geographical area, has been subject to much debate, especially as to its geographical boundaries and essential characteristics. Writing at mid-century, Edna Fergusson considered Arizona and New Mexico unquestionably part of the region and saw the arid desert and presence of Hispanic and Native American cultures as defining aspects of the Southwest. She generally disregarded much of California, Colorado, Oklahoma, Texas, and Utah. Fergusson, *Our Southwest* (New York: Alfred A. Knopf, 1941). Subsequent geographers also have focused on population demographics, cultural influence, and geological character.

This volume defines the Southwest through a set of shared aesthetic characteristics and through a sense of community that seems to have existed between artists from Arizona, Colorado, New Mexico, Oklahoma, and Texas. Emily Ballew Neff has summarized some of those characteristics as "the rugged, sun-drenched plains, framed by distant snow-capped mountains or angular mesas" and "vast empty spaces—combined with sharp geological contours, a vivid, boldly colored palette, and an intense sunlight that flattens forms." Neff, *The Modern West: American Landscapes*, 1890–1950 (New Haven, Conn.: Yale University Press, 2007), 129.

3 The use of the term Abstract Expressionism has been identified chiefly with the New York School, and its use here is complicated, albeit necessary for economy. The term is understood to include a variety of aesthetic approaches commonly known as Action painting or gestural abstraction, Color Field painting, Post-painterly abstraction, and postwar assemblage. Mary Fuller McChesney questioned whether the term applied to painters of the Bay Area, many of whom are included in this study, and she received mixed responses from the artist themselves. McChesney, *A Period of Exploration: San Francisco, 1945–1950* (Oakland, Calif.: The Oakland Museum, 1973), 64–73. Susan Landauer, in her important examination of the Bay Area at mid-century, suggested that the term was applicable, when applied loosely: "At best we can say it was a cultural mood in which artists throughout the United States found their discrete voices, and some, for a time, sang in unison." Landauer, *The San Francisco School of Abstract Expressionism* (Berkeley: University of California Press, 1996), xx.

4 Ansel Adams, letter to Alfred Stieglitz, September 21, 1937, reproduced in Mary Street Alinder and Andrea Gray Stillman, *Ansel Adams: Letters and Images, 1916–1984* (Boston: Little, Brown and Company, 1988), 98.

5 This study would not have been possible without the groundbreaking scholarship of key scholars. Examinations of mid-century modernism in the Southwest are still rare, and most authors focus on developments in individual states. For Colorado, the primary source is Michael Paglia and Mary Voelz Chandler, *Colorado Abstract: Painting and Sculpture* (Albuquerque, N.Mex.: Fresco Fine Arts Publications, Inc., 2009). Mid-century modernism in New Mexico has been examined in Deborah Boll, Peter Walch, and MaLin Wilson, *Albuquerque '50s* (Albuquerque: University of New Mexico Art Museum, 1990), and in David L. Witt's influential study, *Taos Moderns: Art of the New* (Santa Fe, N.Mex.: Red Crane Books, 1992). Texas modernism has received a similar treatment, beginning with Barbara Rose and Susie Kalil, *Fresh Paint: The Houston School* (Austin: Texas Monthly Press, 1985) and followed more recently by Alison de Lima Greene, *Texas: 150 Works from the Museum of Fine Arts, Houston* (New York: Harry N. Abrams, Inc., 2000) and Katie Robinson Edwards, Jim Edwards, and Mark L. Smith, *Texas Modern: the Rediscovery of Early Texas Abstraction* (1935–1965) (Waco, Tex.: Martin Museum of Art, Baylor University, 2007). Recently, Katie Robinson Edwards published an excellent and thorough study on the subject with *Midcentury Modern Art in Texas* (Austin: University of Texas Press, 2014).

6 Dorothy C. Miller, ed., *Fourteen Americans* (New York: Museum of Modern Art, 1946), 7, 8.

7 Frank Gagnard, "Dallas Visited by Director of Guggenheim Museum," *Dallas Morning News*, March 8, 1954.

8 "Work of Three Hangs in Guggenheim Show," *Fort Worth Star Telegram*, sec. 3, 12. Daniel Defenbacher, David E. Brauer, *Artists' Progress: Seven Houston Artists*, 1943–1993 (Houston: The Glassell School of Art, Museum of Fine Arts, Houston, 1993), 10.

9 James Johnson Sweeney, *The Southwest: Painting and Sculpture* (Houston: Museum of Fine Arts, Houston, 1962), n.p.

10 Lester Burbank Bridaham, "Statement of the Juror," in Otto Karl Bach, *57th Annual Exhibition of Western Art* (Denver: Denver Art Museum, 1951), n.p.

11 Bridaham may have had in mind something similar to Pollock's contention, "It seems to me that the modern painter cannot express this age, the airplane, the atom bomb, the radio, in the old forms of the Renaissance or of any other past culture." William Wright, "An Interview with Jackson Pollock," in Francis V. O'Connor, *Jackson Pollock* (New York: the Museum of Modern Art, 1967), 79. The interview was intended for a radio broadcast that never aired, so it is possible that Bridaham had not heard Pollock's comments. Bridaham also may have been summarizing Adolph Gottlieb's statement, "Today when our aspirations have been reduced to a desperate attempt to escape from evil, and times are out of joint, our obsessive, subterranean and pictographic images are the expression of the neurosis which is our reality." Gottlieb, "Statement," *Tiger's Eye* 1, no. 2 (December 1947): 43.

12 Otto Karl Bach, *60th Annual Exhibition of Western Art (Denver: Denver Art Museum,* 1954), n.p.

13 James Thrall Soby, "Foreword . . . New Talent in the U.S.A.," *Art in America* 43, no. 1 (February 1955): 12.

14 David Witt, *Modernists in Taos: From Dasburg to Martin* (Santa Fe, N.Mex.: Red Crane Books, 2002), 135.

15 For more on the Jonson Gallery, see Ed Garman, "The Jonson Gallery: A Significant Decade," *New Mexico Quarterly* 30, no. 1 (Spring 1960): 57. The building served as a home for Jonson and a gallery for his work and that of UNM students. De Kooning quoted in Ed Garmen, *The Art of Raymond Jonson* (Albuquerque: University of New Mexico Press, 1976), xiv.

16 W. Jackson Rushing III has argued that rock art, as well as Native American ceramics and jewelry, was an influence on Jonson and that Jonson employed motifs drawn from the collection his wife Vera assembled. Rushing, *Native American Art and the New York Avant-Garde* (Austin: University of Texas Press, 1995), 83–84.

17 Garmen noted that materiality was a particular concern of Jonson's in the 1950s. Garman, *Raymond Jonson*, 142-45.

18 Richard Diebenkorn, oral history interview by Susan Larsen, Archives of American Art, May 1–December 15, 1987, http://www.aaa.si.edu/collections/interviews/oral-history-interview-richard-diebenkorn-11813. Hereafter cited as AAA.

19 Diebenkorn quoted in James Schevill, "Richard Diebenkorn," *Frontier* 8, no. 3 (January 1957): 22.

20 Ibid.

21 Ibid.

22 Diebenkorn quoted in Larsen interview.

23 For further information on Littler's career, see Andrew Rush and Wayne Entice, *Charles Littler, 1928–1991: A Retrospective Exhibition* (Tucson: University of Arizona Museum of Art, Tucson, 1994). In addition to his study with Hofmann, Littler circulated with the New York School, as well as the Beat poets and Allan Kaprow.

24 For a recent discussion of Hofmann, see Karen Wilkin, *Hans Hofmann: A Retrospective* (New York: George Braziller, Inc., 2003), but for more specific information on his teaching principles and aesthetic theories, see Hofmann, "Excerpts from his Teaching," in Herschel B. Chipp, ed., *Theories of Modern Art: A Source Book by Artists and Critics* (Berkeley: University of California Press, 1968), 536–44.

25 For a history of La Galeria Escondida, see Phyllis F. Dorsett, "La Galeria Escondida," *Artspace* 11, no. 4 (Fall 1987): 43–49.

26 Mandelman quoted in Robert Hobbs, *Beatrice Mandelman: Taos Modernist* (Albuquerque: University of New Mexico Press, 1995), 55. Mandelman's comments were taken from an interview with David Witt, December 23, 1982.

27 Mary Fuller, "When You Are Over Fifty," *Southwest Art Gallery Magazine* (May 20, 1972): 42.

28 Still reportedly visited Corbett's one-man show at La Galeria Escondida in 1951. Dorsett, "La Galeria," 48. Robert Motherwell was a visiting artist at the Colorado Springs Fine Arts Center in 1954 at the invitation of Emerson Woelffer.

29 Dorsett, "La Galeria," 45.

30 Stephen Polcari has argued that Abstract Expressionism regarded life and nature as "a natural continuum of instability, rising, falling, evolving, and struggling." This belief in constant change and the uncertainty of existence was a deliberate contrast to the utopian ideals of the 1930s that believed humankind could eventually solve every natural and social ill, resulting in a perfect civilization. Polcari, *Abstract Expressionism and the Modern Experience* (Cambridge, Mass.: Cambridge University Press, 1991), 52.

31 Corbett, letter to Clay Spohn, n.d., Edward and Rosamond Walling Tirana Corbett Papers, AAA, reel 4382, frame 67. Art historian Susan Landauer has also argued that Corbett's evocative use of black is similar to that of Symbolist Odilon Redon. Landauer, *Edward Corbett: A Retrospective* (Richmond, Calif.: Richmond Art Center, 1990), 23.

32 Landauer, *Edward Corbett*, 26.

33 Mary Fuller, "Edward Corbett, a Profile," *Art Digest* 28, no. 7 (January 1, 1954): 21.

34 Corbett Papers, reel 4382, frame 23, AAA. Most of Corbett's poems from New Mexico are undated.

On the issue of silence in Corbett's work, critic Emily Genauer dubbed him an "Inaction" painter and associated the silence of his works with Zen Buddhism. Genauer, "Now Come 'Inaction' Painters Shouting a Significant Silence," *New York Herald Tribune*, March 15, 1959, sec. 4, 7.

35 Gerald Nordland, *Edward Corbett* (San Francisco: San Francisco Museum of Modern Art, 1969), n.p.

36 Still drove Spohn to Taos in 1951. Spohn, oral history interview by Paul Cummings, January 9 and February 5, 1976, AAA, http://www.aaa.si.edu/collections/interviews/oral-history-interview-clay-spohn-11671. Spohn, untitled writing, September 1954, Clay Spohn Papers, box 8, folder "Notes and Writings," AAA. Although Spohn stated in this writing that his initial reaction was wonder at "the vast feeling of spacelessness; eternal space and therefore spaceless," he had lost much of that feeling by 1954: "But this I feel no more. The horizon is the same as it was—it is in the same place—but it no longer goes on and on, it no longer goes beyond—it is no longer continuous. One now feels hampered, trapped, restrained. Perhaps it is the experience of too many long, dreary winters without break, without change."

37 Spohn discussed his hope that seclusion would benefit his painting in an untitled writing, May 14, 1952, Spohn Papers, box 8, folder "'Notes and Writings,' February–September, 1952," AAA. He listed possible ideas for painting in "Subjective or Idea Material," May 5, 1954, Spohn papers, "'Notes and Writings,' February–March, 1955," AAA.

38 McChesney stated, "The desert and the wilderness, which I truly love and love to be in as much as possible, has influenced me a great deal. Of course, the artist is no different from anyone else in that he is influenced by everything around him visually and psychologically, but he has the ability to digest this and turn it into art." Mary Fuller, *Robert McChesney: From Arena to Barranca, 19 Years* (Hayward: California State University, 1977), n.p. He also noted, "Ed Corbett was very involved in nature and the wilderness, the desert, the mountains, all that sort of thing and I had been too." Mary Fuller McChesney, *A Period of Exploration: San Francisco, 1945–1950* (Oakland, Calif.: The Oakland Museum, 1973), 59.

39 Guidebooks at mid-century noted the caves had formed initially between 60 and 100 million years earlier and were subject to slow but steady changes in physical character. For an example, see John Moseley and W. A. Dunagan, *What A Hole: History Geology of Carlsbad Caverns* (Carlsbad, N.Mex.: printed privately, 1948).

40 For a discussion of Martin's early influences, see Richard Tobin, "Agnes Martin: Before the Grid," in *Agnes Martin: Before the Grid* (Taos. N.Mex.: The Harwood Museum of Art of the University of New Mexico, 2012), 13–37.

41 Mary Fuller McChesney, conversation with author, February 6, 2013. For examples of Martin's early landscapes, see *Agnes Martin: Before the Grid.*

42 Letter from Jack Boynton to Eulalia Emetaz, October 14, 1956, La Galeria Escondida Papers, Folder B, AAA.

43 Art historian Jermayne MacAgy argued that Boynton's paintings are concerned chiefly with "the depiction of the essence of space—this space incorporating aspects of the forces of nature." MacAgy, "Texas—From Blue Bonnet to Blue Streak," *Art in America* 49, no. 2 (1961): 57.

Boynton's use of the horizon compares to that of Gottlieb's *Imaginary Landscape* series, which began in 1951. Lawrence Alloway noted that Gottlieb was alone among the New York School to use the horizon line as a compositional device, but Boynton and other artists in the Southwest employed it regularly. Lawrence Alloway, "Adolph Gottlieb and Abstract Painting," in Sanford Hirsch and Mary Davis McNaughton, *Adolph Gottlieb: A Retrospective* (New York: The Arts Publisher, Inc., 1981), 56.

44 Douglas MacAgy, *James Boynton* (New York: Barone Gallery, 1959), n.p. Charles C. Eldredge has suggested that O'Keeffe's painting *From the Faraway Nearby* (1937; The Metropolitan Museum of Art, New York, The Alfred Stieglitz Collection) encapsulates the metaphysical significance artists perceived in the Southwest. Eldredge, "The Faraway Nearby: New Mexico and Modern Landscape," in Eldredge, Julie Schimmel, and William H. Truettner, *Art in New Mexico, 1900–1945: Paths to Taos and Santa Fe* (New York: Abbeville Press, 1986), 179.

45 Letter from Eulalia Emetaz to Charles Williams, July 5, 1956, Charles T. Williams Papers, reel 1800, frame 755, AAA. Emetaz was interested in seeing more of Williams's work but could not offer him an exhibition until 1957.

46 Fred S. Bartlett, *Taos Painting: Yesterday and Today* (Colorado Springs: Colorado Springs Fine Arts Center, 1952), n.p. For an expanded discussion of the exhibition, see Witt, Taos Moderns, 17-18.

47 For instance, Spohn and Corbett planned a trip to Colorado Springs in late 1955, and it is clear from the correspondence that Woelffer was already friendly with many of the colony artists by this time. Letter from Spohn to Woelffer, August 11, 1955, Emerson Woelffer Papers, box 1, folder "10/30/47–12/10/54," AAA. A letter from the following year notes that Woelffer had called Martin to inform her of the death of Jackson Pollock, who was a mutual friend. Both Woelffer and Pollock's brother Charles had visited Taos in the summer of 1956. Spohn To Woelffer, August 20, 1956, Woelffer Papers, box 1, folder "10/30/47–12/10/54," AAA.

48 Robert Motherwell, "Emerson Woelffer: A Born Painter," *Art News* 77, no. 2 (February 1978): 80. Motherwell suffered a creative block while away from his studio and work.

49 Rothko told Corbett that he would be visiting Santa Fe in August 1955. Letter from Spohn to Woelffer, August 19, 1955, Woelffer Papers, box 1, folder "10/30/47–12/10/54," AAA.

50 Michael Paglia, "Ken Goehring," http://www.westword.com/2007-07-26/culture/ken-goehring/full/, accessed June 23, 2013.

51 Tricia Hurst, "Passing the Torch: Janet Lippincott and Marcia Oliver," *Southwest Art* 10, no. 3 (August 1980): 99.

52 Al Kochka has stated "[Bunnell] studied Far Eastern religion as well as Christianity. These studies provided the impetus for his artistic forays into the metaphysical world dealing with the reasons for mankind's existence." Dord Fitz and Al Kochka, *Charles Bunnell (1897–1968): The Past Remembered, A Retrospective Exhibition* (Amarillo, TX: Amarillo Art Center, 1987), n.p.

Bunnell credited Pollock with a fundamental shift in American art: "I respect Pollock very highly, because I knew Jack personally, and because he freed not only America, he freed the world, to try anything. Lots of it wasn't any good, but he told them not to be afraid to go ahead, and try anything." Tape recorded interview with Charles R. Bunnell, interview by Sylvia Loomis, November 10, 1964, AAA.

For a further discussion of Bunnell's early work and the Rocky Mountains, see Cori Sherman North, *Charles Bunnell: Rocky Mountain Modern* (Colorado Springs: Colorado Springs Fine Arts Center, 2013).

53 Fitz quoted in Fitz and Kochka, *Charles Bunnell*, n.p.

54 Fitz quoted in an untitled manuscript on Bunnell, n.d., Fitz Papers, box 1, folder "Dord Fitz's Writings about Charlie Bunnell," WHC.

55 Kirkland quoted in Hugh A. Grant, *Mysteries in Space* (New York: Genesis Galleries, 1978), 64, 65.

56 Kirkland quoted in Hugh Grant, "Discussions with Vance Kirkland," in Krzystof Stanislawski, Richard R. Bretell, and Hugh Grant, *Vance Kirkland: Malarstwo/Painting* (Sopot, Poland: Panstwowa Galeria Sztuki, 1997), 57.

57 Dianne Perry Vanderlip has observed that "The random chance encounters between oil and water, which deposited an organic pattern of pigment, created textures that simply could not have been made by the artist's brush, or even by mixing oil with mineral spirits or turpentine, as was normally done." Vanderlip, "Vance Kirkland: A Painter's Journey," in Peter Weiermair, ed., *Vance Kirkland*, 1904–1981 (Zurich: Edition Stemmle, 1998), 19.

58 Strong quoted in Jo Farb Hernandez and Paul J. Karlstrom, *Fire and Flux, an Undaunted Vision: The Art of Charles Strong* (Belmont, Calif.: Wiegand Gallery, 1998), n.p.

59 Fitz, "Personal notes," box 5, folder "Gallery Shows 1957," Fitz papers, WHC.

60 Fitz, untitled statement, Fitz papers, box 1, folder "Story of Dord's Artists," WHC. Fitz also stated in that document that he considered Jung "the father of a great creative era that is yet to come."

61 Lawrence Campbell, "Elaine de Kooning Paints a Picture," *Art News* 59, no. 8 (December 1960): 44. The emphasis is de Kooning's.

62 Elaine de Kooning, "Albuquerque Artists Exhibit in New York," *New Mexico Quarterly* 30, no. 1 (Spring 1960): 55.

63 Elaine de Kooning, "New Mexico," *Art in America* 49, no. 4 (1961): 56.

64 For more information on the Great Jones Gallery exhibit, see de Kooning, "Albuquerque," Great Jones Gallery, New York, N.Y., February 2–February 21, 1960, in the William Conger Papers, box 1, folder "Various Items to Early 1970's," AAA. Also see Lawrence Campbell, "Fourteen Albuquerque Painters," *Art News* 58, no. 10 (February 1960): 12, and Boll, Walch, and Wilson, *Albuquerque '50s*, 37–38.

65 Ingrid Evans, "William Vaughn Howard: A Portrait," *Artspace* 12, no. 3 (Summer 1988): 25. The article also discusses the importance of Diebenkorn in Howard's artistic formation.

66 Donald Kuspit and Julie Karabenick, *William Conger: Paintings, 1958–2008* (Chicago: Chicago Cultural Center, 2009), 30.

67 Conger quoted in *William Conger: Paintings and Drawings* (Milwaukee: Alverno College, 1968), n.p.

68 Conger quoted in Kuspit and Karabenick, *William Conger*, 31, and Conger, e-mail message to author, February 7, 2012.

69 Letter from de Kooning to Fitz, 1959, Fitz Papers, box 1, folder "Elaine de Kooning Correspondence and Sales," WHC.

70 Fitz, untitled narrative, Fitz Papers, box 1, folder "Story of Dord's Artists," WHC.

71 Jerry Bywaters, "The Lower Midwest," *Art in America* 43, no. 1 (February 1955): 84.

72 Edwards, *Midcentury Modern Art in Texas*, 207.

73 Thomas Motley, "The Sculptural Works of Charles T. Williams," in Diana R. Block, et. al., Charles T. William, *Retrospective with Friends: Charles T. Williams, Roy Fridge, Jim Love, David McManaway, Gene Owens* (Denton: University of North Texas Press, 1998), 3.

74 G. T. Munson, "Franz Kline," *Art News* 49, no. 7 (November 1950): 48. Munson, it should be noted, believed that the comparison to calligraphy was an error, and Kline was as interested in the white as the black. Elaine de Kooning believed that Kline had more influence on modern Japanese painting than calligraphy had on him: "Indeed, far from being derivative, his black and white image had a wide influence on modern Japanese artists almost immediately after his works were published. The Japanese reevaluation of the great tradition of Zen calligraphy was, in a way, triggered by their special interpretations of Kline's style." de Kooning, *Franz Kline Memorial Exhibition* (Washington, D.C.: Washington Gallery of Art, 1962), 17.

75 Edwards, *Midcentury Modern Art in Texas*, 212.

76 Hatchett remained at TU until 1964. For further biographical information on Hatchett, see David Hatchett and Richard Huntington, *Duayne Hatchett: Form, Pattern, and Invention—A Retrospective* (Buffalo, N.Y.: Burchfield Penny Art Center, Buffalo State College, 2009). Williams and Hatchett seem to have met in 1959–60, as suggested in a letter from Hatchett dated November 27, 1960. Williams Papers, reel 1801, frame 734.

77 Douglas MacAgy, *one i at a time* (Dallas: Pollock Galleries, Meadows School of the Arts, Southern Methodist University, 1971), 10.

78 David Hatchett, "My Father," in *Duayne Hatchett*, 14.

79 Dan Wingren, *Ben L. Culwell* (San Antonio: Marion Koogler McNay Art Institute, 1977), n.p.

80 For further information on the growth of Dallas after WWII, see Royce Hanson, *Civic Culture and Urban Change: Governing Dallas* (Detroit: Wayne State University Press, 2003), 31–45.

81 Thomas McEvilley, *Richard Stout: Approaching the Limits of Space* (Houston: printed privately, 2004), 17.

82 MacAgy, "Texas—From Blue Bonnet to Blue Streak," p. 57.

83 For a discussion on MacAgy's career as a curator and a complete list of her exhibitions, see Dominique de Menil, A *Life Illustrated by an Exhibition* (Houston: University of St. Thomas, 1968).

84 Edwards, *Midcentury Modern Art in Texas*, 187.

85 For a thorough history of the de Menils and their involvements in the arts in Houston, see William A. Camfield, "Two Museums and Two Universities: Toward the Menil Collection," in Josef Helfenstein and Laureen Schipsi, eds., *Art and Activism: Projects of John and Dominique de Menil* (New Haven, Conn.: Yale University Press, 2010), 49–73.

86 Marcia Brennan, "Seeing the Unseen: James Johnson Sweeney and the de Menils," in Brennan, Alfred Pacquement, and Ann Temkin, *Modern Patronage: de Menil Gifts to American and European Museums* (New Haven, Conn.: Yale University Press, 2007), 22, 25.

87 James W. Boynton, Louise Ferrari, Jim Love, Richard Stout, and Dick Wray, oral history interview by Sandra Curtis, AAA, November 28, 1979, http://www.aaa.si.edu/collections/interviews/oral-history-interview-james-w-boynton-louise-ferrari-jim-love-richard-stout-and-dick-wray-12521, accessed April 29, 2012.

88 Wray saw Pollock and de Kooning for the first time in the *New American Painting* exhibition at the Musee d'Art Moderne. David E. Brauer, *Artists' Progress: Seven Houston Artists, 1943–1993* (Houston: The Glassell School of Art, Museum of Fine Arts, Houston, 1993), 20.

Patrick Lopez recalled that Wray had met a Danish woman in Paris and eventually followed her home to Denmark. He also began painting seriously during this time. Patrick Lopez, e-mail message to author, May 16, 2014.

89 Shirley Pfister, "Artist Dorothy Hood," *Houston Chronicle*, May 5, 1974, sec. 7, p. 6.

90 The connection to NASA space exploration was first made in Ann Holmes, "D. Hood's Vivid Imagery," *Houston Chronicle*, March 24, 1969, sec 4, p. 7. Later sources also noted the influence of 2001, namely Brauer, *Artists' Progress*, 14, and Lauraine Miller, *Dorothy Hood: A Pioneer Modernist* (Corpus Christi: South Texas Institute for the Arts, 2003), 7.

91 Hood quoted in James Harithas, *Dorothy Hood: Recent Paintings* (Houston: Contemporary Arts Museum, 1970), n.p.

92 O'Neil quoted in "O'Neil Painting Bidding Closes April 1 at OU," *Norman Transcript*, March 19, 1964, p. 5.

93 Sam Olkinetzky, "John O'Neil: An Appreciation," *Crosscurrents* 11, no. 1 (January/February 1998): 3. The quote is drawn from a 1963 issue of the Copenhagen journal Kunst.

94 O'Neil, "Beginnings: Personal Notes About Art at Rice University (1965–1970)," *Rice Sallyport* (Fall 2005): 1. Oklahoman Elinor Evans encouraged O'Neil to accept the position at Rice. Evans had taught formerly at Oklahoma State University but had joined the architecture department at Rice.

95 O'Neil quoted in Olkinetzky, "John O'Neil," 6.

96 O'Neil assisted Winston and Ada Eason in collecting Italian and American modernist work during a sojourn to Italy 1961–62. The collection was eventually exhibited at OU as "Selections from the T. Winston Easton Collection," from January 5 to January 27, 1964. O'Neil also exhibited at the M-59 Galleries in Copenhagen in 1960. Carolyn G. Hart, "For Art's Sake," *Sooner Magazine* 32, no. 10 (November 1960): 11.

97 Polcari has interpreted Tomlin's late work such as *No. 8* (1952; The Phillips Collection; Washington, D.C.) as a response to the vivacity of nature: "They consist of a vitalism of layered spots in continual flicker and flux . . . a unique vitalist continuum of renewing, flowering, energetic force—quintessential Abstract Expressionist thought and response to history realized in a haunting elegiac pastoral." Polcari, *Abstract Expressionism*, 326, 328.

98 Eugene Bavinger, interview by Tom Toperzer, July 16, 1986, transcript, Fred Jones Jr. Museum of Art artist files, University of Oklahoma, Norman, p. 7.

99 Marty Avrett and Dean Bloodgood, conversation with author, January 18, 2011.

100 Ibid.

101 Fitz, untitled narrative, Fitz Papers, box 1, folder "Story of Dord's Artists," WHC. Through Fitz, McVicker also associated with other artists in the region. For example, he was included in the *13 Man Show: Drawings and Paintings* at Dord Fitz Galleries, which ran from October 18 to 31, 1959, and included with Bunnell, Boynton, Elaine de Kooning, and John Grillo.

102 McVicker gave Avrett a copy of Richard Maurice Bucke, *Cosmic Consciousness: A Study in the Evolution of the Human Mind* (Philadelphia: Innis & Sons, 1901). Avrett and Bloodgood, conversation with author, January 18, 2011.

103 Polcari, *Abstract Expressionism*, 52.

104 Mandelman quoted in Robert Hobbs, *Beatrice Mandelman: Taos Modernist* (Albuquerque: University of New Mexico Press, 1995), 2.

105 Hobbs has argued that Mandelman became interested in Zen in the 1950s after Betty Parsons and Kenzo Okada visited Taos. Ibid, 79.

106 Landauer noted Corbett's disinterest in Action painting and has referred to his paintings as "antiphysical." Landauer, *Edward Corbett*, 23.

107 Gerald Nordland, *Edward Corbett* (College Park, Md.: The Gallery, University of Maryland, 1979), n.p. and Landauer, *Edward Corbett*, 39.

108 Genauer, , "Now Come 'Inaction,'" 7.

109 This painting is undated, but McKinney's stylistic approach, which employs the same layers as *By-Product of Silence*, is consistent with his work in the 1950s. By 1962, McKinney turned his attention to light and kinetic works and painted less. Although *Spring* likely dates from the 1950s, a date of ca. 1960 has been proposed as based on comparisons to other works of equal sophistication, such as an untitled painting dated 1964 in the collection of the Oklahoma State University Museum of Art.

110 Henkle was hired at OU in 1951, but cutbacks led him to the private sector in 1952. He worked at Dave Chapman Industrial Design in Chicago until the fall of 1953, when he was invited to return to the faculty. For further information on Henkle's career, see Susan Havens Caldwell, *Oil and Wood: Oklahoma Moderns George Bogart and James Henkle* (Norman: Fred Jones Jr. Museum of Art, University of Oklahoma, 2014).

111 http://www.dallasnews.com/obituary-headlines/20130204-bill-verhelst-founder-of-southern-methodist-university-sculpture-program-dies-at-89.ece, accessed September 23, 2013.

112 Verhelst's 1958 solo exhibition at the Barone Gallery in New York City was compared to that of Lipton. Hugo Munsterberg, "Wilbert Verhelst," *Arts* 33, no. 1 (October 1958): 59. For more information on Lipton and his interest in growth and germination, see Lori Verderame, *An American Sculptor: Seymour Lipton* (University Park, Penn.: Palmer Museum of Art, Pennsylvania State University, 1999), and Albert Elsen, *Seymour Lipton* (New York; Harry N. Abrams, Inc., 1970).

113 Flowers was included in the *Exhibition Momentum, Midcontinental* held in Chicago later that spring that was juried by Philip Guston. The exhibition was an annual protest against the policies of the Art Institute of Chicago. Flowers was included that same year in an exhibition at the cooperative Wells Street Gallery, coincident with John Chamberlain's first exhibition there. Stout, e-mail message to author, July 8, 2014.

114 The title, inscribed on the verso, is in Fitz's handwriting, so it is possible the title was Fitz's and not Bunnell's, who infrequently titled his paintings. Mary Alice Gibner, e-mail message to author, July 14, 2014.

115 Fitz, untitled narrative, Fitz papers, box 1, folder "Story of Dord's Artists," WHC. Prior to his 1988 retrospective, Fitz retitled *Gathering One* as *Revelation*. The painting is one of a series, *The Way*, which includes the painting of the same name. The spiritualist beliefs expressed in *Gathering One* were drawn from Fitz's knowledge of Hinduism and Buddhism. The artist had a theosophical approach to religion and found truth in various metaphysical traditions. Carolyn Fitz, e-mail message to author, July 14, 2014.

116 Edwards, *Midcentury Modern Art in Texas*, 194.

117 Daniel L. Rust, *Flying Across America: The Airline Passenger Experience* (Norman: University of Oklahoma Press, 2009), 158.

118 Diebenkorn quoted in Nordland, *Richard Diebenkorn* (New York: Rizzoli International Publications, 1987), 47. Mark Lavatelli has argued that both Gorky's example and the flight led to the changes in Diebenkorn's work. Norland, Lavatelli, and Charles Strong, *Richard Diebenkorn in New Mexico* (Santa Fe: Museum of New Mexico Press, 2007), 32.

119 Bernard de Voto, "Transcontinental Flight," *Harper's Magazine* 205, no. 1226 (July 1952): 47–50.

120 Alyson B. Stanfield discusses Bavinger's piloting experience in "Eugene A. Bavinger, 1919–1997," *Crosscurrents* 10, no. 5 (September–October 1997): 5. For the history of municipal airport creation in the U.S., see Janet R. Daly Bednarek, *America's Airports: Airfield Development, 1918–1947* (College Station: Texas A&M University Press, 2001), 163. The skyways are addressed briefly in Carl R. Markwith, "Skyway Beneath the Clouds," *National Geographic* 96, no. 1 (July 1949): 88–89.

121 Bavinger, interview with Toperzer, p. 2.

122 Robert Smithson discusses entropy as a theme in "Entropy and the New Monuments," *Artforum* 4, no. 10 (June 1966): 26–31.

123 Robert Meier and Reginald Fisher, *Art and the Atom: An Exhibition of Contemporary Art Used in Scientific Advertisements* (Taos, N.Mex.: The Stables Art Gallery, 1963), n.p. A geological reading of *Suspension* is supported in part by Donald O. Strel, who argued that Ribak was "searching for the bigger meaning of rocks, crevices, canyons" in his mature work. Strel, *Ribak: Louis Ribak Retrospective* (Santa Fe: Museum of Fine Arts, Museum of New Mexico, 1975) n.p.

124 The ads appeared in *Scientific American* 205, no. 4 (October 1961): 205, and *Chemical and Engineering News* 39, no. 40 (October 2, 1961): 27.

125 Both Ribak and Mandelman were committed to an art of social engagement while living in New York. According to Witt, the couple was under Federal Bureau of Investigation surveillance for two decades after two residents of Taos accused them of being subversives. Witt, *Taos Moderns*, 108 n. 33. By the 1960s, both artists were practicing abstractionists, but occasionally social themes appeared prominently in their works. Most notable is Mandelman's collage *Untitled (Free Speech)* (ca. 1960s; Harwood Museum of Art).

126 F. Barrows Colton, "Man's New Servant, the Friendly Atom," *National Geographic* 105, no. 1 (January 1954): 71–90.

127 For a discussion on the visual impact of the Atomic Age on American culture, see Brooke Kamin Rapaport, et. al., *Vital Forms: American Art and Design in the Atomic Age, 1940–1960* (New York: Brooklyn Museum of Art, 2001).

128 Richard Huntington, "Duayne Hatchett's Well-Ordered Universe" in *Duayne Hatchett: Form, Pattern, and Invention—A Retrospective* (Buffalo, N.Y.: Burchfield Penny Art Center, Buffalo State College, 2009), 36. Hatchett created *Sputnik I* the year Sputnik 5 successfully returned from space with living plants and animals. For an extended discussion of the impact of Sputnik, see Paul Dickson, *Sputnik: the Shock of the Century* (New York: Walker and Co., 2001).

129 Fitz kept a file on UFOs and followed reports closely. Fitz Papers, box 10 "Mind Control and UFOs," WHC. UFOs were first defined by Air Force regulation 200-2, issued in 1953. Several incidents occurred relatively close to Amarillo, including Woodward, Oklahoma, and Levelland, Texas. The latter took place on November 2–3, 1957, and multiple witnesses reported a glowing egg-shaped object. Multiple motorists experienced allegedly engine and headlight failure during the event, only to have power return after.

130 See n. 60.

131 Kendrick Oliver, *To Touch the Face of God: The Sacred, the Profane, and the American Space Program* (Baltimore, Md.: Johns Hopkins University Press, 2013), 89.

132 James Harithas, *Dorothy Hood Paintings* (Syracuse, N.Y.: Evenson Museum of Art, 1972), n.p.

133 Ann Holmes, "Dorothy Hood's New Work: Brilliant Episodes in Space," *Zest*, May 17, 1970, in Dorothy Hood Papers, reel 2153, frame 709, AAA.

134 Grant, *Mysteries in Space*, 66.

135 For example, see Rennie Taylor, "Stars, Age 24 Billion, Found by Astronomers," *The Washington Post*, December 29, 1959, p. A10.

136 Vanderlip, in Weiermair, *Vance Kirkland*, 19.

Publication Notes

Copyright © 2014 The University of Oklahoma

This catalogue has been published in conjunction with the exhibition
Macrocosm / Microcosm:
Abstract Expressionism and the American Southwest.

Fred Jones Jr. Museum of Art
October 3, 2014, through January 4, 2015

No part of this publication may be reproduced or used in any form without the written consent of the Fred Jones Jr. Museum of Art.

Catalogue author: Mark Andrew White
Catalogue designer: Jeff Price
Copy editor: Jo Ann Reece

Fred Jones Jr. Museum of Art
The University of Oklahoma
555 Elm Avenue, Norman, Oklahoma 73019-3003
Phone: 405.325.3272; Fax : 405.325.7696
www.ou.edu/fjjma

Emily Ballew Neff, Wylodean and Bill Saxon Director and Chief Curator
Mark A. White, Eugene B. Adkins Senior Curator and Curator of Collections
Gail Kana Anderson, Deputy Director and Liaison to University President

Library of Congress Control Number: 2014948685
ISBN: 978-0-9851609-7-5

This catalogue was printed by the University of Oklahoma Printing Services and is issued by the University of Oklahoma. 1,000 copies have been printed and distributed at no cost to the taxpayers of Oklahoma.

The catalogue cover includes the following works:

COVER:
Eugene "Gene" Bavinger (U.S., 1919–1997)
Red Earth [detail], 1971
oil on canvas, 69 x 69 in.
Philbrook Museum of Art, Tulsa, Oklahoma

Duayne Hatchett (U.S., b. 1925)
Landscape West [detail], 1962
steel, 17 x 15 x 2 in.
Collection of the artist; reproduction permission courtesy of the artist

Janet Lippincott (U.S., 1918–2007)
Southwest Landscape, 1962
oil on canvas, 60 x 60 in.
Fred Jones Jr. Museum of Art, the University of Oklahoma, Norman, Oklahoma; reproduction permission courtesy of the Karan Ruhlen Gallery

J. Jay McVicker (U.S., 1911–2004)
Yellow Green [detail], 1967
acrylic on canvas, 48 x 48 in.
Collection of Jonathan and Talitha Nichols

Vance Kirkland (U.S., 1904–1981)
Painting No. 3 [detail], 1961
oil and water on linen, 75 x 108 in.
Collection Kirkland Museum of Fine and Decorative Art, Denver; reproduction permission courtesy of the Kirkland.

TITLE PAGE:
Beatrice Mandelman (U.S., 1912–1998)
Untitled (60.SP.4.39), ca. 1960
mixed media collage on paper, 10 x 12 in.
Fred Jones Jr. Museum of Art, the University of Oklahoma, Norman, Oklahoma; gift of the Mandelman-Ribak Foundation, 2014.

PREFACE PAGE:
Emerson Woelffer (U.S., 1914–2003)
Morning Earth, 1955
oil and collage on canvas, 36 x 28 in.
Manny Silverman Gallery, Los Angeles, CA; Artwork Courtesy of the Otis College of Art and Design Emerson Woelffer Collection.

About the Venue

Fred Jones Jr. Museum of Art, University of Oklahoma
Norman, Oklahoma

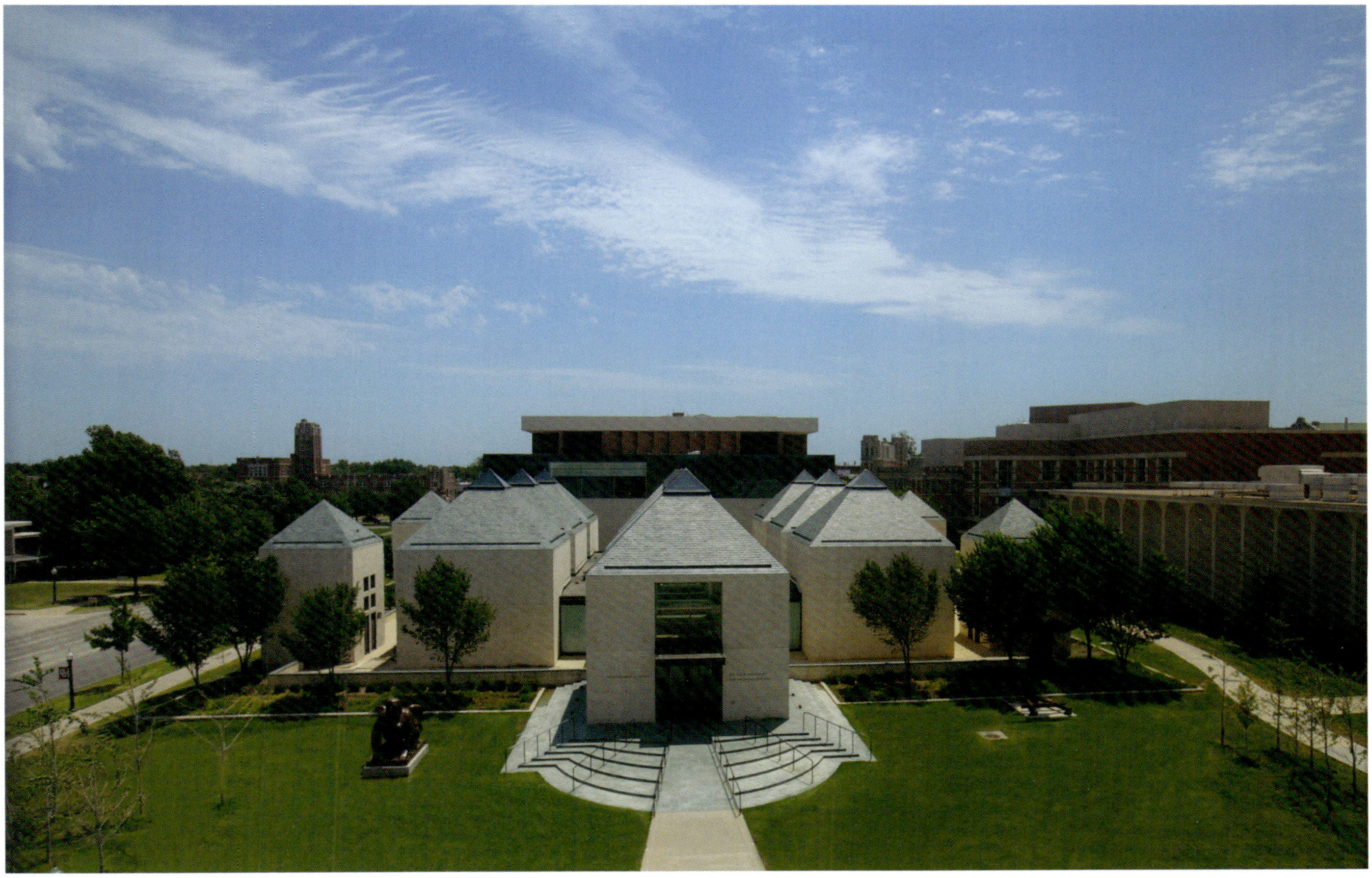

Photo: Eric H. Anderson

The University of Oklahoma's Fred Jones Jr. Museum of Art is widely regarded as one of the finest university art museums in the United States. The museum's growing collection features nearly 17,000 objects. Highlights include the Weitzenhoffer Collection of French *Impressionism*, the Eugene B. Adkins Collection of art of the American Southwest and Native American art, the James T. Bialac Native American Art Collection, twentieth century American painting and sculpture, ceramics, photography, contemporary art, Asian art, and works on paper from the sixteenth century to the present.